Images of Immigrants and Refugees in Western Europe

Images of Immigrants and Refugees in Western Europe

Media Representations, Public Opinion, and Refugees' Experiences

Edited by
Leen d'Haenens, Willem Joris, and François Heinderyckx

LEUVEN UNIVERSITY PRESS

Published with the support of the
KU Leuven Fund for Fair Open Access
and
Belspo (Belgian Science Policy Office), as part of the framework programme BRAIN-be (Belgian Research Action Through Interdisciplinary Networks), contract nr BR/165/A4/IM2MEDIATE.

Published in 2019 by Leuven University Press / Presses Universitaires de Louvain / Universitaire Pers Leuven. Minderbroedersstraat 4, B-3000 Leuven (Belgium).

Selection and editorial matter © Leen d'Haenens, Willem Joris, and François Heinderyckx, 2019
Individual chapters © The respective authors, 2019
Every effort has been made to contact all holders of the copyright in the visual material contained in this publication. Any copyright-holders who believe that illustrations have been reproduced without their knowledge are asked to contact the publisher.

This book is published under a Creative Commons Attribution Non-Commercial Non-Derivative 4.0 Licence.

The license allows you to share, copy, distribute, and transmit the work for personal and non-commercial use providing author and publisher attribution is clearly stated. Attribution should include the following information:
Leen d'Haenens, Willem Joris, and François Heinderyckx (eds.). *Images of Immigrants and Refugees in Western Europe: Media Representations, Public Opinion, and Refugees' Experiences*. Leuven, Leuven University Press. (CC BY-NC-ND 4.0)

Further details about Creative Commons licenses are available at http://creativecommons.org/licenses/

ISBN 978 94 6270 180 9 (Paperback)
ISBN 978 94 6166 281 1 (ePDF)
ISBN 978 94 6166 282 8 (ePUB)

https://doi.org/10.11116/9789461662811

D / 2019/ 1869 / 15
NUR: 741, 811

Layout: Crius Group
Cover design: Frederik Danko
Cover illustration: Ruslan Shugushev/Shutterstock.com

Contents

Chapter 1. Images of Immigrants and Refugees in Western Europe: Media Representations, Public Opinion, and Refugees' Experiences   7
Leen d'Haenens and Willem Joris

Part I – Policy on migration and integration in Europe

Chapter 2. Migration and integration policy in Europe: Comparing Belgium and Sweden   21
Paul Puschmann, Ebba Sundin, David De Coninck, and Leen d'Haenens

Part II – Media representations

Chapter 3. The Refugee Situation as Portrayed in News Media: A Content Analysis of Belgian and Swedish Newspapers – 2015-2017   39
Rozane De Cock, Ebba Sundin, and Valériane Mistiaen

Chapter 4. Depiction of Immigration in Television News: Public and Commercial Broadcasters – a Comparison   57
Valériane Mistiaen

Chapter 5. Agency and Power in the Dutch-Language News Coverage of the Summer 2015 Refugee Situation in Europe: A Transitivity Analysis of Semantic Roles   83
Lutgard Lams

Chapter 6. A Diverse View on the Promotion of Tolerance and Cultural Diversity through the Eyes of Journalists: Focus on Belgium and Sweden   101
Stefan Mertens, Leen d'Haenens, Rozane De Cock, and Olivier Standaert

Part III – Public opinion

Chapter 7. Discordance between Public Opinion and News Media Representations of Immigrants and Refugees in Belgium and Sweden   123
   David De Coninck, Hanne Vandenberghe, and Koen Matthijs

Chapter 8. Online News Consumption and Public Sentiment toward Refugees: Is there a Filter Bubble at Play? Belgium, France, the Netherlands, and Sweden: A Comparison   141
   Stefan Mertens, Leen d'Haenens, and Rozane De Cock

Chapter 9. The Effects of Dominant versus Peripheral News Frames on Attitudes toward Refugees and News Story Credibility   159
   Willem Joris and Rozane De Cock

Part IV – Refugees' experiences

Chapter 10. Beyond Victimhood: Reflecting on Migrant-Victim Representations with Afghan, Iraqi, and Syrian Asylum Seekers and Refugees in Belgium   177
   Kevin Smets, Jacinthe Mazzocchetti, Lorraine Gerstmans, and Lien Mostmans

Conclusion   199
   François Heinderyckx

List of authors   203

Chapter 1
Images of Immigrants and Refugees in Western Europe: Media Representations, Public Opinion, and Refugees' Experiences

Leen d'Haenens and Willem Joris

There are no simple solutions to the European migration crisis

Europe has always been a continent of migration, but the numbers of refugees who entered the European Union reached an all-time high in 2015 and 2016 and have remained elevated ever since. In 2015 EU member states received over 1.3 million applications for international protection—more than twice the previous year's figure (Eurostat, 2018a). In 2016 more than 1.2 million asylum seekers entered the EU. In 2017, the number of applications (705,705) started to decline. Most applicants are male: 72 percent in 2015; 68 percent in 2016; and 67 percent in 2017 (Eurostat, 2018a). Since at least the summer of 2015, we Europeans have been struggling with the question of *how many* and *which migrants* we are willing to welcome to our welfare states. And we are faced with ethical questions: how can we reconcile our choices with our ethical standards? One crucial, albeit fraught distinction is that which separates 'economic' migrants—looking for better living conditions—from refugees, who must leave a politically unsafe, war-torn country simply to survive.

The current refugee issue has turned on its head our complacent view of migration owing to the sheer numbers of people fleeing across the Mediterranean Sea or through Southeast Europe, seeking shelter in EU member states. Most immigrants entering 'Fortress Europe' from the South are political refugees fleeing war or persecution in their home countries. The top three origins of applicants are countries in an ongoing state of civil war, i.e., Syria, Afghanistan, and Iraq (Eurostat, 2018a). In addition, most 'economic migrants' come from parts of Africa, Asia, and Eastern Europe in search of a better life (Park, 2015). Given the dual nature of this migration wave, the EU and its citizens have been of two minds over the issue, depending on the moment in time, the country, its absorption capacity, and its government's political hue. Despite the desperate state most refugees find themselves in, starting with the humanitarian disaster taking place in the Mediterranean, many developed countries in Europe have been reluctant to take them in and provide them with shelter, safety, employment, education, and permanent residence. Moreover, the overlapping gray areas in the categorization of migrants made it even more difficult for policy makers in the EU member states to take a clear stance with regard to refugees. According to the United Nations High Commissioner for Refugees (UNHCR), a refugee is "any person forced to flee his or her country because of persecution, war or violence." The organization estimated in 2016 that more than half of all the 65.6 million refugees worldwide came from just three countries—Syria, Afghanistan, and South Sudan (UNHCR, 2018).

Governments, the news industry, and public opinion in Europe have been increasingly preoccupied with refugees seeking access to Europe. Highly interconnected with political agendas and audience perceptions, media depictions affect the public perceptions of both refugees/migrants and integration and migration policies (among others, Entman, 1993; Orgad, 2012). Public opinion is split (if not wholly negative) and generally uninformed or misinformed (e.g., Ceobanu & Escandell, 2010; Hainmueller & Hopkins, 2014; Jacobs, Hooghe, & de Vroome, 2017; Meuleman, Davidov, & Billiet, 2009; Rustenbach, 2010), while policies and politicians seem ineffectual when not downright hostile in the face of such dire needs.

There are no simple solutions because migration is a complex matter, perceptions of it are fraught with emotions, and it cannot be met with coldly 'rational' decisions—while involving both national and international rules. The actors in this complex interplay are not only the people on the move, governments, and NGOs, but also often ruthless refugee smugglers. So solutions will need to be creative and multifaceted. Although some progress has been made since the crisis in the autumn of 2015, the fault lines within Europe have so far prevented any revision of the Dublin Regulation,[1] which was never meant to cope with massive migration anyway.

In Germany, by June 2018, the refugee and irregular migration issue had poisoned relations between Chancellor Merkel's Christian Democratic Union (CDU) and the latter's Bavarian sister party, the CSU, whose leader insisted migrants arriving in Germany should be returned to the European country where they were first registered. Merkel pleaded for a European-wide approach

---

1   Regulation establishing the criteria and mechanisms for determining the Member State responsible for examining an asylum application lodged in one of the Member States by a third-country national.

and managed to work out an arrangement with the other EU member states at the June 2018 European summit (see also Henley, 2018). An agreement was reached to set up 'migrant control centers' on European territory, where 'economic' migrants are to be separated from 'refugees', after which the latter can be transferred to a member state other than the one where they first landed. Both the opening of such centers and the integration of refugees having entered the EU through a border state such as Italy or Greece will happen on a voluntary basis. There is also talk of 'disembarkation platforms' to be set up outside Europe under the supervision of the United Nations and financed with European money, where refugees will be able to apply for asylum. The decision of member states to spread migratory pressure through new reception centers over more countries than Greece and Italy only while reinforcing Frontex (the EU border security forces) is a positive outcome. However, the voluntary character of the arrangement is disturbing, as it shows once again that the EU does not have the political will to give fair and equal treatment to each and every refugee while breaking the business model of the people smugglers.

Attitudes toward migrants and refugees

The research we present in this book explores both the ways refugees—those fleeing the Syrian and Iraqi civil war and the continuing armed conflicts plaguing Afghanistan—are being received by the general populations and the perceptions of the people surrounding the resettlement of Syrians in Belgium and Sweden. We compare the attitudes of the public as well as the determinants—both individual-level opinions and macro-level social and economic factors—that may be shaping these attitudes.

For contextualization purposes we bring together selected evidence of opposing sentiments regarding the notion of accepting large numbers of refugees in a variety of countries as reported through polling results (see Table 1.1) as well as motives behind this reluctance to share one's country with additional refugees. In a 2015 global survey on immigration attitudes conducted by Gallup for the International Organization for Migration, 52 percent of respondents across Europe stated that the number of immigrants should be reduced in their countries (Esipova et al., 2015). The largest percentages were found in Northern and Eastern Europe (56 percent in each case). Thirty-nine percent of Western Europeans also favored a decrease in immigration numbers (Esipova et al., 2015). Eurobarometer results (EB 85, fieldwork May 2016) show that immigration is the main concern at European level according to 48 percent

Table 1.1: Research results – opposing sentiments to accepting large numbers of refugees in Western European countries

	ESS	Ifop	Ipsos MORI	Pew Research Center	Ipsos
Too many immigrants in my country				FR: 63%	NL: 63%
Obligation of country to admit refugees				FR: 54% NL: 61%	
Refugees will take our jobs	BE: 43% FR: 37% SE: 21%			FR: 5% SE: 4%	
Refugees do not integrate into society				SE: 40% FR: 23%	
Sympathy for Syrian refugees coming to the country				SE: 57% FR: 27%	
Diversity makes a country a better place to live	NL: 59% SE: 51% BE: 41% FR: 21%			SE: 36% FR: 26% NL: 17%	SE: 31% BE: 18% FR: 16%
Refugees are a threat to country		FR: 26% SE: 15%		FR: 45% NL: 36% SE: 24%	
Refugees increase terrorism likelihood				NL: 61% SE: 57% FR: 46%	
Date	2014-15	2015	2016	2016	2017
Sample size	2,000 in each of 22 countries	1,000 in each of 7 countries	12,646 in 12 countries	1,000 in each of 10 countries (on average)	17,903 in 25 countries
Design	Survey	Online Survey	Online survey	Telephone Survey/Interviews	Interviews
Author	ESS	Ifop	Ipsos MORI	Pew Research Center	Ipsos

of Europeans, followed by terrorism and the economic situation (European Commission, 2016). This indicates a rapid change in public perception, as immigration was ranked only fourth on the concern list in 2014. In the EU28 countries a majority of respondents (58 percent) have a negative feeling about immigration of people from outside the EU.

Several studies reveal an increase in negative attitudes toward refugees in EU countries (e.g., De Coninck, Matthijs, Debrael, Joris, De Cock, & d'Haenens, 2018). While such attitudes may have been relatively favorable at the start of the crisis, they grew more negative with increased numbers, demands for increased resources to assist the refugees, and increased (perceived) threats to the destination countries' way of life and economic prosperity. The literature on surveys of attitudes toward migrants and refugees tends to demonstrate that individual-level variables are the most important factors explaining negative or positive reception of refugees (e.g., De Coninck et al., 2018). In particular, age, occupation, education, and income levels are important. In general, the younger, better educated, and more professional respondents tend to be more accepting.

Do news media depictions influence public concern?

This book sets out to investigate the dynamic interplay between news media depictions of the current non-EU immigrant situation with a specific emphasis on the refugee situation on the one hand, and both governmental and societal (re)actions on the other. Policies have been put in place at both European and national levels to relocate and resettle asylum seekers among the EU member states, which generated more hostility toward migrants and their purported negative impact, while other voices were more supportive of such policies.

Refugees have taken a prominent place in news production, political discussions, policy formation, and public concern around the world in recent years. According to Gabrielatos and Baker (2008: 9) the print media should be viewed as "an excellent source of data for the examination of the construction of refugees and asylum seekers" because of their power "over the selection, extent, frequency, and nature of their reporting" and "the reciprocity of influence between readers and newspapers." By way of an example, Gamson and Modigliani (1989: 2) argued that the media use their power of influence by interpreting 'the reality', emphasizing specific frames that help control the agenda based on "interpretive packages." Our analysis of news stories departs from the idea that media makers "make conscious or unconscious framing judgments in deciding what to say, guided by frames" (Entman, 1993:

52). The news text "contains frames, which are manifested by the presence or absence of certain keywords, stock phrase(s), stereotyped images, sources of information, and sentences that provide thematically reinforcing clusters of facts or judgments" (Entman, 1993: 52). One such frame in the unfolding humanitarian drama was the iconic image of Alan Kurdi, the Syrian toddler whose lifeless body washed up on a Turkish beach in September 2015. This shocking image brought the European refugee crisis into the spotlight and—at least for a while—generated more empathy for the refugees' tragic journey. Previous agenda-setting research related the prominence of topics in news media (media agenda) to their ranking on the public agenda. In Belgium, a study by Jacobs (2017) showed a positive relationship between the amount of television news attention dedicated to migration and the public perception of this topic as an important societal issue in Belgium, with both variables fluctuating simultaneously in the 2003-2014 period.

As a complement to previous research on immigration, refugees, public opinion, and news media in Belgium, the field will benefit from an integrated approach given the currently fragmented content analysis view, with a focus on only one specific medium or news brand, time period, or media language. Moreover, asylum seekers framing data are now outdated (e.g., Van Gorp, 2005), and inaccurate measuring of crucial media variables should be remedied: the European Social Survey includes no more than two questions on television, and it relies on wide frequency use indicator categories, while the Eurobarometer ignores media variables altogether. Based on the combination of public opinion data and newspaper stories on the topic of immigration to the UK, a study by McLaren, Boomgaarden, and Vliegenthart (2018) shows that by emphasizing two concrete issues associated with immigration—the economy and education—the media appear to increase concerns about immigration. On the other hand, emphasis on more abstract themes elicits scant attention among the British public.

To our knowledge, this book is the first on this topic to incorporate all parts of the classic communication model: sender (journalistic culture), content (news messages), receiver (public), media effects—as well as an oftentimes forgotten group: giving a voice to the refugees who are themselves subjects of the news content makes it possible to reveal an endogenous side of the refugee situation alongside the official narrative.

Focus on Belgium and comparison with Sweden

Although our focus is on Belgium, the research evidence presented in the chapters will always be placed in an international perspective, Sweden being the key country of comparison. The strong increase in asylum claims in Belgium since 2015 requires looking at good practices and long-term approaches. While population figures are comparable (9.9 million Swedes versus 11 million Belgians), Belgium and Sweden differ greatly in terms of migration policy and integration indicators, as illustrated in Table 1.2 by the 2015 Migrant Integration Policy Index (MIPEX). Both countries are also faced with a different reality when it comes to the actual number of incoming refugees. For Belgium, this meant an increase in 2015 of 178 percent compared to 2014 (38,990 applications), for Sweden a rise of 108 percent (156,110 applications). Both countries also differ as to their populations' responses. Sweden (62 percent) is one of the EU28 countries (together with Ireland, Luxemburg, Portugal, and Spain) in which a clear majority of inhabitants have positive feelings about non-EU immigrants (European Commission, 2018). In contrast, the Belgian population (43 percent) is less positive toward non-EU immigrants.

Sweden is also the European country *par excellence*, with a generous welcoming policy, a long history of tolerance and openness, and the highest

Table 1.2: 2015 Migrant Integration Policy Index (MIPEX) scores (in %).

	Belgium	Sweden
Overall MIPEX-score	67	78
Labor Market Mobility	64	98
Family Reunion	72	78
Education	61	77
Health	53	62
Political Participation	57	77
Permanent Residence	86	79
Access to Nationality	69	73
Anti-discrimination	78	85

Note. Meaning of the scores: 0% Critically unfavorable; 1-20% Unfavorable; 21-40% Slightly unfavorable; 41-59% Halfway to Best Practice; 60-79% Slightly favorable; 80-99% Favorable; 100% Best practice (MIPEX, 2015).

score on the Migration Integration Policy Index (MIPEX). The 2015 MIPEX is a tool created to cover eight policy areas based on 167 policy indicators which map out a migrant's trajectory toward full citizenship in all European Union countries as well as several others. We will use the scores from both countries in this study to compare government policy with individual attitudes toward refugees. These policies cover labor market mobility, family reunion, education, health, political participation, permanent residence, access to nationality, and anti-discrimination. Comparing six integration indices, Jedwab and Soroka (2014) argue that MIPEX offers the most comprehensive set of economic and social indicators, although it captures the 'best practices' in regard to policies and not actual integration outcomes.

With its 78 percent score Sweden is at the top of the MIPEX list, which is made up of 38, mostly Western, countries. Belgium ranks seventh with a 67 percent score. The average score of integration policies is 52 percent, which means such policies remain major obstacles for immigrants keen to fully participate in economic, social, and democratic life. The EU migrant integration indicators (Eurostat, 2018b) also clearly show that Sweden does much better than Belgium in most respects. For example, policy in Sweden results in higher activity rates among immigrants (i.e., non-EU citizens by birth) (Sweden: 77.0 percent; Belgium: 60.3 percent) and fewer immigrants at risk of poverty and social exclusion (Sweden: 40.8 percent; Belgium: 52.6 percent).

Sweden's policy approach and results with respect to media depictions and public opinion building will thus be essential input for Belgian policy makers, helping them do what is possible and/or needed to guarantee equal access and opportunities to the refugees in terms of targeted employment, education, and health support. At the same time, higher public trust levels should be gained and media workers should be inspired to produce less biased news.

How the refugee issue was studied

The theme and focus of this book are the result of a collaborative research project, *Images of Immigrants in the Media: Thought-provoking Effects (IM²MEDIATE)*, which combines four complementary multi-stakeholder group perspectives:
1) analyzing the policy related to national governmental (re)actions across countries with emphasis on Belgium and Sweden as divergent cases;
2) analyzing the news media content in the context of a journalism culture;
3) studying societal reactions of the general public;
4) studying the push and pull factors in migration from a refugee perspective.

It is the book's ultimate goal to inventory the multiple public, policy, and media voices heard in Belgium on this crucial issue, while learning from practices abroad (with a focus on Sweden), and to formulate recommendations toward a more encouraging integration policy, while lowering anti-immigration and anti-refugee sentiment.

To study the interplay and the possibly pivotal role of the media in this complex societal challenge, the book compares the news media representations of non-EU immigrants—with a special emphasis on refugees in Dutch- and French-speaking Belgium and in Sweden—as potentially powerful public opinion-formation drivers on the issue. Based on their news selection, gatekeeping, and (re)presentation of the situation and the individuals involved, news media can choose to either connect people or to sharpen differences by stressing 'otherness'. The precise framing and reconstruction of everyday reality can shape public opinion in terms of evaluation of the present situation and the necessity of action, appropriate policy initiatives, and solutions. The news media under study include audiovisual and online media; both verbal and visual content are analyzed. The particularities of linguistic representation in each language under study (Dutch, French, and Swedish) are mapped and compared. In addition, qualitative in-depth interviews with journalists serve as a reflective feedback loop complementing the content analysis results. Comparisons with available cross-country data from the Worlds of Journalism project on the professional culture of journalism being influential in the media framing of immigrants with a focus on refugees are added.

To assess public opinion on non-EU immigrants and refugees, we conducted a survey among a representative sample of adults (aged between 18 and 65, accurately reflecting the Belgian population as to gender, SES, and education) as well as adolescents (aged between 15 and 18) in the regions under study. To investigate potential links between the content of news media (Chapter 3) and public opinion on the refugee situation in particular (Chapter 7), an experimental research design was set up (Chapter 9). News stories typical of the various news frames on refugees (based on content analysis results) were turned into experimental material including counter-frames so as to test the potential effects of various framing approaches on the public's mental pictures.

Further to the content analysis and the public opinion survey, Chapter 10 is built around data collected among refugees in Belgium to inductively reconstruct their potentially manifold views on Belgium and Europe and explore their motivations for choosing this country as a temporary or final destination in their search of a new future. Based on the proportionate number of first-time asylum applicants in the EU (Eurostat, 2018a), the focus is on interviewees coming from Syria (29 percent of total number in 2015), Afghanistan (14 percent), and Iraq (10 percent). These are the three largest groups of refugees who have arrived in Belgium since the latest immigration peak (summer of 2015). Issues related to religion will receive significant attention. This includes questions of perceived 'islamophobia' and the potential of faith-based group identities.

Book structure

The book is divided into four sections. The first section addresses the policy on migration and integration in Europe (Chapter 2); the second section focuses on media representations (Chapters 3-6); the third section looks at public opinion toward immigrants, refugees, and asylum seekers (Chapters 7-9); and the final section focuses on the refugees' experiences (Chapter 10).

The first section investigates the policy on migration and integration in the light of the refugee issue. In Chapter 2, Paul Puschmann, Ebba Sundin, David De Coninck, and Leen d'Haenens compare different migration and integration policies in Europe, with a focus on Belgium and Sweden.

The second section of this book examines the media representations of the European refugee crisis. In Chapter 3 Rozane De Cock, Ebba Sundin, and Valériane Mistiaen analyze the portrayal of the refugee issue in news media through a content analysis of Belgian and Swedish newspapers between 2015 and 2017. Furthermore, Valériane Mistiaen (Chapter 4) examines the differences between Belgian French-language public and commercial television broadcasters regarding the refugee issue. In Chapter 5 Lutgard Lams investigates the verbal processes associated with the refugee as well as the non-refugee actors, such as political elites, governmental institutions, or NGOs. In Chapter 6 Stefan Mertens, Leen d'Haenens, Rozane De Cock, and Olivier Standaert study the journalists' views on their role to promote tolerance and cultural diversity in societies with diverging migration and integration policies.

The third section analyzes public opinion toward immigrants, refugees, and asylum seekers. In Chapter 7 David De Coninck, Hanne Vandenberghe, and Koen Matthys examine the impact of news media consumption and trust on attitudes about immigrants and refugees in both Belgium and Sweden. Moreover, the chapter analyzes if and to what extent the level of importance of the migration issue and the presence of intergroup contact are mediators of news consumption. Chapter 8 investigates the filter bubble. Stefan Mertens, Leen d'Haenens, and Rozane De Cock test the assumption that online news users will hold more outspoken viewpoints on refugees due to a more segregated, likeminded news consumption. Next, in Chapter 9, Willem Joris and Rozane De Cock analyze the possible effects of a set of commonly used and peripheral, atypical news frames on individuals' opinions and attitudes on refugees. The effect study is based on a survey experiment among the general public of between 18 and 65 years old in Flanders (Dutch-speaking part of Belgium).

The fourth section explores the refugees' experiences. This section gives voice to those who often remain voiceless, and reflects on representations of migration. In Chapter 10 Kevin Smets, Jacinthe Mazzocchetti, Lorraine Gerstmans, and Lien Mostmans concentrate on how asylum seekers and refugees make sense of how they are represented, and how those representations connect to broader issues of victimization, recognition, and identity.

Lenses of the research team differed across the chapters. At times the scope of the research presented in this book involves a comparison of four countries (C6, C8), or two with a focus on Belgium and Sweden (C2, C3, C7). Some chapters focus on news production or reception in one language area: the Dutch-speaking press in Flanders and the Netherlands (C5), Flanders (C9), or the French-speaking part of Belgium's broadcast news (C4). The last chapter in the book (C10) looks at Belgium as a 'host country' for Afghani, Iraqi, and Syrian refugees from the perspective of the latter.

References

Ceobanu, A. M., & Escandell, X. (2010). Comparative analyses of public attitudes toward immigrants and immigration using multinational survey data: A review of theories and research. *Annual Review of Sociology, 36*, 309–328.

De Coninck, D., Matthijs, K., Debrael, M., Joris, W., De Cock, R., & d'Haenens, L. (2018). The relationship between media use and public opinion on immigrants and refugees: A Belgian perspective. *Communications: The European Journal of Communication Research, 43*(3), 403–425.

Entman, R.M. (1993). Framing: Toward clarification of a fractured paradigm. *Journal of Communication, 43*(4), 51–58.

Esipova, N., Ray, J., Pugliese, A., Tsabutashvili, D., Laczko, F., & Rango, M. (2015). *How the World Views Migration*, International Organization for Migration with Gallup. Retrieved from https://publications.iom.int/system/files/how_the_world_gallup.pdf June 13, 2018.

European Commission (2016). *Standard Eurobarometer 85. Public opinion in the European Union. Report.* Brussels: European Commission.

European Commission (2018). Eurobarometer Interactive. Retrieved from http://ec.europa.eu/commfrontoffice/publicopinion/index.cfm/Chart/index July 17, 2018.

European Social Survey (2015). *ESS Round 7 (2014/2015) Technical Report.* London: ESS ERIC.

Eurostat (2018a). *Asylum and first time asylum applicants by citizenship, age and sex.* Retrieved from http://ec.europa.eu/eurostat/data/database July 1, 2018.

Eurostat (2018b). *Migrant integration database*. Retrieved from http://ec.europa.eu/eurostat/web/migrant-integration/data/database July 17, 2018.

Gabrielatos, C., & Baker, P. (2008). Fleeing, sneaking, flooding: A corpus analysis of discursive constructions of refugees and asylum seekers in the UK press, 1996-2005. *Journal of English Linguistics, 36*(1), 5–38.

Gamson, W., & Modigliani, A. (1989). Media discourse and public opinion on nuclear power: A constructionist approach. *Journal of Sociology, 95*(1), 1–37.

Hainmueller, J., & Hopkins, D. J. (2014). Public attitudes toward immigration. *Annual Review of Political Science, 17,* 225–249.

Henley, J. (2018, June 29). EU migration deal: What was agreed and will it work?, *The Guardian*. Retrieved from https://www.theguardian.com/world/2018/jun/29/eu-summit-migration-deal-key-points July 16, 2018.

Ifop (2015). *Les Européens face à la crise des migrants*. Retrieved from https://jean-jaures.org/sites/default/files/redac/commun/113347_presentation_-_fondation_jean_jaures_v2.pdf July 18, 2018.

Ipsos (2017). *Global views on immigration and the refugee crisis*. Retrieved from https://www.ipsos.com/sites/default/files/ct/news/documents/2017-09/Global_Advisor_Immigration.pdf July 18, 2018.

Ipsos MORI. (2016). *Public attitudes towards refugees in Europe*. Retrieved from https://www.ipsos.com/ipsos-mori/en-uk/public-attitudes-towards-refugees-europe July 18, 2018.

Jacobs, L. (2017). *The role of immigration news as a contextual-level factor for anti-immigrant attitudes: The effect of tone and threat frames.* Leuven: KU Leuven (Doctoral Dissertation).

Jacobs, L., Hooghe, M., & de Vroome, T. (2017). Television and anti-immigrant sentiments: The mediating role of fear of crime and perceived ethnic diversity. *European Societies, 19*(3), 243–267.

Jedwab, J., & Soroka, S. (2014). *Indexing integration: A review of national and international models*. A report prepared for the Department of Citizenship and Immigration Canada. Montreal: Association for Canadian Studies (Canadian Institute for Identities and Migration).

McLaren, L., Boomgaarden, H., & Vliegenthart, R. (2018). News coverage and public concern about immigration in Britain, *International Journal of Public Opinion, 30*(2), 173–193.

Meuleman, B., Davidov, E., & Billiet, J. (2009). Changing attitudes toward immigration in Europe, 2002–2007: A dynamic group conflict theory approach. *Social Science Research, 38*(2), 352–365.

MIPEX (2015). *Migrant Policy Index*. Retrieved from www.mipex.eu July 15, 2018.

Orgad, S. (2012). *Media representation and the global imagination*. Cambridge: Polity.

Park, J. (2015). *Europe's migration crisis*. Retrieved from http://cfr.org/refugee-and-the-displaced/europes-migration-crisis/p32874 July 17, 2018.

Pew Research Center. (2016). *Europeans fear wave of refugees will mean more terrorism, fewer jobs*. Retrieved from http://assets.pewresearch.org/wp-content/uploads/sites/2/2016/07/14095942/Pew-Research-Center-EU-Refugees-and-National-Identity-Report-FINAL-July-11-2016.pdf July 18, 2018.

Rustenbach, E. (2010). Sources of negative attitudes toward immigrants in Europe: A multi-level analysis. *International Migration Review, 44*(1), 53–77.

UNHCR (2018). *Refugee facts. What is a refugee?* Retrieved from https://www.unrefugees.org/refugee-facts/what-is-a-refugee July 16, 2018.

Van Gorp, B. (2005). Where is the frame? Victims and intruders in the Belgian press coverage of the asylum issue, *European Journal of Communication, 20*(4), 484–507.

PART I

POLICY ON MIGRATION AND INTEGRATION IN EUROPE

Chapter 2
Migration and integration policy in Europe: Comparing Belgium and Sweden

Paul Puschmann, Ebba Sundin, David De Coninck, and Leen d'Haenens

The events that followed the Arab Spring—the civil war in Syria, the rise of Islamic State, and the power struggle in Libya following the death of Gaddafi—were among the factors that triggered the largest refugee crisis since the Second World War. Other events such as the political crisis in the Democratic Republic of Congo, the persecution of the Rohingya in Myanmar, and the exodus that resulted from Venezuela's economic collapse have since made matters even worse. As a result, some 68.5 million people worldwide have been on the move through no choice of their own according to the UNHCR's latest figures; 25.4 million of those are refugees and 3.1 million are asylum seekers. Currently, the largest numbers of refugees worldwide originate from Syria (6.3 million), Afghanistan (2.6 million), and South Sudan (2.4 million). While most people who flee war and persecution remain within their country's borders, a majority of asylum seekers and refugees —fugitives who had to cross a national border—move to neighboring countries. In relative terms, Lebanon is the country that hosts the largest number of refugees: one out of six inhabitants of this small eastern Mediterranean country is a refugee. With some 3.5 million refugees, Turkey is the number one host country of refugees in absolute terms (UNHCR, 2018).

While 85 percent of the world's displaced persons are located in developing countries, the West has not remained unaffected. As a consequence of armed conflicts, political and religious persecutions, and poverty, hundreds of thousands of refugees and economic migrants—including vulnerable groups such as minors, pregnant women, and disabled, diseased and elderly people—from the Middle East, Africa, and South Asia have attempted to reach Europe in recent years. This has led them on a long and deadly journey across land and sea. Starting in 2011 the numbers of asylum applicants in EU member states grew significantly, from 309,040 in 2011 to 1,322,844 in 2015, after which a gradual decline set in (Eurostat; Asylum statistics 2018).

In absolute terms Germany has been Europe's premier host country. In 2015 (the year with the highest number of asylum-seeker applications in the EU) it registered 476,508 asylum applications, which is more than a third of all applications in the EU that year. With respectively 177,134 and 162,451 asylum applications in 2015, Hungary and Sweden were the EU's number two and three host countries. In 2017, Germany remained the number one host country, while Hungary and Sweden became less attractive than Italy and France, among others (Eurostat, 2018).

Rising numbers of refugees in Europe have spurred diverging political responses from national governments, as member states are affected in different ways and the EU remains unable to come up with a coherent migration policy. Some countries have been openly welcoming of refugees, including Germany and the Nordic countries, especially Sweden. The political attitude toward refugees in these countries is mostly characterized by concerns for solidarity and responsibility and can be summarized by German chancellor Angela Merkel's words: "Wir schaffen das!" (We can do this!). Despite taking in and retaining relatively few refugees, Portugal might be described as even more liberal, as its government has actively tried to attract more refugees. This political attitude is in strong contrast with that of the Italian, Hungarian, Austrian, and Greek governments, for instance, who have attempted to cut down the numbers of asylum seekers flocking to their countries through measures such as the creation of hundreds of kilometers of fences on the EU's external frontiers, between Greece and Turkey or Hungary and Serbia, making it more difficult for asylum seekers to reach a safe haven and strengthening the notion of a 'Fortress Europe'. Walls have also gone up between EU member states, however, between Slovenia and Croatia, for instance, and even within the Schengen area, between Austria and Slovenia.

The rise of border fences and the temporary reinstatement of border controls within the Schengen area show that the refugee crisis has strongly divided the European member states, leading to a political crisis. As a majority of refugees enter the European Union through Italy (central Mediterranean route) and Greece (eastern Mediterranean route), these countries have felt the strongest migratory pressures under the Dublin Convention, which allocates responsibility for an asylum seeker to the country of entry, so that all other member states would be legally justified in sending most asylum seekers back to Italy and Greece. The Convention thus creates a huge imbalance in responsibilities between Northern and Southern European States. In order to reduce this migratory pressure on the latter, plans have been made by the European institutions to relocate refugees across the EU. This has been thwarted by Eastern EU member states—mostly Hungary, Slovakia, and Poland—which added an East-West divide within the EU. In practice, the number of refugees who have been relocated has remained small owing to disagreements on quotas as well. Nevertheless, the number of resettled persons increased from 6,550 in 2014 to 24,155 in 2017 (Eurostat, 2018).

As the crisis deepened, support for accepting refugees declined everywhere in Europe, including in initially very welcoming countries such as Germany and Sweden. This is related to the election victories of nationalist and populist parties, who used the refugee crisis to their advantage. In Germany, for instance, the far-right AFD (Alternative für Deutschland) grew rapidly on the strength of its anti-refugee rhetoric, and so did the Sweden Democrats in Sweden, forcing governments to alter their liberal course and move to the right, which in practice mostly meant limiting the numbers of refugees being admitted. At the European level this move to the right is illustrated by the agreement negotiated with Turkey, according to which the latter agreed to take in refugees who refuse to apply for asylum in Greece or are ineligible for asylum within the EU. The overall aim of this agreement was to curb the influx of refugees and undocumented migrants. The same goes for the Migration Partnership Framework, which aims to handle asylum applications outside Europe, fight human trafficking, and avoid dangerous sea crossings, in which thousands of migrants have died over the previous years (Castillejo, 2017; UNHCR, 2018). However, all these measures also show that Europe is increasingly shifting responsibility to third countries, many of which—Turkey included—are already shouldering a heavier load than EU countries.

The refugee crisis is in many ways related to the European integration process itself. The will to foster peace, liberty, and economic prosperity has driven European nations closer to one another since the Second World War. As a result of intensive political cooperation, the creation of a common market and a free-travel zone, Europe has turned into one of the best places in the world to live in terms of GDP per capita and perceived quality of life. Thanks to the dominance of liberal democracy, economic growth and stability, universal health care and social welfare provisions, it has increasingly become an attractive destination for migrants. While the world has not become more migratory over the last half a century—the share of people who live in a country where they were not born has remained close to 3 percent of the global population—Europe has absorbed an ever-larger share of the world's international migrants (Czaika & De Haas, 2014). While this creates plenty of opportunities for further economic growth, it has also caused fears as national governments have partially lost control of those who enter their territory owing to the opening of borders within the Schengen area. This problem was acknowledged long before the refugee crisis. The Schengen Treaty provides for a uniform visa system, and steps were taken to strengthen the EU's external borders. Later, Frontex was established to monitor and control the latter. The refugee crisis has shown, however, that these borders are permeable, which fuels xenophobia and racism and bolsters Eurosceptic parties.

The immigration threat is fivefold. First of all, there is a fear that Europe will be overrun by political refugees and economic migrants from developing countries, notably Africa and the Middle East. This 'invasion' notion, which has even taken hold in some academic circles (e.g., Collier, 2014; Betts & Collier, 2018), is reinforced by images of boats overflowing with refugees and economic migrants desperate to reach European shores, as well as reports on the number of migrants and refugees entering Europe that fail to contextualize the situation (cf. Lucassen & De Haas, 2017). Second, some national citizens fear that the arrival of large groups of refugees will be too costly. Refugees receive shelter, clothing, education, medical treatment, etc., while draining social welfare funds due to their low level of labor market participation. This fear is especially present in North-Western European states with a strong welfare system—rich countries which many migrants want to reach once they set foot in Italy or Greece. Third, there is anxiety that terrorists might hide among the refugees. This security threat has to be viewed in the context of 9/11, the rise of the Islamic State, and the recent terrorist attacks in European cities—Madrid (2004), London (2005/2017), Paris (2015/2016), Brussels (2016), Nice (2016), Barcelona (2017), Berlin (2016), and Stockholm (2017), the last two being committed by (rejected) asylum seekers. Fourth, there is a fear that European values might crumble: many newcomers are Muslims, and Islam is often viewed as incompatible with Western values (separation of church and state, gender equality, etc.). The mass assaults on women that took place in Cologne, Hamburg, and other German cities on New Year's Eve 2016 had a profound impact in this respect. The fifth and final fear is that refugees will turn out to be 'unassimilable elements' in European societies in the long run (Lucassen, 2005).

European countries must deal with highly conflicting forces. On the one hand globalization, free markets, and international treaties—e.g., the 1951 Refugee Convention, the Schengen Agreement and the European Convention on Human Rights—push for open borders and the welcoming of newcomers for work, study, family reunification, and asylum purposes. On the other hand, there is a desire to control and curb migration and close borders, as the unrestrained influx of immigrants weighs on welfare systems, poses security threats (there may be criminals and terrorists among them), and might create a divide between 'insiders' and 'outsiders' (Favell & Hansen, 2002). The latter is especially true for non-Western immigrants who score consistently worse on integration scores compared to Western immigrants. Previously, these problems were mostly handled through visa policies—making it difficult or even impossible for economic migrants from developing countries to enter European territory, while keeping the Union's external borders tightly shut. This system has proved unsustainable in recent years under much increased migratory pressures, so that many member states started to act on a more individual basis. This led to divergent approaches, and a combination of short-term, mainly ad hoc measures intended to deal with immediate problems rather than develop a long-term solution. The Global Compact for Safe, Orderly and Regular Migration, a document negotiated and prepared by the United Nations, constitutes, by contrast, a long-term vision on migration policies on an international scale. The compact lists 23 objectives and commitments related to migration, highlighting migrant rights and the need for evidence-based migration policies (International Organization for Migration, 2018). Although nonbinding under international law, the compact was widely debated in several countries as many politicians feared its endorsement would stimulate migration, and criticized the compact for its lack of distinction between documented and undocumented migration. In Belgium, tensions related to the country's approval of the compact caused a collapse of the federal government in December 2018. Nonetheless, Belgium (and Sweden) endorsed this compact mere days later at the UN General Assembly, along with 150 other countries (Segers & Kerckaert, 2018).

In this chapter we will describe and compare the current immigration and integration policies of two Schengen member states: Belgium and Sweden, with a focus on economic migrants, asylum seekers, and refugees. Also, we will describe how these countries have dealt with the recent refugee crises. Subsequently, we will make a systematic comparison of migration and integration in Belgium and Sweden today, using key policy areas from the Migrant Integration Policy Index. Finally, we will make an inventory of key similarities and differences, and draw some general conclusions. The comparison between Belgium and Sweden is interesting as the latter has often been perceived as the ultimate immigration-friendly nation, with top integration scores, while Belgium scores considerably worse and the Belgian government has used a much more negative discourse on immigration, and has even launched social media campaigns to discourage potential asylum seekers from coming to Belgium.

Unless otherwise stated, we define asylum seekers as migrants who have applied for asylum and who are awaiting a decision; refugees as migrants whose asylum application has been approved; and economic migrants as people who were in no particular danger in their country of origin and whose main motivation was to improve their socio-economic position. These are ideal types, in the Weberian sense, as economic and political motives are often mixed up in practice. Asylum seekers from Syria or Iraq who arrive in Greece or Italy, but continue their journey to North-western Europe, have in fact political and economic motives.

The Belgian case

Belgium has responded to the refugee crisis in an ambivalent way. Theo Francken, the Secretary of State for Asylum, Migration, and Administrative Simplification at the time of the refugee crisis up until the governmental collapse in December 2018, has described Belgium's policy toward asylum seekers 'as strict, but fair, [and] not too gentle'. This presupposes that the Belgian government has gone to great lengths to curb the influx of asylum seekers and economic migrants, and to return those who have no right to live in Belgium to their country of origin or a responsible third country. Francken has used tough public discourse. Concerning undocumented immigrants Francken used wording such as 'chasing them' or 'cleaning up', for instance. Furthermore, he wants to fight human traffickers and supports both the creation of asylum centers and the relocation of application procedures outside Europe as a way to end undocumented immigration. Francken has also criticized what he calls 'Europe's open border policy' as it might—in his eyes—imply the end of the Union. Moreover, he has launched campaigns on social media directed toward Iraqis to discourage them from coming to Belgium. There have been several incidents in which Francken's policy was criticized as too harsh or lacking humanity, such as the case of Sudanese refugees who refused to apply for asylum and were repatriated, after which some of them were allegedly tortured once back in Sudan. This sparked a political crisis in Belgium. Francken maintained his position, however. Public protests also arose against Francken and Belgium's interior minister Jan Jambon (also N-VA) when a Kurdish-Iraqi toddler was killed by a police bullet in the spring of 2018. The girl and her family had been removed from the United Kingdom and were chased by the Belgian police as they tried to return to the UK in a van with other transit migrants (Austin & Rankin, 2018).

The way Francken is portrayed in news media and the type of discourse he maintains seem to suggest that Belgium's immigration and integration policy is in essence a one-man show, and it suggests that a breach in Belgium's immigration and integration policy has appeared in recent years; one from a very liberal to a very restrictive policy. However, there seems to be a large discrepancy between Belgium's actual migration and asylum policy and the way Francken and his administration frame and report on it, the latter being largely tailored for the electorate of the N-VA, a nationalist party (of which Francken is a member) which favors a strict policy on immigration. This discrepancy has been noted both by the left and the far-right (cf. Buxant, 2017). While the policy is presented as extremely strict, statistics from the Belgian Immigration Office and Fedasil, as well as reports by Myria, suggest the opposite: Belgium has become in fact more liberal toward refugees than under Francken's (liberal) predecessor, Maggie De Block. Statistics show that the refugee crisis led to an increase in first-time asylum applications in Belgium from about 1,000 in January 2014 to 6,360 in September 2016, after which a decline set in. From March 2016 on, the number of first-time asylum applications was back to its January 2014 level.

In the 2014-2016 period, most asylum applications were made by Syrians (15,540), Iraqis (10,950), and Afghans (10,760). In 2016, 63 percent of all asylum seekers were male and 37 percent female, with a clear over-representation of men in the 18-34 age category. However, distributions by ethnicity show that the over-representation of (young) males is mainly caused by some refugee groups, first of which are the Afghans (86 percent male). For the Syrians there was only a slight over-representation of men (52 percent male) among the asylum seekers, from which one may assume that many Syrians arrived with their families (Myria, 2017: 90).

The increase in asylum applications in 2014 and 2015 was considerable and required action. It was met by an increase in the number of reception centers. The figures show that the Belgian authorities made sufficient efforts to give shelter to all applicants. On January 1, 2014, reception centers had the capacity to receive 20,182 individuals, with a 73 percent occupancy rate. This number rose to 33,659 on January 1, 2016 when 96 percent of the actual capacity was in use. Subsequently a decline set in, and by January 2018 the number of openings had decreased to 23,283, of which 76 percent were in use (Fedasil, 2018). Also interesting is the evolution of the acceptance rate of asylum applications, which has increased strongly and is very high in the case of Syrians. Next, it seems that with regard to the humanitarian visa, priority was given to Christian Syrians and other religious minorities over Muslims (Myria, 2017). Moreover, there were some rescue actions, e.g., in Aleppo in 2015, which specifically targeted Christians (Decreus, 2015).

A special challenge in Belgium is caused by transit migrants who want to reach the United Kingdom. Many transit migrants used to settle in a self-constructed camp in Calais, Northern France, at a stone's throw from the Belgian border. However, after this so-called 'Jungle of Calais' had been dismantled, security measures were taken to prevent refugees from trying to reach the UK through the port or the Eurotunnel. As a result, migration routes have shifted and Brussels' North station—from where buses depart to Great Britain—has become a new hub to embark on a dangerous trip across the English Channel. Consequently, many refugees cluster in the nearby Maximilian park and live in very poor conditions. This has led to controversy because this is happening only a few kilometers from the European institutions. While the Belgian authorities want the transit migrants to apply for asylum, the targeted group of refugees refuses as they aim to continue their journey—often facilitated by human traffickers—to the United Kingdom, while they lack legal status in Belgium. In order to solve these problems, Belgium and the UK aim to cooperate more intensively (Torfs, 2018).

In late 2018, the United Nations unveiled the Global Compact for Safe, Orderly and Regular Migration which lists 23 objectives and commitments related to migration, highlighting migrant rights and the need for evidence-based migration policies (International Organization for Migration, 2018). The Belgian federal government was involved in its development, and initially agreed to endorse the compact at the UN General Assembly in December 2018. However, in the weeks leading up to this endorsement, majority parties clashed over the contents of the compact, as they did in several other countries. N-VA, citing issues with the compact's content and fearing a new wave of migrants, no longer wanted to endorse the compact and requested that Belgium would abstain from the vote in the General Assembly. Other majority parties disagreed with this stance, and wanted to go ahead with the earlier agreed-upon endorsement. This tension eventually led to the collapse of the Belgian federal government in December 2018. Despite this, Belgium endorsed the compact at the UN General Assembly some weeks later (Segers & Kerckaert, 2018).

The Swedish case

Sweden was one of Europe's main receivers of asylum seekers during the recent refugee crisis. In 2015, Sweden reached a historical high in the number of asylum seekers: almost 163,000 applications were made in that year (Krzyżanowski, 2018; Swedish Migration Agency, 2019). Afterwards the government took action in order to limit the influx of asylum seekers and to minimize potential negative impacts of the refugee crisis on Swedish society. Among the measures taken were the temporary reinstallation of border checks, restrictions on the attainment of residence permits, and attempts to facilitate the repatriation of rejected asylum seekers to their countries of origin. Notwithstanding these restrictive measures, Sweden agreed in 2017 on the relocation of 2,800 refugees who applied for asylum in Italy or Greece. This underlines the willingness of the Swedish government to cooperate with other European administrations regarding migration and integration issues (Swedish Ministry of Justice, 2018).

Notwithstanding the restrictive measures taken from the end of 2015 on, the highest number of granted asylum applications was reached in 2016—due to the time-lag caused by the asylum procedure itself—when, according to the Swedish Migration Agency, 30,863 persons obtained asylum over the months of October, November, and December. In 2017, the number of granted applications started to drop and in 2018 it reached numbers (somewhat more than 10,000 for the whole year), which were actually lower than before the refugee crisis (Swedish Migration Agency, 2019).

The population composition of the asylum-seekers and refugees in Sweden resembles that of Belgium to a very large degree. The greatest numbers of refugees in Sweden are of Syrian, Afghan, and Iraqi origin. For 2016, the numbers of asylum applications for individuals of those origin countries were respectively 5,459, 2,969, and 2,758. Overall, about 60 percent of the applicants were male and some 40 percent were female. The majority of asylum seekers are young: more than half of them were below the age of 25 (Swedish Migration Agency, 2019).

Traditionally, the Nordic countries have the reputation of having generous welcoming policies toward all groups of migrants, including refugees. According to Tanner (2016) this attitude has changed to become more hostile since the rise of populist parties. In Sweden, the Sweden Democrats were founded in 1988 but were paid little attention to in the political debate for almost two decades. In the election of 2010, the party gained enough votes to become represented in the parliament with 20 of the 349 seats. Since then the party has grown in popularity and the anti-multicultural and anti-integration arguments have remained high on the party's agenda. In the elections of 2014 and 2018, the party has consistently gained more votes, the latest outcome being that it holds 62 seats. In the most recent election, the two main parliamentary blocs gained an even number of seats, resulting in 'deadlock' for months. After four months of negotiations between parties it was clear that a new government could be approved and installed in January 2019.

Even in the years prior to the 'refugee crisis' in 2015, the increasing numbers of refugees from Syria and Iraq led to frictions in Swedish society. In August of 2014, the Swedish Prime Minister, Fredrik Reinfeldt, addressed the importance of showing tolerance in his summer speech, a few weeks before the election: "*I know this will cause friction. I therefore call on the Swedish people to show patience and open their hearts*" (quoted in The Local, August 16, 2014). A year later, at the beginning of September, the new Prime Minister, Stefan Löfven, called for the same at a rally for refugees. For the election in 2018, opinion polls showed that immigration and integration were the main issues of concern for voters.

Since turning from being a poor country with a major emigration to North America in the nineteenth and early twentieth centuries to a rich country in the second half of the twentieth century, Sweden has welcomed immigrants and refugees in record numbers. Labor immigration was crucial for the country to develop and become the welfare state it has been recognized as. Back then, an ageing population was not an issue, but now it is one of the top societal challenges for Sweden and many other countries worldwide. The changing demography, due to immigration, has been highlighted as one way to meet this challenge. Integration is seen as one of the key factors in this discussion (cf. Bengtsson & Scott, 2011).

Comparing Belgium and Sweden

While the previous sections drew a more general picture of how the Belgian and Swedish governments have dealt with the refugee crisis, a more systemic comparison of the countries' immigration and integration policies will be discussed in this section. We will focus on key policy areas from the Migrant Integration Policy Index (MIPEX): family reunification, permanent residence, labor market mobility, anti-discrimination, education, political participation, health, and access to nationality. This index is a tool specifically designed to compare the integration policies of all 28 EU member states, along with those of 10 other countries (Australia, Canada, Iceland, Japan, South Korea, New Zealand, Norway, Switzerland, Turkey, and the USA). Through 167 policy indicators, this index attempts to create a multi-layered picture of migrants' opportunities to participate in their new environment. Sweden, with an overall score of 78 percent at the time of the most recent measurement in 2015, is the highest-scoring country in the index. Belgium ranks 7th with a score of 67 percent (see also Table 1.2).

When breaking down the overall integration policy score by policy area, we note that Sweden scores very high on **labor market mobility**, while Belgium's score is much lower. Key aspects in this regard are the fact that in Sweden migrants can look for employment from the day they arrive as there are no distinctions made between Swedish and non-Swedish citizens in labor market regulations. In Belgium, migrants have to obtain citizenship to gain equal rights to public sector jobs, and other regulations also restrict access to the private job market for noncitizens. Access to general support is high in both countries, but it is in terms of targeted support for newcomers that Sweden distinguishes itself from Belgium. In particular the 2009 Labor Market Introduction Act in Sweden laid out a framework which made it easier for newcomers to learn Swedish and find jobs that match their skills (MIPEX, 2015).

In terms of **family reunion**, we find that Sweden and Belgium have similar policies, as newcomers with (at least) one-year permits can be reunited with their partners. In Belgium, members of low-income groups (with an income <120 percent of minimum 'social integration' income level) are not allowed to reunite with their partners. Such an income restriction on family reunion is present in only seven other EU countries. In Sweden, a basic fee per family member is required, with lower fees in effect for refugees and permanent residents. The procedure through which reunion is decided is usually short in both countries, and family members can mount a legal challenge in case of rejection. In Sweden, spouses and adult children admitted under family reunification provisions enjoy near-equal social rights to the Sweden-based families, while in Belgium labor market integration for reunited family members is delayed (MIPEX, 2015).

Sweden has the best policy on **education** for newcomers, particularly in terms of targeting the needs of immigrant pupils and making sure schools facilitate these as much as possible. Schools also receive compensation for extra costs related to bilingual pupils. Furthermore, the Swedish government encourages schools to seize new opportunities in terms of skills that these migrant pupils bring to their education. For pupils it is sometimes possible to choose courses in their mother tongue. Belgium lags somewhat behind in this policy area, as economically disadvantaged pupils often receive insufficient support, and there are no systematic solutions to socio-economic concentration or related problems of high turnover of teachers in disadvantaged schools. A lack of evidence-based policy in this area is also notable in Belgium (MIPEX, 2015).

Neither Belgium nor Sweden scores particularly highly on **health** policy for newcomers. Both countries make efforts to ensure that all newcomers are entitled to the same health benefits as citizens, and access policies are in place to ensure migrants know about these entitlements and other health benefits. In Belgium, it appears problematic that reporting undocumented migrants is not explicitly prohibited in professional codes of conduct. Health services are only partially responsive to the needs of migrants in both Belgium and Sweden—and many other countries in the EU (MIPEX, 2015).

When considering **political participation**, we find a large divide between the two countries. Sweden ranks 7th in this area, and has slightly favorable opportunities for political participation. We note this regarding voting rights (some of the most inclusive in Europe), the strong position of NGOs, and cities' constant experimenting with new methods of democratic and participatory methods for migrants. Voting rights in Belgium are more restricted, having become open to foreigners only since the 2006 local elections. It also appears that in regional elections in Brussels, Flanders, and Wallonia, non-EU citizens do not have voting rights. The consultative bodies (that represent migrants) from Belgium are some of the weakest in Europe. Political liberties are the same in both countries, as non-EU citizens are guaranteed the right to join or form associations or political parties (MIPEX, 2015).

The policy area of **permanent residence** for newcomers is the only one in which Belgium ranks higher than Sweden, even topping all other countries. Here, EU and non-EU citizens are treated equally in their path to permanent residence, simply requiring that they have a basic income. The procedure to obtain permanent residence is often short and clear, but in Sweden there is some cause for concern as this procedure is less discretionary than in most EU countries. In both Belgium and Sweden, any permanent resident may work, study, and live in the country, enjoying the same rights as other citizens. Associated with permanent residency is **access to nationality**. Here, we find that both countries tolerate dual citizenship for both immigrants and emigrants. The eligibility standards are fairly similar, as migrants need to be long-term residents first (e.g., having lived in the country for at least five years, attained permanent residency). Following this, they must also pass 'good character' requirements and pay a basic fee. In Belgium, an additional employment requirement—one of the most demanding in Europe—is also in effect, making the path to obtaining nationality harder (MIPEX, 2015).

The final policy area under consideration in MIPEX is that of **anti-discrimination**. The definition of discrimination in both countries is fairly comprehensive, ensuring that actors cannot discriminate based on ethnicity, religion, nationality, etc. The procedures to enforce these regulations are robust, with legal aid, NGO support, etc. The Interfederal Centre for Equal Opportunities (Belgium) and the Equality Ombudsman (Sweden) are strong institutions which support victims of discrimination. In Sweden, more effort is undertaken to inform the public about discrimination, and to include anti-discrimination clauses in public contracts than in Belgium (MIPEX, 2015).

In any event, the MIPEX evaluates written policy. If the multicultural project does not run deeper than words in official documents, there is a much greater likelihood of failure (see also Michael Adams, 2017).

Similarities and differences

In the course of the twentieth century both Belgium and Sweden transformed from emigration into immigration countries. Both countries faced strong immigration in the post-war era owing to the economic boom they were experiencing. However, after some period of strong labor influx, the governments of both countries felt the urge to curb immigration; in Sweden from the mid-1960s on, and in Belgium in the early 1970s following the oil crisis (Borevi, 2012; Lesthaeghe, 2000). They were successful in reducing immigration in the short run—for some time immigration fell even below emigration—but failed in the long run. Immigration barriers turned temporary migrants into permanent migrants, and as a result of family reunification, family formation, and the influx of refugees, immigration soon started to rise again, and reached figures during the last two decades which have never been registered before (Grönberg, 2013). The recent refugee crises have added to this, but an important structural component is formed by intra-European immigration, which has gone up ever since the Schengen Zone was established and the EU was systemically extended.

Belgium and Sweden have made efforts to receive and integrate newcomers, and both countries strive for a multicultural society, which means that they prefer a salad bowl over a melting pot model (Martens & Caestecker, 2001; Tawat, 2014). This implies that in the imagined ideal society, newcomers enjoy equal opportunities, while they are able to maintain their heritage culture, religion, and identity. In both countries this ideal is only partially put into practice, and it turns out to be a far greater challenge for non-Western immigrants when compared to Western immigrants—but our systematic analysis of the MIPEX scores showed that Sweden out-performs Belgium in all domains of migrant integration, except for the field of obtaining permanent residency. Sweden scores especially well in terms of labor market integration.

The different performances in terms of migrant integration can be partly ascribed to the fact that Sweden developed a comprehensive integration policy much earlier on in the twentieth century, while Belgium kept viewing post-war immigrants as 'temporary elements' in Belgian society until the late 1970s. It was only during the 1990s that a real integration policy was being formulated, when in practice huge disparities between natives and immigrants had already come into being (Martens & Caestecker, 2001). This means that Belgium has been overtaken by events and policies developed since the 1990s aimed largely at healing old wounds, while integration policy should be forethoughtful. The late reaction of the Belgian government is a missed opportunity, but it has above all given incentives to frame immigration in a negative way and to curb it as much as possible, although with no success. During the previous government's tenure, immigration and acceptance rates for asylum seekers have increased further, notwithstanding the strong anti-immigration discourse maintained by the Secretary of State for Asylum, Migration, and Administrative Simplification.

In general, Sweden is a more immigrant-friendly nation than Belgium, and it offers newcomers the same superb social welfare provisions as native-born Swedes. This reveals that Sweden is very generous and regards immigrants as highly valuable. This might be partially related to the fact that Sweden is a relatively large country with a small population, while Belgium is a small country with a relatively large population, but it also signifies cultural differences (Sweden aims to be a leading nation in terms of humanitarian aid and social equality), and a failure of Belgium's government to identify and use immigrants' human capital in an efficient way. More generally, immigration is framed in Sweden in terms of opportunities, while the Belgian government has presented immigration more as a challenge or even a burden. In fact, immigration can be both—an opportunity and a burden—and much depends on the willingness of immigrants to adapt to the host society, and the willingness of the receiving society—both the government and the native population—to assist them in this difficult process. This is rewarding, also economically. The better immigrants perform, for instance, in the labor market, the less they drain from social welfare provisions, and the more they contribute to the maintenance of the social system itself.

No matter what attempts from right-wing parties will be launched to curb immigration, and no matter what kind of sophisticated policy on the European level will be developed, immigration into European member states will continue as long as Europe remains safe and prosperous. It is therefore better and wiser to put the greatest efforts into the integration of immigrants and to develop policies which counteract segregation and discrimination in all domains of society. This requires a positive, open attitude toward newcomers from the receiving society, no matter what reason migrants may have had to move to the receiving country. Governments set an example for society at large by the type of policies they develop and apply, but maybe even more so by the language which politicians use in public. In this respect, Sweden cannot serve only as an example for Belgium, but for the majority of European societies. Government policy should not be guided by fear, but by thoughtfulness, intelligence, foresight, and courage.

References

Adams, M. (2017). *Could it happen here? Canada in the age of Trump and Brexit*. New York: Simon & Schuster.
Austin, R., & Rankin, J. (2018, May 18). Belgian authorities admit two-year old girl was shot after police chase. *The Guardian*.
Bengtsson, T., & Scott, K. (2011). Population aging and the future of the welfare state: The example of Sweden. *Population and Development Review, 37*(Supplement), 158–70.
Betts, A., & Collier, P. (2018). *Refuge: Transforming a broken refugee system*. London: Penguin Books.
Borevi, K. (2012). Sweden: The flagship of multiculturalism. In: G. Brochmann, A. Hagelund, K. Borevi, H. Vad Jønsson (Eds.), *Immigration policy and the Scandinavian welfare state, 1945-2010* (pp. 1–24). Houndmills, Basingstoke, Hampshire & New York: Palgrave Macmillan.
Buxant, M. (2017, December 27). "Avec Francken, on est arrivé à la limite de ce qui est supportable". *L'Echo*.
Castillejo, C. (2017). The EU migration partnership framework. Time for a rethink? *Discussion Paper 28/2017*. German Development Institute.
Collier, P. (2014). *Exodus. Immigration and multiculturalism in the 21st Century*. London: Penguin Books.
Czaika, M., & De Haas, H. (2014). The Globalization of Migration: Has the World Become more Migratory? *International Migration Review, 48*(2), 283–323.
Decreus, T. (2015, July 9). Ernstige vragen bij reddingsactie Syrische Christenen. Dewereldmorgen. be http://www.dewereldmorgen.be/artikel/2015/07/09/ernstige-vragen-bij-reddingsactie-syrische-christenen.
Eurostat (2018). *Asylum and first time asylum applicants by citizenship, age and sex*. Retrieved from http://ec.europa.eu/eurostat/data/database July 1, 2018.
Favell, A., & Hansen, R. (2002). Markets against politics: Migration, EU enlargement and the idea of Europe. *Journal of Ethnic and Migration Studies, 28*(4), 581–601.
Grönberg, P. (2013). Sweden, migration 19th Century to present. In I. Ness (Ed.) *The Encyclopedia of Global Human Migration*. Hoboken, N.J.: Wiley-Blackwell.
International Organization for Migration. (2018). *Global Compact for Migration*. Retrieved from https://www.iom.int/global-compact-migration January 2019.
Krzyżanowski, M. (2018). "We Are a Small Country that Has Done Enormously Lot": The 'Refugee Crisis' and the hybrid discourse of politicizing immigration in Sweden. *Journal of Immigrant & Refugee Studies, 16*(1-2), 97–117.
Lesthaeghe, R. (2000). Transnational Islamic communities in a multilingual secular society. In R. Lesthaeghe (Ed.), *Communities and generations: Turkish and Moroccan populations in Belgium*. Brussel: Vrije Universiteit Brussel – Steunpunt Demografie.
Lucassen, L. (2005). *The immigrant threat. The integration of old and new migrants in Western Europe since 1850*. Urbana and Chicago: University of Illinois Press.
Lucassen, L., & De Haas, H. (2017, October 28). De 'opvang in eigen regio'-mantra is voorlopig niets meer dan een holle Leus. *Trouw*.
Martens, A., & Caestecker, F. (2001). De algemene beleidsontwikkeling sinds 1984. In J. Vrancken, C. Timmerman, & K. Van der Heyden (Eds.), *Komende generaties. Wat we (niet) weten over allochtonen in Vlaanderen*. Leuven: Acco.
MIPEX (2015). *Migrant Policy Index*. Retrieved from www.mipex.eu July 15, 2018.
Myria (2017). *Migratie in cijfers en in rechten*. Brussels: Myria Federal Migration Centre.
Segers, F., & Kerckaert, P. (2018, December 19). VN-migratiepact goedgekeurd in New York: 152 voor, 12 onthoudingen, 5 tegen [UN-migration pact approved in New York: 152 for, 12

abstentions, 5 against]. *VRT NWS – Flanders News.be*. Retrieved from https://www.vrt.be/vrtnws/nl/2018/12/19/belgie-stemt-keurt-vn-migratiepact-in-new-york-goed/ January 2019.

Swedish Migration Agency (2019), Asylum. Retrieved from https://www.migrationsverket.se/English/About-the-Migration-Agency/Statistics/Asylum.html/ January 2019.

Swedish Ministry of Justice (2018). 'Sweden's Migration and Asylum Policy', Factsheet February 2018. Retrieved from https://www.government.se/491b2f/contentassets/84c1ec8c729f4be384a5ba6dddeb0606/swedens-migration-and-asylum-policy January 2019.

Tanner, A. (2016). Overwhelmed by refugee flows, Scandinavia tempers its warm welcome. Migration Policy Institute, Washington. Retrieved from https://www.migrationpolicy.org/article/overwhelmed-refugee-flows-scandinavia-tempers-its-warm-welcome August 27, 2018.

Tawat, M. (2014). Danish and Swedish immigrants' cultural policies between 1960 and 2006: Toleration and the celebration of difference. *International Journal of Cultural Policies*, *20*(2), 202–220.

The Local: *Reinfeldt Calls for Tolerance to Refugees*. (2014, August 16). Retrieved from https://www.thelocal.se/20140816/reinfeldt-calls-for-tolerance-to-refugees on August 27, 2018.

Torfs, M. (2018, February 27). UK to help out Belgium to clamp down on transit migration. *VRT NWS – Flanders News.be*. Retrieved from https://www.vrt.be/vrtnws/en/2018/02/27/u_k_to_help_out_belgiumtoclampdownontransitmigration-1-3154282/ August 2018.

UNHCR (2018, August 03). UNHCR sounds alarm as Mediterranean Sea deaths pass 1,500 mark. Retrieved from http://www.unhcr.org/news/press/2018/8/5b6476bd4/unhcr-sounds-alarm-mediterranean-sea-deaths-pass-1500-mark.html August 2018.

PART II

MEDIA REPRESENTATIONS

Chapter 3
The Refugee Situation as Portrayed in News Media: A Content Analysis of Belgian and Swedish Newspapers – 2015-2017

Rozane De Cock, Ebba Sundin, and Valériane Mistiaen

Introduction

In the fall of 2015, one of the most common images carried by the European news media was that of refugees walking along train tracks in the hope of reaching various destinations in Europe. Their faces showed tiredness, worry, but also relief. For many of them the long journey by foot was par for the course after the dangerous crossing of the Mediterranean Sea.

The media expounded on many themes—the journey itself, the political reactions in the various European countries, the European Union's ponderous scramble for solutions likely to help these people seeking the safety of the EU borders, and civil society's response to what has been referred to as the refugee crisis.

In this chapter we compare the portrayal of the refugee crisis in Swedish and Belgian newspapers from 2015 to 2017: news reporting, features, debates, columns, and letters to the editors. The portrayal touches on many facets of the European situation in the three years in question: from compassion and humanitarian concerns to racism and xenophobia.

News reporting on refugees

Studies that pertain to refugees and immigration can be found within the 'agenda setting' research field. Many have their starting-point in specific cultural areas and countries. In Belgium and Sweden the issue has attracted many researchers over a long period of time, since both nations have a history of immigration.

In a recent report Strömbäck, Andersson, and Nedlund (2017) conclude that Swedish studies focus on various aspects of the refugees and immigration issue, such as historical overviews, stereotyping, and racism, adding that few studies look at the way the news media are portraying this issue—especially from 2010 on. What they found in their literature overview was that the news media are problem-orientated and that they tend to focus on the point of view of the authorities (see also Chapter 5). In their study of newspaper reporting between 2010 and 2015, they conclude that negative portrayals of refugees are more common than positive ones. This is in line with older research by Van Gorp (2005) indicating that in Belgian newspapers refugees were most often portrayed as victims or intruders and the existence of a negativity bias in Flemish television news (Jacobs, Meeusen, & d'Haenens, 2016). De Cleen et al. (2017) stress the discursive continuity of negative discourse on migration-related topics in Flanders and thus also in the latest 'refugee crisis'. This discourse is, according to them, only adapted to the current situation and is therefore still portraying refugees as a cultural, economic, or security threat.

Furthermore, Strömbäck et al. (2017) mention a UNHCR report that focuses on news reporting on the refugee situation (Berry, Garcia-Blanco, & Moore, 2016). This report highlights differences in coverage of the refugees/migrants issue in five EU countries, and concludes that the most positive reporting is that of Swedish newspapers as compared to coverage in Spain, Italy, Germany, and the UK. Compared to Strömbäck et al. (2017), this shows that while negative portrayal of refugees dominated in the Swedish newspapers, it was still more positive than that to be found in the press of other European countries.

The UNHCR report devotes one chapter to the Swedish press coverage. Written by Askanius and Linné (2016), this chapter is based on a sample of circa 300 articles from a nine-month period in 2014-2015. Immigration figures, mortality statistics, mafia/trafficking, and political response/policy are among the themes that score high for all three Swedish newspapers. Both Strömbäck et al. (2017) and Berry et al. (2016) provide descriptions of the media representation of the refugee situation up to 2015—that is almost our study's starting point. Furthermore a number of studies review previous research on the portrayal of refugees/migrants in European and Scandinavian countries. For example, Camauër (2011) lists some of the early works of the 2000s and concludes as follows:

> Generally, the reviews suggest that a majority of the studies have concluded that ethnic minority groups, refugees and migrants often appear in the reporting as unadjusted, marginalized, crime perpetrators and/or 'threats', and are stereotypically represented. (Camauër, 2011: 38)

Horsti, Hultén, and Titley (2014) contribute to the field with their work on national public service media (PSM) as well as a comparison between some European countries, including Belgium and Sweden (Flemish Public Broadcasting and Swedish Public Service media and their policies and programs on cultural diversity). The study targets the policy question among the national PSM companies. The Belgian perspective has its own complexity owing to the country's multilingual structure. Nevertheless, Dhoest (2014: 119) concludes that "the presence of ethnic minorities in Flemish public broadcasting is problematic but not hopeless". As for the Swedish study, it highlights a lack of focus on diversity issues in the policy documents (Hultén, 2014).

Chouliaraki and Zaborowski (2017) conducted a content analysis of 1,200 articles selected in the newspapers of countries that lay on the migratory routes used during the 2015 refugee crisis: Greece, Serbia, Hungary, Czech Republic, and Germany. It is worth mentioning that politicians' voices dominate the press coverage at the expense of citizens and refugees, which "reconstitutes and re-legitimizes their exclusion" (p. 629). According to Chouliaraki and Zaborowski (2017) this is done by silencing them as well as through decontextualization and collectivization, e.g., including refugees into collective referents such as nationality. Moreover the authors argue that using humanitarian and security-oriented terminology and portraying refugees as victims or threats contributes to the 'refugee misrecognition'. The work of Sumuvuori et al. (2016) comparing Finnish, British, and Belgian newspapers (the quality papers *Le Soir* and *De Morgen*) on their reporting on refugees during early 2016 also concludes that politicians and experts are given a forum in the press, whereas refugees remain voiceless (see also Chapter 5).

The last two arguments are put forward by the Council of Europe report *Media Coverage of the 'Refugee Crisis': A Cross-European Perspective*, by Georgiou and Zaborowski (2017), who content-analyzed the quality press of eight European countries (Czech Republic, France, Germany, Greece, Hungary, Ireland, Serbia, and UK) from July to November 2015 to pinpoint any evolution in the news coverage. They labeled a first period as 'careful tolerance' in connection with the mass drownings in the Mediterranean Sea (July). A second period was titled 'ecstatic humanitarianism' as Europe appeared for once as "a place of (relative) solidarity to the plight of asylum seekers" (Georgiou & Zaborowski, 2017: 8) after Alan Kurdi's death. The last month of the study (November) coincided with an increase of 'fear and securitization' in the wake of the Paris terrorist attacks. Although briefly discussed, this study also stressed that differences in coverage depend on various factors such as historical, socioeconomic, and political context, press culture, media regulation, ideology, and freedom (Georgiou & Zaborowski,

2017: 11-14). In this respect, it is important to set up multicultural comparative studies such as the IM2MEDIATE project. Not only are totally opposing media cultures worth an in-depth analysis; countries belonging to the same type of media system can also show intriguing differences and similarities. Within the widely used taxonomy of media systems by Hallin and Mancini (2004), Belgium and Sweden, along with the other Nordic countries, are part of the democratic corporatist section. Nevertheless, of all these countries, Belgium is the closest to the polarized pluralist model (Hallin & Mancini, 2004, p. 169), which turns the comparison between the two countries' news reporting on refugees into an interesting case study.

Methodology

This chapter is based on the findings of a quantitative content analysis of Belgian and Swedish newspapers' representations of the refugees and immigration issue in the years 2015-2017. The study was divided into 11 periods spanning between March 21, 2015 and July 4, 2017. Period 1 runs from March 21 to April 4, 2015. The idea here was to look at a period predating the summer of 2015, generally seen as the start of the so-called refugee crisis. Period 2 runs from August 24 to September 20, 2015 and corresponds to the start of the 'crisis' period, which encompasses the appearance of refugee camps in Brussels' Maximilian Park, the drowning of Alan Kurdi, and German chancellor Angela Merkel's "Wir schaffen das". The third period is the week of September 21-27, 2015. This was when European leaders reached an agreement on the settlement of refugees in the various EU member states as proposed by François Hollande and Angela Merkel. Only Hungary, Romania, Slovakia, and the Czech Republic voted against the agreement. Period 4 runs from October 7 to November 6, 2015 (the start of the resettlement in other EU member states of refugees having entered the EU through Greece and Italy). The fifth period revolves around the Cologne incident (January 1-7, 2016), in which many women were sexually assaulted during the German city's New Year's Eve celebrations. In the news this incident was linked by officials to refugees and migrants, sparking a heated debate on crime, refugees, cultural threats, and racism. It was in period 6 (March 17-23, 2016) that a highly controversial agreement was struck between the EU and Turkey, under which Turkey would prevent refugees from entering the EU in exchange for the cash needed to shelter them in Turkish camps as well as relaxed visa rules for Turkish people. The seventh period is that of the Olympic Games (August 5-22, 2016), which saw teams of refugee athletes enter the competition. Period 8 includes the key moment of the Hungarian referendum (October 2 to 9, 2016), which asked the following question: *"Do you want the European Union to be entitled to prescribe the mandatory settlement of non-Hungarian citizens in Hungary without the consent of Parliament?"* A clear signal was sent to the EU when 98 percent of the voters answered in the negative, even though quorum requirements (participation of at least 50 percent of registered voters) were not met. The ninth period (October 17-30, 2016) is that of the 'dismantlement of the Calais Jungle'—the forcible evacuation of a long-established refugee camp in Calais, a French town close to the Belgian border and the gateway to the UK. Adoption by the Hungarian Parliament of a law making it possible to detain asylum seekers upon arrival corresponds to our tenth period (March 7-13, 2017). Finally, period 11 runs from June 28 to July 4, 2017, a time when Italy considered closing its ports to NGO ships.

For the purposes of this study a total of 1,832 articles on refugees published by four Belgian newspapers (two Dutch-language and two French-language titles) and two Swedish newspapers were content-analyzed. Data collection was done using the GOPress, Europresse, and Factiva archives as well as online news media subscriptions (Belgium), and Media Archive Retriever (Sweden). For each media landscape, the main national quality newspaper and the largest popular newspaper were content-analyzed. All articles were at least 300 words long and contained the word *refugee* and/or the local language variants and synonyms.

The two Swedish newspapers are *Dagens Nyheter* and *Aftonbladet*. *Dagens Nyheter* can be described as an independent liberal daily newspaper (seven issues a week), founded in 1862. It is the quality paper with the highest circulation rates among national newspapers (over 600,000 copies—TS, 2016). *Aftonbladet* is a popular daily (seven issues a week), founded in 1830 and described as independent and social democratic. It ranks among Sweden's major national popular papers, with a circulation of circa 550,000 copies (TS, 2016). In total, 977 Swedish items were content-analyzed. The distribution between the two papers was: *Dagens Nyheter* (606) and *Aftonbladet* (371).

The Belgian Dutch-language newspapers include *De Standaard* and *Het Laatste Nieuws*. *De Standaard* was founded in 1918 as part of a Catholic-conservative tradition. In 2014-2015, according to the Belgian Information Center on Media (CIM), it was Flanders' most read quality newspaper (16.9 percent of total coverage) while *Het Laatste Nieuws* reached 36.4 percent of the overall newspaper readership (CIM, 2018). Created in 1888 to support the Liberal Belgian Party, this paper is part of the *Persgroep* publishing company and is the most popular daily in Flanders. *Le Soir* is the most read broadsheet in French-language Belgium. In 2014-2015, it reached 18.7 percent of the total newspaper readership. *Le Soir* was founded in 1887 by Emile Rossel as a politically independent paper within a liberal tradition. It is now part of the powerful *Rossel* group. The last newspaper in our study is the French-language *L'Avenir*, whose audience reach is 15.6 percent (CIM 2018). It is a Catholic daily first published in 1918. Today, *L'Avenir* is also the name of a Wallonia-oriented media group of nine newspapers—a major name in Belgium. In total, 855 articles were studied for Belgium: 298 articles from *De Standaard*, 267 from *Het Laatste Nieuws*, 81 from *Le Soir*, and 209 from *L'Avenir*. Different article genres such as news reports, interviews, in-depth documentaries, editorials, columns, and letters to the editors are included in the sample as the selection of all these genres is part of the inclusion versus exclusion decisions taken by news professionals in a newsroom resulting in a final news product: the newspaper.

The research team developed a coding instrument (inspired by Berry, Garcia-Blanco, & Moore, 2016) that went through multiple rounds of adjustments before pre-testing. The quantitative analysis was based on 51 variables. Some of the variables and variable values are the same as those of the UNHCR report, which will contribute to more comparable analyses. Twenty-two different themes were identified (number 23 was labeled "other" and mainly included articles about culture or art). The themes ranged from immigration figures to (human) rights to journey-related matters (search and rescue, mafia/traffic, mortality figures, aid supplies, humanitarian issues, rejection rate, etc.), to the immigration issue itself (civil and political response, racism), to all aspects pertaining to arrival and settlement (reception, post-arrival integration, economic threat, threat to national security, cultural threat, health risk for the country of destination, crime against/by refugees, success stories, etc.). Intercoder reliability was measured on a sample of Swedish ($n = 30$) and Belgian news articles ($n = 30$). Cohen's kappa showed perfect reliability for some variables such as *mentioning immigration figures* and *mentioning success stories*. Other variables had a reliability score higher than .90 (for example, *gender*), or higher than .80 (among others, *post-arrival integration, educational and occupational background*). The *religion, racism, mentioning humanitarian dimensions,* and *degree of collective portrayal* variables scored above .70, with only a few variables scoring between .60 and .70 (such as *family background*).

In each news story the first three refugees mentioned were coded by gender in order of appearance. The total number of refugee and non-refugee actors quoted or paraphrased was also calculated. We recorded all mentions of religion—e.g., Christian, Muslim. The degree of *collective portrayal* was coded on a scale from 1 (highly collective portrayal) to 5 (highly individual portrayal) based on plural nouns, personal pronouns, statistics, and figures or metaphoric language used (e.g., floods, wave).

Research question and hypotheses

For comparison purposes between the Swedish and Belgian newspapers, we formulated the following research question and hypotheses as guidelines for the comparative content analysis, based on the literature as presented above.
RQ: *What were the most important thematic topics pertaining to refugees in the Swedish and Belgian newspapers in 2015-2017?*
H1: *Swedish newspapers pay more attention (expressed as prominence in the news, number and length of articles) to refugees than the Belgian press does.*
H2: *As time goes by, newspapers will devote less attention (expressed as a decrease in newsworthiness based on number and length of articles) to refugees.*
H3: *'News domestication' results in the newspapers referring to the home country as the most important location of the news story—this for Sweden as well as Belgium.*
H4: *The 'most important country of origin' ranking does not match that of the asylum seekers registered in the two countries under study.*
H5a: *In news articles refugees are mostly presented as a collective rather than as individuals.*
H5b: *The Swedish press is less likely to portray refugees in a collective way than the Belgian press.*

Results

First of all, we compared Swedish and Belgian newspapers with respect to the major thematic topics applied to refugees. When comparing the whole sample, we clearly see resemblances and differences between the two countries (Table 3.1). In both countries the papers primarily focus on political responses to the refugee situation and they both do so in nearly a quarter of all articles. Where they diverge is with the second most important theme: while the Belgian dailies zoom in on the aid supplies, the Swedish newspapers point at civil society's response. Post-arrival integration is the third most common theme in the Belgian press, while in the Swedish press this place is taken by pieces on the refugees' ordeal on land and at sea. Remarkably, the 'journey' theme is four times less frequent in the Belgian press. Welfare related events are reported on twice as often in Swedish newspapers, which also mention human rights more often. The 'threat to national security' theme is mentioned six times more often in Belgium as compared to Sweden. This might be explained by the March 2016 terrorist attacks in Brussels' subway and airport. A refugee as an economic threat, however, is not a commoner theme in Belgian newspapers. Crimes committed by refugees, mortality figures, and mafia/

Table 3.1: Most important themes in news articles on refugees in per cent (N = 1832)

Theme	Belgium	Sweden
1. Immigration figures	3.2	2.0
2. Welfare	1.9	5.2
3. Aid supplies	18.9	5.3
4. Human rights	1.6	4.2
5. Refugee success stories	1.2	2.0
6. Civil society response	4.1	12.6
7. Political response/policy	25.3	26.1
8. Receiving refugees	5.3	3.2
9. Post-arrival integration	8.5	6.4
10. Humanitarian	3.7	2.5
11. Economic threat	1.5	2.5
12. Threat to national security	1.9	0.3
13. Cultural threat	0.8	0.5
14. Health risk for country of destination	0.2	0.1
15. Crime by refugees	2.3	0.9
16. Mortality figures	2.8	0.5
17. Search and rescue	1.1	0.7
18. Mafia/traffic	2.3	0.6
19. Journey	2.7	10.6
20. Rejecting	4.3	3.6
21. Crime on refugees	1.5	2.3
22. Racism	2.1	5.3
23. Other	2.7	2.5

Note: $X^2 (22) = 249, p < .001$

traffic are more present in the Belgian than in the Swedish press. Crimes and racist acts against refugees are more readily condemned by Swedish journalists than by their Belgian counterparts.

Newspaper attention, region, and evolution throughout time

Looking at the number of articles written on the refugee issue in the three years under study, we see that overall the two Swedish newspapers devote more attention to refugees (53.3 percent, $n = 977$) than all four Belgian newspapers combined (47.6 percent, $n = 855$), expressed both in percentages and absolute numbers. Concerning Belgium, taking regional differences into account the Dutch-language press devotes twice as many articles to refugees (30.8 per cent, $n = 565$) as its French-language counterpart (15.8 percent, $n = 290$).

Another indicator of prominence in the news is word count. To compare word count in our three language regions (Sweden as well as Dutch- and French-language Belgium) an ANOVA test was performed, combined with a post-hoc Gabriel test for unequal group sizes ($F(2,1828) = 29.9, p < .001$). This showed that Swedish newspapers not only outweigh their Belgian counterparts in sheer number of published pieces pertaining to refugees, but also that Swedish articles are on average much longer ($M = 813$) than Dutch-language ($M = 663$) and French-language articles ($M = 516$). The Dutch-language articles are also significantly longer than the French-language ones.

Prominence in the news can also be shown by studying the layout of newspapers in terms of item priority. An ANOVA test shows that, on average, news stories on refugees appear on page 10 of Belgium's French-language papers, on page 12 in Swedish newspapers and even further back in Dutch-language newspapers (M = page 17); $F(2,1828) = 59.6, p < .001$. In other words our three regions are quite different with respect to the location of the relevant articles. Our data thus confirm Hypothesis 1, which states that Swedish newspapers pay more attention to refugees than the Belgian press does, except for article position, with French-language newspapers tending to be more upfront with their stories on refugees.

News cycle attention research predicts a decrease in newsworthiness as a topic gradually loses urgency. In other words our second hypothesis is that as time goes by newspapers will pay less attention to the refugee issue. This will be indicated by a decrease in news prominence—fewer articles published in a specific time period and smaller word count. Table 3.2 shows that in the spring of 2015 refugees bound for Europe already faced untold dangers—without the press feeling the need to report on this. Based on the total number of days content-analyzed as part of our study (10.1 percent), period 1 is clearly underreported (only 1.7 percent of the total number of published articles). However, reality indicators (see literature review) show that large numbers of refugees were already coming to Sweden and Belgium—a reality newspapers failed to reflect at the time. Seen from this perspective, period 7 (12.2 percent

Table 3.2: Published articles on refugees (in n and %) per time period (2015-2017) in Swedish and Belgian newspapers compared to percentage of days in data collection period.

Period	Percentage of days in data collection period	Frequency published articles	Percentage of published articles
1	10.1	32	1.7
2	19.0	656	35.8
3	4.7	115	6.3
4	20.3	398	21.7
5	4.7	80	4.4
6	4.7	88	4.8
7	12.2	106	5.8
8	4.7	69	3.8
9	9.5	161	8.8
10	5.4	70	3.8
11	4.7	57	3.1
Total	100.0	1832	100.0

versus 5.8 percent coverage) is underreported as well. Looking at period 3 through 6, and 8 through 11, we notice that news coverage is in line with the expected, proportional attention expressed in number of days. Period 2 encompasses no less than 35.8 percent of all articles in the sample, while time period length would lead us to expect a more proportionate amount of news attention—about 19 percent.

Indeed, news attention suddenly peaks when the events of the summer of 2015 place the refugee issue squarely in the spotlight, with almost 36 percent of all articles published between 2015 and 2017. When plotting all articles on a graph (figure 3.1), what emerges is the typical pattern of a news wave as described by Wien and Elmelund-Præstekær (2009) and Vasterman (2005): the news cycle attention peaks in period 2, 4, and 9, reaching its highest level at first in period 2. This is followed by a calmer period 3, then by a second but lower peak in period 4. News attention ebbs before rising for the third time in period 9—a curve far less steep—before fading away throughout periods 10 and 11. Since our data collection stops at the beginning of July 2017 and reporting follows the typical pattern of a structural news wave (Vasterman, 2005), a new theme within the general refugee issue might generate another

Figure 3.1: Evolution in news attention expressed as number of published articles on refugees per studied time period (2015-2017) in Swedish and Belgian newspapers.

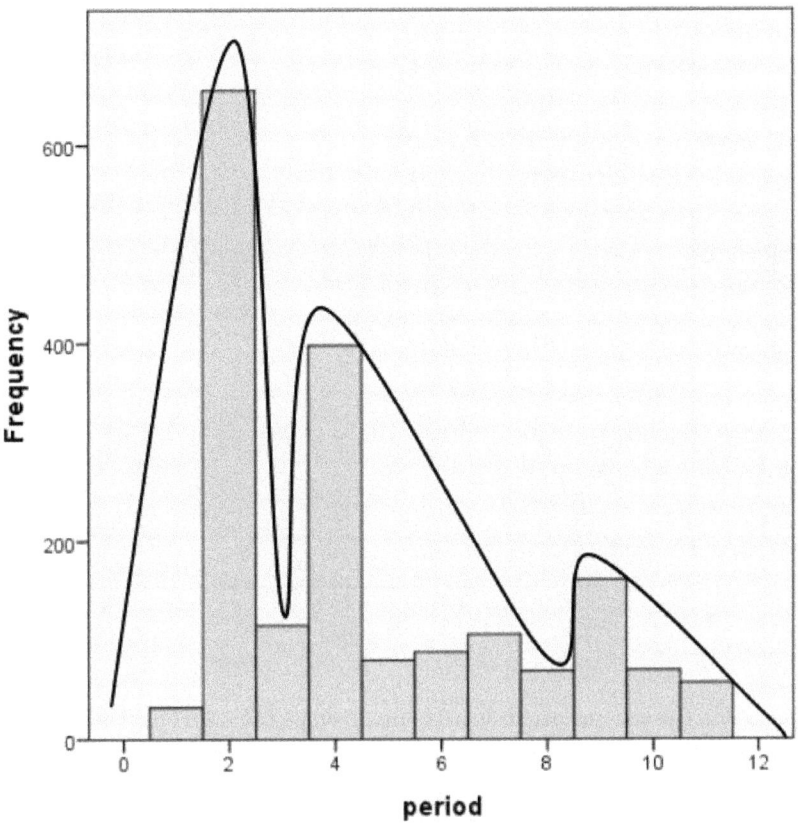

news cycle, although the starting peak is unlikely to reach the intensity of the one generated in the summer of 2015 (period 2).

As already mentioned, an article's word count is another indicator of a topic's prominence. Throughout our eleven periods there is only one significant increase in word count ($F(10,1820) = 3.34, p < .001$), namely in our fifth period (see Figure 3.2). In this period negative news stories focused on the New Year's Eve mass sexual assaults that took place in Cologne and other German cities, with links to crimes committed by migrants and refugees, often drawing on information given by officials. The length of these negative stories increases to an average of 1,022 words, to be contrasted with the word count of stories published in the summer of 2015 (the first news peak). These were no more than 653 words long on average, which is more in line with the overall average word count of the news articles ($M = 720, SD = 621$). Period 8

Figure 3.2: Evolution of average article word length during the studied periods in Swedish and Belgian newspapers

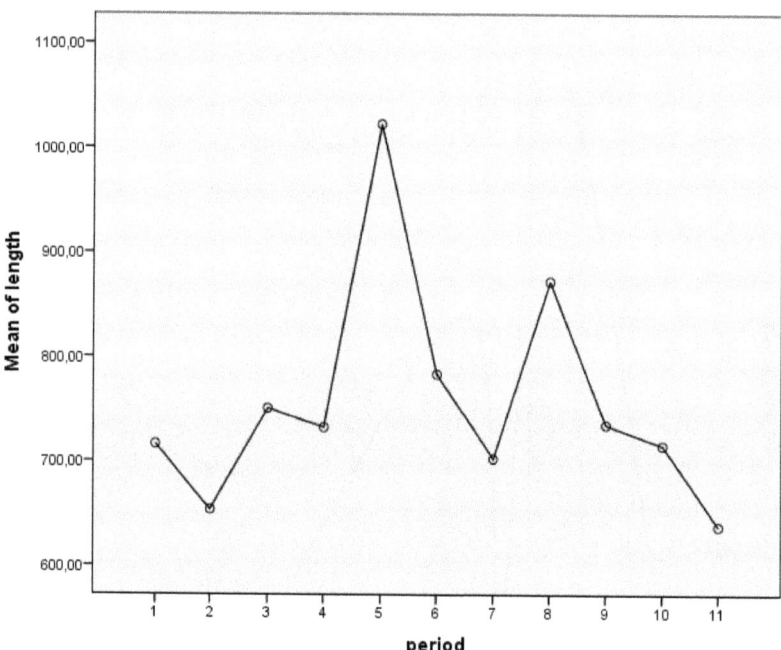

generated the second largest word count average ($M = 871$) but the post hoc test does not show a significant difference from the other time periods. The stories in period 8 focus on the popular rejection of the mandatory settlement by the EU of "non-Hungarians" (i.e., refugees) in Hungary. Period 11 has the shortest articles ($M = 637$), but our hypothesis that news articles on refugees may become shorter in time is refuted.

Focus of news location

As per Hypothesis 3, the newspapers under study primarily focused on events that took place in their own country. In the case of Belgian newspapers nearly 60 percent of all stories on refugees are resolutely Belgian-centric. In Swedish newspapers Belgium is mentioned in only about 1 percent of all articles. Sweden is the first and most-often-mentioned location of news stories on refugees throughout the whole Swedish sample (circa 65 percent), while Sweden is only mentioned as most important location in less than 1 percent of the Belgian pieces. This is a significant difference between the two countries ($X^2(18) = 1190, p < .001$), in line with the 'news domestication'

Table 3.3: Real world percentage of asylum seeker applications by country of origin (top3) compared to newspaper world share of attention for asylum seekers by country of origin for Belgium and Sweden in 2015 – 2017.

Year	Country of origin	EU-28 %	% share Belgium	Newspaper % Belgium	% share Sweden	Newspaper % Sweden
2015	Syria	29	26	29.0	33	29.3
	Afghanistan	14	20	3.6	26	3.1
	Iraq	10	24	5.2	13	2.6
2016	Syria	28	16	20.4	21	17.3
	Afghanistan	15	16	6.3	10	3.9
	Iraq	11	5	4.1	9	1.4
2017	Syria	16	19	23.6	24	6.9
	Afghanistan	7	7	3.6	< 7	5.6
	Iraq	7	< 6	10.9	7	2.8

Note: 2015: $X^2(7) = 386$; $p < .001$; 2016: $X^2(6) = 73$; $p < .001$; 2017: $X^2(6) = 16$; $p < .001$ (Source for EU-28 and percentage share for Belgium and Sweden: Eurostat 2016b, 2017 and 2018c)

hypothesis, which states that a newspaper's home country is the main location mentioned in its articles. The EU in general is the second most mentioned location in both Belgian and Swedish newspapers (circa 10 percent). The balance is equally made up by neighboring countries. No peak in percentages occurs in mentions of Italy, Greece, and Turkey, even though most refugees entered the EU through these countries' borders. The same can also be said for Syria, Afghanistan, and Iraq: less than 2 percent of the articles have these countries as main location.

Hypothesis 4 states that the 'most important country of origin' ranking does not match the country of origin ranking of asylum seekers registered in the two countries under study. To test this hypothesis, in addition to each country's ranking of the countries of origin, we also determined specific shares in the total number of asylum applications filed in Belgium and in Sweden (Eurostat, 2016b; 2017; 2018c). Generally speaking, with respect to actual shares of asylum seekers from the main countries of origins (for both Belgium and Sweden), the ranking follows the top 3 throughout 2015-2017, as shown in Table 3.3.

While this ranking is mostly respected in the newspaper articles, the prominence attributed to the share of nationalities of refugees in reality does not correspond to their visibility in newspaper articles. The main focus of both Belgian and Swedish articles is on Syrian refugees. They do remain the largest share of refugees throughout the years under study, but this intense focus on Syrians in newspaper reporting is at the expense of other nationalities such as Afghanis and Iraqis. In 2015 almost one third of the news articles concentrated on Syrian refugees in Belgium and Sweden. This makes sense as the actual share of Syrian refugees is more or less the same in the two countries. Afghan and Iraqi refugees can be considered to have been overlooked as they are underrepresented in the newspaper world: with a share of only about 3 percent in Belgian and Swedish newspapers in 2015, Afghanis are heavily underrepresented compared to their share of a quarter to a fifth of the total number of asylum seekers in Belgium and Sweden. The same holds true for Iraqis, with an actual share of 24 percent in Belgium and 13 percent in Sweden, while their newspaper share is only a few percent. This phenomenon recurs in 2016 and 2017, with the Belgian press over-representing the Syrian refugees as compared with the official Eurostat statistics. Such is not the case for Sweden: Syrians are underrepresented in the newspaper share, as seen in Table 3.3.

Individual or collective portrayal?

Representing refugees as a faceless throng fleeing a foreign land while facing death tends to deny them any individuality. Based on previous studies of 'refugee reporting', we expect the news articles to portray refugees more as a massive group rather than individuals. For the whole sample in general the slant of the articles is indeed moderately to highly collective ($M = 1.51$, $SD = 1.07$). Three quarters (76.5 percent) of all Belgian and Swedish articles represent refugees as a massive, undifferentiated group—an unending stream. On the other end of the continuum, less than 4 percent of all articles portray refugees in an individual fashion. Finally, about 20 percent of the articles mix collective and individual portrayals.

We expected the Swedish press to portray refugees in a less monolithic manner. For these statistical results we looked at the Swedish versus the Belgian articles (t-test) and then separately at the Dutch-language articles, the French-language articles, and the Swedish articles (ANOVA-test). Both tests showed that our hypothesis was not supported. We measured 'collectivity' on a scale from 1= very collective to 5= very individual. The Swedish press portrays the refugees in a significantly more collective manner ($M = 1.35$) as compared with the Belgian press ($M = 1.69$) ($t(1505,1830) = 6.74, p < .001$). Of the three regions under study Sweden ($M = 1.35$) remains the one whose press has the most collective outlook on refugees, with Belgium's French-language (M = 1.8) and Dutch-language (M = 1.63) papers tending to favor individual points of view more ($F(2, 1829)=26.5, p < .001$).

Conclusion

This study's overall research question was an attempt to define the most important themes to be found in Swedish and Belgian newspapers in the years 2015-2017 regarding the refugee crisis. To answer this question we content-analyzed 1,832 news articles published in six newspapers over 11 periods based on major events.

As indicated by our results there were many different themes accompanying both the coverage of the crisis and the debates it provoked. In both countries political responses—both negative and positive—focused on domestic points of view. Our first four hypotheses were confirmed. Swedish newspapers published more numerous and longer articles on the topic. We identified three peak attention periods (period 2, period 4, and to a smaller extent period 9) but the summer of 2015 (period 2) remains the most important period in terms of news production. This period corresponds to what Georgiou and Zaborowski (2017) labeled "ecstatic humanitarianism". Our fourth hypothesis shed light on the fact that the actual ranking of the countries of origin of registered asylum seekers did not reflect the press's attempts at classification. The main focus in both Belgian and Swedish newspapers is on Syrian refugees. This is a problem inasmuch it could lead to public misperception of the "real" and "good" refugees (Szcepanik, 2016) coming from Syria as they embody the "dreamed archetype of the refugee" (Akoka, 2011) and deserve media attention, as opposed to "the others" coming from other countries and being underexposed.

The results also showed differences between Belgian and Swedish news coverage, however. Our last hypothesis was not confirmed as our findings did not point to a more individualized portrayal of refugees in the Swedish press as compared to Belgium. Future research can look at new trends of news attention with respect to refugees, as well as possible links with recurring news waves. An interesting, extra time period would be the one defined by the Aquarius controversy (a humanitarian ship whose attempts to bring refugees ashore were repeatedly thwarted by the Italian government) as well as the welcoming attitude of the Spanish government (June 2018). In the first seven months of 2018 Spain was the country through which the most refugees entered the EU, with the support of a European Commission intent on managing the growing migratory flows across the Mediterranean and the shift from Italian to Spanish harbors (Reuters, 01/08/2018).

References

Akoka, K. (2011). L'archétype rêvé du refugié. *Plein droit, 90*, 13–16.

Askanius, T., & Linné, T. (2016). Sweden. In M. Berry, I. Garcia-Blanco, & K. Moore. *Press coverage of the refugee and migrant crisis in the EU: A content analysis of five European countries.* Geneva: United Nations High Commissioner for Refugees.

Berry, M., Garcia-Blanco, I., & Moore, K. (2016). *Press coverage of the refugee and migrant crisis in the EU: A content analysis of five European countries.* Geneva: United Nations High Commissioner for Refugees.

Camauër, L. (2011). 'Drumming, drumming, drumming': Diversity work in Swedish newsrooms. In K. Eide & K. Nikunen (Eds.), *Media in motion. Cultural complexity and migration in the Nordic region.* Surrey: Ashgate Publishing Limited.

Chouliaraki, L., & Zaborowski, R. (2017). Voice and community in the 2015 refugee crisis: A content analysis of news coverage in eight European countries. *The International Communication Gazette, 79*(6-7), 613–635.

CIM, Information Center for Media (2018). *Press audience in Belgium.* Retrieved July 17, 2018, from https://www.cim.be/fr/presse/press-audience.

De Cleen, B., Zienkowski, J., Smets, K., Dekie, A., & Vandevoordt, R. (2017). Constructing the 'refugee crisis' in Flanders. Continuities and adaptations of discourses on asylum and migration. In M. Barlai, B. Fähnrich, C. Griessler & M. Rhomberg (Eds.), *The migrant crisis: European perspectives and national discourses* (pp. 59–78). Berlin: LIT Verlag.

Dhoest, A. (2014). Struggling with multiculturalism? Cultural diversity in Flemish public broadcasting policies and programmes. In K. Horsti, G. Hultén, & G. Titley (Eds.), *National Conversations. Public Service Media and Cultural Diversity in Europe.* Bristol: Intellect.

Eurostat (2016a). *Asylum in the EU Member States. More than 410 000 first time asylum seekers registered in the third quarter of 2015.* Retrieved September 7, 2017, from http://ec.europa.eu/eurostat/statistics-explained/index.php/Asylum_quarterly_report.

Eurostat (2016b). *Asylum in the EU Member States. Record number of over 1.2 million first time asylum seekers registered in 2015 Syrians, Afghans and Iraqis: top citizenships.* Retrieved July 16, 2018, from http://ec.europa.eu/eurostat/documents/2995521/7203832/3-04032016-AP-EN.pdf/790eba01-381c-4163-bcd2-a54959b99ed6.

Eurostat (2017). *Asylum applicants in the EU: 2016.* Retrieved July 16, 2018, from http://ec.europa.eu/eurostat/news/themes-in-the-spotlight/asylum2016.

Eurostat (2018a). *Number of asylum applicants: drop in 2017.* Retrieved July 16, 2018, from http://ec.europa.eu/eurostat/statistics-explained/index.php/Asylum_statistics#Number_of_asylum_applicants:_drop_in_2017.

Eurostat (2018b). *Citizenship of first time applicants: Most from Syria and Iraq.* Retrieved July 16, 2018, from http://ec.europa.eu/eurostat/statistics-explained/index.php/Asylum_statistics#Citizenship_of_first-time_applicants:_most_from_Syria_and_Iraq.

Eurostat (2018c). *Asylum in the EU Member States. 650 000 first-time asylum seekers registered in 2017. Syrians, Iraqis and Afghans continued to be the top citizenships.* Retrieved July 16, 2018, from http://ec.europa.eu/eurostat/documents/2995521/8754388/3-20032018-AP-EN.pdf/50c2b5a5-3e6a-4732-82d0-1caf244549e3.

Georgiou, M., & Zaborowski, R. (2017). *Media coverage of the "refugee crisis": A cross-European perspective.* Council of Europe.

Hallin, D.C., & Mancini, P. (2004). *Comparing media systems: Three models of media and politics.* New York: Cambridge University Press.

Horsti, K., Hultén, G., & Titley, G. (2014). *National conversations. Public service media and cultural diversity in Europe.* Bristol: Intellect.

Hultén, G. (2014). A vulnerable diversity: Diversity policies in Swedish public service media. In K. Horsti, G. Hultén, G., & G. Titley (Eds.), *National conversations. Public service media and cultural diversity in Europe.* Bristol: Intellect.

Jacobs, L., Meeusen C., & d'Haenens, L. (2016). News coverage and attitudes on immigration: Public and commercial television news compared. *European Journal of Communication, 31*(6), 642–660.

Reuters (2018, August 1). EU to support Spain, Morocco on migration, but funds limited. Retrieved August 6, 2018, from https://www.reuters.com/article/us-europe-migrants-spain/eu-to-support-spain-morocco-on-migration-but-funds-limited-idUSKBN1KM5FI.

Szcepanik, M. (2016). The 'good' and 'bad' refugees? Imagined refugeehood(s) in the media coverage of the migration crisis. *Journal of Identity and Migration Studies, 10*(2), 23–33.

Strömbäck, J., Andersson, F., & Nedlund, E. (2017). *Invandring i medierna – hur rapporterade svenska tidningar åren 2010-2015?* [Immigration in Media – How did Swedish newspapers report during the years 2010-2015?] Delmi Rapport 2017, 6.

Sumuvuori, J., Vähäsöyrinki, A., Eerolainen, T., Lindvall, J., Pasternak, R., Syrjälä, M., & Talvela, A. (2016). *Refugees and asylum seekers in press coverage. A comparative content analysis of texts published in Helsingin Sanomat and Aamulehti (FI), The Guardian and The Times (UK) and Le Soir and De Morgen (BE) newspapers in the time period from 1 January to 31 January 2016.* London: The Finnish Institute in London.

Van Gorp, B. (2005). Where is the frame? Victims and intruders in the Belgian press coverage of the asylum issue. *European Journal of Communication, 20*(4), 484–507.

Vasterman, P.L.M. (2005). Media-hype self-reinforcing news waves, journalistic standards and the construction of social problems. *European Journal of Communication, 20*(4), 508–530.

Wien, C., & Elmelund-Præstekær, C. (2009). An anatomy of media hypes. Developing a model for the dynamics and structure of intense media coverage of single issues. *European Journal of Communication, 24*(2), 183–201.

Chapter 4
Depiction of Immigration in Television News: Public and Commercial Broadcasters – a Comparison

Valériane Mistiaen

Introduction

The media play an important role in mental representations as they constitute the main source of knowledge about many issues, contributing to the "common sense" understanding of the world (e.g., d'Haenens & Mattelart, 2011: 237). They affect the way in which the local population will act and react. As is demonstrated in this book, this is even truer for reporting about immigration, as most people will never meet refugees in person but will instead refer to real-life experiences communicated to them by the media. In this sense Tétu (2004) argues that even if there is a break in the timing of the broadcast and discordance between the original context and the reception context, the 'direct' aspect of the news automatically turns the viewer into a witness.

Regarding immigration news, many content and discursive analyses focus on European newspapers (Baker et al., 2008; Chouliaraki & Zaborowski, 2017). These studies either concentrate on how minority groups are represented in the news (Van Dijk, 1991), on the framing used to depict the immigration processes (Van Gorp, 2005; De Cleen et al., 2017), or on the linguistic patterns (Gabrielatos & Baker, 2008; Holmes & Castañeda, 2016; Calabrese & Mistiaen, 2018).

Given the difficulties associated with gathering TV news items, fewer studies focus on TV channels. Only a few concentrate on the framing of the language of TV news items pertaining to immigration and its impact on opinions (see for instance Lecheler, Bos & Vliegenthart, 2015). In the Dutch-speaking part of Belgium, recent studies have looked at the way public and commercial broadcasters deal with immigration topics (Jacobs, Meeusen & d'Haenens, 2016; Meeusen & Jacobs, 2017), but, as far as we know, no comparable study was executed in the French-speaking part. This chapter contributes to these efforts by studying Belgian French-language immigration TV news.

We believe that different processes are used by each media platform to report an external situation to the news audience, and that these different processes will trigger different reactions. Based on images and language interfaces, different media will also organize their own rhetoric according to what they think their audience expects (Tétu, 2004: 9-10).

In this chapter, we intend to investigate, through a lexical analysis, whether and, if so, how public and commercial Belgian French-language TV newscasts diverge in their coverage of the refugee crisis. We hypothesize that the distinct logic of both types of broadcasters (public and commercial) will be reflected in news items on immigration.

We shall first describe the Belgian media context and our hypotheses, corpus partition, and methodology, before moving to findings and discussion.

Public service and commercial broadcasting in Belgium

"Media systems are embedded in their social environment which is also culturally—and nationally—shaped" (Thomass & Kleinsteuber, 2011: 25). This is why it is necessary to acquire a deeper insight into both French-language Belgian TV channels under study within their own specific environment.

Established in 1977, the RTBF (*Radio Télévision belge de la Fédération Wallonie-Bruxelles*—Belgian radio and television of the French-language community-Brussels) in July 1997 became by decree an autonomous state enterprise with a cultural remit. This decree "emphasizes the importance of producing programs of its own, reflecting the cultural heritage and identity of the French-speaking community in Belgium" (De Bens, 2004: 23). The RTBF offers six radio stations and five TV channels: *La Une* (main channel), *La Deux* (events, discovery programs; targets minority groups), *La Trois* (cultural programs for a youth audience), *OUFtivi* (for young people), *PureVision* (thematic channel available on cable) and *ARTE Belgium* as well as an audio and video content-on-demand digital platform, *Auvio*. The public service is funded up to 75 percent by the Belgian French-language Community. Other revenue is derived from sponsorship and advertising.

On its website the public service broadcaster states that its goal is to be a "leader for expression and fulfillment for everyone, by everyone and everywhere". Its mission statement is: "[to meet] the needs and expectations of Belgian French-language citizens as well as to inform, entertain and educate. Its first mission is to confirm and verify information before explaining it and

Figure 4.1: TV audiences in French-speaking Belgium in 2017 (in %)

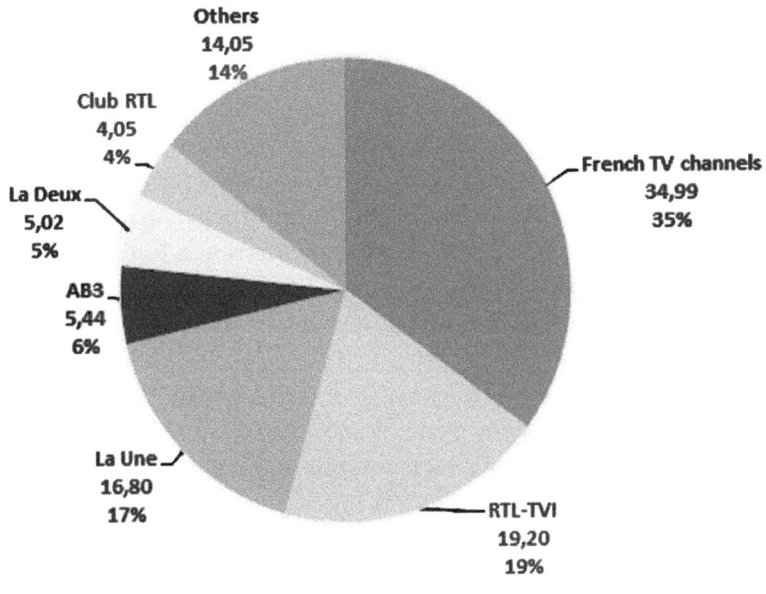

Source: CIM TV – Sud, 1/1 – 31/12/2017, 02-26h, 4+, Live+7+Invités – GfK Belgium NV.

putting it into perspective". Since 2016 the RTBF has organized activities and training sessions in order to foster cultural diversity amongst its programs and employees (RTBF, 2017: 71).

RTL-TVI (*Radio Télévision Luxembourg – Télévision Indépendante*—Luxembourgish Independent Radio and TV), the commercial French-language counterpart owned by the RTL Group, was established in 1987. RTL Belgium operates four radio stations and three TV channels: *RTL-TVI* (main channel), *Club RTL* (for young people) and *Plug RTL* (for teenagers). It focuses on innovation, production, and distribution of "the best audio-visual content". Nonetheless, its Internet website specifies that RTL Belgium's goal is to be a "link within community life, through the production of news and proximity programs". As far as we know, nothing comparable to the diversity focus of the RTBF exists for RTL-TVI.

As shown by Figure 4.1, in 2017, *RTL-TVI* and *La Une* were the two most watched Belgian TV channels by Belgium's French-language audiences.

We should emphasize that Belgium's French-language TV operators face stiff competition from France's TV channels (mostly *TF1, France 2, & France 3*) and have been struggling to retain/increase their viewership (Raeymaeckers & Heinderyckx, 2018: 15). On a national level, "*La Une* (…) is in direct competition with *RTL-TVI* during prime time. The RTBF offers more and longer newscasts than does RTL-TVI" (De Bens, 2004: 24). In June 2018 the RTL-TVI evening newscast was more watched (15.8 percent of the audience) than the RTBF evening newscast (13.6 percent) (CIM, 2018).

The main differences between public service and commercial broadcasters is that the former do not depend on advertising revenue and are thus expected to play at democracy-building through "a 'public logic', characterized by universal service, public value, quality and diversity as key values, whereas the commercial news production process is dominated by a market-oriented logic and is characterized by audience maximization" (Jacobs et al., 2016: 643). Owing to market competition, commercial broadcasters are more likely to dwell on soft news and sensationalist stories to boost ratings (McManus, 1994; Bird, 2000).

As seen in the RTBF mission statement, *La Une* has a public commitment to put issues into perspective, provide more background information (i.e., more experts, interviews of direct protagonists), and depict minorities in a more positive light (Van den Bulck & Broos, 2011). Moreover, commercial broadcasters are expected to be of lower quality as they tend to use "more sensational features in their news compared to public service broadcasters" (Kleemans & Hendriks Vettehen, 2009: 236). Commercial newscasters are also expected to feature less "hard news" (e.g., politics, economics) and more "soft news" (e.g., sleaze, scandal, sensation, and entertainment) (Esser, 1999: 293). Popular media cultivate viewer empathy by interviewing eyewitnesses with whom they can easily identify in order to trigger a more emotional reaction (Hendriks Vettehen, Nuyten & Peeters, 2008: 320). Research by Tink (1998: 102) showed that "the RTBF and *France 2* select some topics according to educational rather than commercial criteria and ... address news topic in a more diverse way than private channels".

More differences among newspapers than among TV stations

The third chapter of this book deals with the portrayal of migrants by Belgian and Swedish newspapers. It concludes that Belgian French-language newspapers show a clear tendency to represent the refugees as a nondescript mob, giving them very few opportunities to express themselves—and when given a voice, most of the refugees presented are male adults. In our previous studies (Joris et al., 2018; Mistiaen, 2017) focusing on the Belgian French-language press, we conclude that politicians are overrepresented and are invited to express their views very often. The education or family background of the refugees is barely mentioned. And the most frequent origins of the refugees, when indicated, are Syrian and Iraqi, while the main theme covered refers to political solutions to the refugee crisis.

These findings concur with Georgiou and Zaborowski's cross-country study (2017: 3) of European media coverage of the refugee crisis, and confirm the general lack of voice given to (female) refugees, although it would help to adopt a broader perspective. A study by Chouliaraki and Zaborowski (2017) states that politicians are present in 66 percent of the sample, compared to only 16.6 percent of migrants and refugees (p.620), which ties in with the newspaper coverage findings presented in this book's Chapter 3.

The preliminary results of our quantitative analyses of French-language television news items in Belgium follow the same patterns, with the exception that refugees are somehow interviewed more frequently on TV than quoted in newspapers (Mistiaen, 2018).

From these quantitative analyses we conclude that overall differences between French-language tabloids and broadsheets are greater than between public and commercial French-language TV channels. Previous studies confirm that similarities between the two TV channels stand out. A combination of quantitative and qualitative analysis carried out during seven months in 2007 shows no difference between the public and the commercial broadcasters in French-language Belgium (Daclette, 2007). For Flanders, after analyzing 140 newscasts from 2003 through 2007, Van den Bulck and Broos (2011) concluded that there was barely any difference in the way minority groups were stereotyped by Flemish commercial (VTM) and public (VRT) broadcasters, notwithstanding the fact that the latter had developed a diversity charter.

Given that so few differences are found between public and commercial broadcast news reports on immigration issues, all journalists may share similar personal values, beliefs, and social capital when it comes to minority representation (Van den Bulck & Broos, 2011: 212). As a result differences might not be dictated by market logic but by the personal beliefs and experiences of the journalists processing immigration news.

Our exploratory study of the corpus analyzed in this chapter (Mistiaen, 2018) shows similar patterns. Firstly, politicians are overrepresented and there is a general lack of voice given to refugees, with the exception that refugees are somehow interviewed more frequently on TV than quoted in newspapers. Secondly, the exploratory research also concludes that overall differences between French-language regional newspapers and broadsheets are greater than between public and commercial French-language TV channels. Thirdly, even though our preliminary analysis did not highlight any statistical significance, we noticed that the public broadcaster (*La Une*) mentions the origin of the refugee more often, and more often presents a solution angle to the crisis. However, this channel seems to neglect the families and occupational background of refugees. Moreover, commercial broadcaster *RTL-TVI* seems to give more importance to individuals and shows many more children (8 percent for 2 percent on *La Une*).

This chapter goes deeper than the former analyses, offering a quantitative and qualitative analysis of the differences found between both Belgian French-language TV channels with respect to immigration topics.

Hypotheses

To investigate the divergences between public and commercial Belgian French-language TV newscasts pertaining to the immigration issue, we formulated the following hypotheses:

H1: *The public broadcaster presents more news related to immigration, and the sequences are longer compared to the commercial broadcaster.*
H1a: *La Une explains the causes of immigration and some concepts linked to it. For a better understanding, the refugee crisis is more often put into perspective using figures, graphs, and tables than on RTL-TVI, which focuses more on sensationalistic aspects.*
H2: *The public broadcaster makes fewer references to cultural, economic, security, or health threats as compared to the commercial broadcaster.*
H2a: *As a consequence, more references to welfare, cultural enrichment, and a general positive tone will be found on La Une.*

Corpus and Methodology

What follows is a short quantitative analysis giving a global picture of the corpus and an in-depth qualitative analysis of 300 segments of the Belgian evening newscasts of the public and commercial TV channels, respectively *La Une* (50,928 words) and *RTL-TVI* (50,923 words). The period of analysis spans from March to September 2015. We first browsed databases of both channels to extract news items dealing with *migrants* or *refugees* in the context of the refugee crisis. Then, we watched each item twice and coded the sequences in a SPSS file before transcribing all segments, with special attention to interviews and mention (or omission) of sources with respect to figures, charts, or graphs. The process was impeded by the fact that queries in the search engine are limited to descriptors provided by RTBF or RTL archivists, not the whole

Table 4.1: Corpus description

Events		Number of *La Une* sequences	Number of *RTL-TVI* sequences
21 March to 4 April 2015	- Bart De Wever's (Mayor of Antwerp and the leader of Nieuwe-Vlaamse Alliantie (N-VA), a nationalist Belgian Dutch-speaking political party) declaration on integration (24/03/15) - Visa not allowed for five Yezidi women who were expected to give testimony at the European parliament (23/03/15)	3	0
24 August to 20 September 2015	- Bart De Wever's declaration on the revision of the refugee status (26/08/15) - Discovery of 71 deaths in a lorry in Austria (27/08/15) - Tensions in Eastern Europe (Hungary, Croatia, Serbia, Macedonia) - Emergency measures taken in Belgium - Citizens initiatives - Various shipwrecks in the Mediterranean Sea - Eurostar traffic interruption (02/09/15) - Alan Kurdi's death (02/09/15) - Queue in front of the Belgian Foreign Office - Maximilian park (Brussels) - Calais jungle - Liesbeth Homans's (N-VA politician, Vice-minister and Flemish Minister of Home Affairs, Housing, Administrative Affairs, Integration, Social Economy, Equality and Poverty) declaration on social housing for refugees - Various European summits and meetings on refugee distribution and quotas (05,09,14/09/15) - More than 17,000 migrants arrived in Germany (05-06/09/15) - Petra Laszlo's incident in Hungary (08/09/15) - European marches in favor of refugees (12/09/15)	109	151
21 to 27 September 2015	- The N-VA declares that they want to reduce family allowances for refugees (21/09/15) - Hungary allows police to open fire on refugees who illegally cross the border (21/09/15) - Bart De Wever (N-VA) states that "Schengen is clinically dead" (22/09/15) - European extraordinary meeting (23/09/15) - Tensions in Eastern Europe (Hungary, Croatia, Serbia)	21	16
Total		133	167

contents of the newscasts. As a result, some segments may have been omitted. Furthermore, we completed a first exploratory reading to detect the main patterns, and highlighted the main events marking our corpus.

Then, our analysis consists of a lexical analysis complemented by Corpus Linguistics (CL) tools. Adopting a CL methodology "allows for a higher degree of objectivity—that is, it enables the researcher to approach the texts (relatively) free from any preconceived notions regarding their linguistic or semantic/pragmatic content" (Gabrielatos & Baker, 2008: 7).

After cleaning our corpus of all unnecessary information (Née, 2017), we processed it using a concordance software (AntConc), determined the relevance (i.e., keyness) of the corpus (which determines the keywords, e.g., the most frequent lemmas), and used the concordance tool. The concordance tool facilitates the study of every occurrence of a term in its immediate lexical context—its co-text—based on various rankings (alphabetical order of the right or left context, chronological order of the corpus).

Results

Number and length of the news items

Before looking at the way the story is told, we asked ourselves whether the crisis was dealt with in Belgian French-language TV newscasts. To do so, we looked at the frequency of immigration news items on both TV channels and the length of each segment. On a strictly numerical level, *RTL-TVI* presents more news dealing with immigration than *La Une* for the period under study. But surprisingly, a close look at the division by period (see Table 4.1) did not single out any news item for the first period on *RTL-TVI* (but three on *La Une*), while for the last period, *La Une* broadcast five more segments than *RTL-TVI*. This is significant as the span was a one-week period, thus making it a noticeable difference. Moreover, *RTL-TVI* produced 41 more news items during the second period, which has been identified as the peak in the mediatization of the refugee crisis (Berry et al., 2016).

At this point of the analysis, we must mention some differences regarding the selection of broadcast segments. Although *La Une* presents a lower number of news items on immigration for the period under study, there is only one theme it did not address (see Appendix 4.1) when *RTL-TVI* did: the French artists' mobilization after Alan Kurdi's dramatic death (September 6, 2015). Likewise, we found eleven themes that were not touched upon by *RTL-TVI*

Table 4.2: All immigration news entirely dedicated to immigration figures, contextualization and legal context

La Une	RTL-TVI
- 25/08/15: Immigration figures and graphs - 01/09/15: Immigration figures - 04/09/15: Germany's immigration figures and graphs - 14/09/15: Schengen space - 15/09/15: European financial support - 23/09/15: Geneva convention - 24/09/15: Toughening of residence conditions (limitation of residence permit and family reunification)	- 03/09/15: Myria report - 24/09/15: Toughening of residence conditions (limitation of residence permit and family reunification)

but were covered by *La Une* (e.g., Yezidi women at the European Parliament (March 27, 2015), the "golden song" (August 25, 2015), possible health threat (September 4, 2015 and September 24, 2015), possible presence of terrorists in the crowds of refugees (September 10, 2015)).

To understand the extent to which *La Une* gives viewers more 'keys' to understanding the situation, we counted all the segments entirely dedicated to immigration figures or contextualization and the complex legal tools regarding immigration.

We noted seven instances aimed at helping citizens to understand the refugee crisis on *La Une* compared to two on *RTL-TVI*. Hence, we argue that *La Une* produces more documentary work than *RTL-TVI*. As to the sequence duration, each news item lasts an average of one minute and 24 seconds on *RTL-TVI* and two minutes and one second on *La Une*. During the first period under study news items dealing with refugees were mainly broadcast after the tenth news item. In contrast, during the second and third periods news items regarding refugees were at the beginning of the news broadcast (among the first five topics). This clearly shows that immigration topics were given prominent media coverage at the end of the summer of 2015, and especially at the end of August and the beginning of September. This was a period when many upsetting images could be seen on European media (Berry et al., 2016). Nonetheless, we did not notice any particularity or common denominator that might justify the broadcasting of news item in the second part of the newscast (see Appendix 4.1), so it is probably due to the reporting of other newsworthy events that occurred in that period (start of the school year, VW scandal, closing of the Caterpillar plant).

Our first hypothesis is thus only partially validated as we noticed that *La Une* presented fewer news items related to immigration during our period of analysis but addressed a wider variety of topics than *RTL-TVI*. *La Une*'s news items are longer than those of the commercial broadcaster and the segments appear more often at the beginning of the newscast than on *RTL-TVI*.

Mention of threats

To examine our second hypothesis, i.e., whether the public broadcaster makes fewer references to threats (cultural, economics, security, or health threats), we examined the language used in the newscast. To identify the segments using terminology linked to threats, we studied the lexical fields surrounding three terms: conflict, security, and terrorism, using both thesaurus dictionaries and our own experience. As required by the concordance program, the lists were lemmatized.

For both broadcasters, the most prominent lexical field was *security* (435 occurrences in *La Une* corpus; 384 occurrences in *RTL-TVI* corpus), followed by *conflict* (respectively 259 and 278 occurrences) and *terrorism* (respectively 227 and 195 occurrences). From these three related lexical fields, we grouped the most frequent terms and analyzed them in concordance in Table 4.3.

From a strictly numerical point of view, we could claim that *La Une* focused more on security, conflict, and terrorism, but our reading of the corpus invited us to look further into these news items. To understand how these terms were used in context, we undertook a deeper analysis of all the occurrences previously mentioned.

From the first lexical field, the terms *fight,* *conflict,* and *war* mainly focus on the Syrian war and the "brave" refugees who flee conflicts and fight for their lives. On *La Une*, we also found two occurrences of *fighters*, which were used to refute the idea that ISIS fighters infiltrate refugee migration flows. Fewer references to the Syrian war appear in the *RTL-TVI* corpus and the broadcaster does not address the idea that Islamic fighters might arrive in Europe within refugee migration flows. It actually focuses on what ISIS fighters do to civilians and on funds raised by the European Union to stop the war.

We discovered that the only *RTL-TVI* news item in which the term *attacks* was mentioned told the story of an Iraqi couple and their baby who decided to leave Iraq after being victims of an attack. Here *RTL-TVI* focused on the human side, choosing to end the sequence with sentences such as: *Their lives were in danger. They saved their baby's life. A hope for another life starts* (September 9, 2015). Within the eight items mentioning the term *attack* in the *La Une* corpus, two referred to suicide attacks in Afghanistan and four to the Paris, Brussels, and Thalys attacks. These items explained that the authors of these attacks were not newcomers but people who had been living in Europe for a long time.

Regarding the term *weapon** (or *arms*), half of the sequences of *La Une* and one third of *RTL-TVI* sequences dealt with the Hungarian law that

Table 4.3: Frequencies of terms belonging to the lexical fields of conflict, terrorism, and security (Translation in Appendix 4.2)

		Number of occurrences in a security context (*La Une* corpus)	Number of occurrences in a security context (*RTL-TVI* corpus)
Security	*Mesure** (*measure*)	21 (2 emergency measure – 1 safety measure – 3 retaliatory measure) (...) a security measure immediately criticized by humanitarian organizations. (31/08/15)	24 (3 emergency measure – 3 restrictive measures – 2 drastic measures) (...) Belgians are in favor of more border controls (...). (27/08/15)
	*Polic** (*police*)	49 (...) Belgians are in favor of more border controls (...). (14/09/15)	57 Policemen arrest them (...). (16/09/15)
	*Problèm** (*problem, trouble, difficulty*)	40 The problem is that they number around 1,000 and there is only space for 260 people in the waiting room. (31/08/15)	23 This raises an issue, police inform us that they were many looters in the camp (...). (05/09/15)
	*Protection** (*protection*)	14 (...) refugee status is then a protection which is difficult to obtain. (23/09/15)	3 This grants refugees social security which is similar to that of national citizens belonging to the destination country. (22/09/15)
	*Sécurit** and *sûreté* (*security and safety*)	26 Must the city of Brussels manage the influx of asylum seekers, with all the issues linked to security, health and administration? (11/09/15)	18 Because of the lack of security, police back-up was called for at Maximilian Park. (04/09/15)
	*Urgence** (*emergency*)	18 It is here that Croatia set up an emergency registry and transit center. (19/09/15)	18 All the British, German and French political leaders agree on the need to act urgently. (03/09/15)
	Total	168	143

		Number of occurrences in a security context (*La Une* corpus)	Number of occurrences in a security context (*RTL-TVI* corpus)
Conflict	***Arme**** (*weapon, arms*)	13 (...) *a coastguard takes out his gun and opens fire in the sky.* (12/09/15)	19 *And we stay in Greece where many policemen and even the army were mobilized.* (06/09/15)
	Attentat* (*attack*)	8 *Indeed, numerous suicide attacks threaten citizens every day.* (24/08/15)	2 *They left Baghdad because they were victims of an attack (...).* (09/09/15)
	Combat* (*fight*)	10 *A child who, with his family, is continually fleeing conflicts in Syria.* (03/09/15)	8 *She recounts her detention in the company of five other captives in a house where fighters pass by every day.* (03/09/15)
	Conflit* (*conflict*)	9 *(...) people who flee conflicts ask for asylum (...).* (23/09/15)	10 *The European Union prefers to invest in supporting countries near conflict zones.* (24/09/15)
	Danger* (*danger*)	17 *Thus, to recall, they are protected people welcomed because their lives were in danger in their country.* (23/09/15)	11 *(...) an often very dangerous journey to get to Europe (...).* (08/09/15)
	Dram* (*drama*)	18 *(...) open Europe's eyes on the human tragedy that takes place at its doors.* (03/09/15)	15 *Once again in the Mediterranean Sea, another similar tragedy.* (28/08/15)
	Guerre* (*war*)	42 (mostly references to wars in Middle Eastern countries) *(...) these migrants who flee wars and conflicts.* (30/08/15)	41 (mostly references to wars in Middle Eastern countries) *In this humanitarian crisis unprecedented since WWII.* (30/08/15)
	Mort* (*dead*)	24 *IOM estimates that the death toll could exceed 4,000 deaths in 2015.* (01/09/15)	22 *According to the International Organization for Migrations, since the beginning of the year, more than 2,500 refugees have died in the Mediterranean Sea.* (13/09/15)
	Total	141	128

		Number of occurrences in a security context (*La Une* corpus)	Number of occurrences in a security context (*RTL-TVI* corpus)
Terrorism	Djihadiste* (jihad)	9 So, are there any jihads among the asylum seekers? (10/09/15)	6 They are trapped: between the government and jihads who both persecute them. (14/09/15)
	Islam* (Islam)	33 (among which 25 *Islamic State*) (...) *Islamophobia files are the ones that achieve the greatest increase.* (29/08/15)	20 (among which 16 *Islamic State*) *Islamist humanitarian organizations, close to the Gulf States and Qatar, to name one, would / could encourage refugees to join Europe.* (03/09/15)
	Menac* (threat)	15 *It is a provisional measure which is authorized when a serious threat to public order and national security is suspected.* (14/09/15)	8 *The Prime Minister ends his speech on the issue of security when faced with terrorist threat.* (06/09/15)
	Terroris* (terrorist – terrorism)	8 (among which 2 ISIS – Islamic State of Iraq and the Levant – terrorist organizations/groups) (...) *the dismantling of the Verviers terrorist group would have contributed to the diffusion of racist comments.* (29/08/15)	13 (among which 8 ISIS terrorist organizations/groups) (...) *kidnapped and imprisoned by Islamic State terrorists.* (03/09/15)
	Total	65	47
TOTAL		374	318

allows the shooting of migrants who illegally enter the territory. From our reading, *La Une* tended to focus more than *RTL-TVI* on the justifications and consequences of this law, while adopting a more critical point of view (*The debate is more urgent than ever* (September 14, 2015); *The following images attest that some migrants flee bombs* (September 22, 2015); *Many in Europe are still shocked after Hungary's announcement to allow its army [to shoot]* ... (September 22, 2015).

In both corpuses, *danger** mostly refers to the risks of staying in a country at war and the difficulties refugees come across on their journey to Europe. *Drama** also echoes the tragic way in which some journeys end. Interestingly, usage of the terms *drama* and *dead* peaks at the very beginning of September 2015 with Alan Kurdi's death and the discovery of 71 dead migrants in a lorry in Austria.

An important term mentioned in the second lexical field (*security*) is *police*. *La Une* mainly uses it in connection with Eastern European police forces threatening refugees (complete with tear gas, truncheons, handcuffs…) or attempting to secure borders. *RTL-TVI* refers only twice to police abuses. Police are mainly depicted as usefully maintaining calm and order and investigating and jailing smugglers.

With respect to the third lexical field under study, *terrorism*, it almost always refers directly or indirectly to the Islamic terrorist group ISIS and its threats. Only once does *RTL-TVI* mention that Hungarian policemen are seen as a threat to refugees, while *La Une* addresses the question of whether jihadists might hide within migration flows. We should add that *La Une* is the only channel which discusses the refugees' arrival as a possible threat for Europe while clarifying that these are always the words of far-right politicians (*Others, on the extreme right-wing, think that migrants are simply a threat for Europe.* September 9, 2015).

Regarding the term *problem*, half of the occurrences on *La Une* refer to the problems generated by the arrival of refugees. On three occasions it is linked with medical issues newcomers are facing, and twice with infrastructure problems. On *RTL-TVI*, surprisingly, the emphasis is placed on the problems generated by the wave of solidarity seen in Belgium. In these news items we found an unusual sentence punctuating vox pop interviews: *The problem and the truth being that many Belgian citizens are afraid to see so many foreigners arriving in our country* (September 3, 2015). As with most vox pops, it is regrettable that an editorial team should make such a generality with no other basis than chance encounters with three random passers-by in this case. This example also echoes two other instances previously quoted: *… Belgians are in favor of more border controls …* (August 27, 2015) and *… Islamist humanitarian organizations, close to the Gulf States and Qatar, to name one, would / could encourage refugees to move to Europe* (September 3, 2015). These examples found in *RTL-TVI* corpus attracted our attention because they generalize opinions or state unverified information without any caution.

The term *measure* is always used in the political sense of establishing new means to tackle the refugee crisis: The emergency of *crisis* is underlined by the widespread use of the terms *emergency measure, emergency places, emergency aid, summoned in emergency* (*La Une*); *emergency shelters, opened in emergency* (*RTL-TVI*). Concerning *La Une* all occurrences of *protection*, except one related to border protection, refer to the Geneva refugee status. On the contrary *RTL-TVI* does not broach the subject of refugee protection, which is surprising in a corpus of news items dealing with refugees.

Generally speaking the term *security* refers to European security on *La Une* and to Belgian security on *RTL-TVI*. *Social security* was mentioned a few times after Bart De Wever stated that he wanted refugees to be deprived of social

Table 4.4: References to cultural, economic, and health threats (translation in Appendix 4.3)

		Number of occurrences in a security context (*La Une* corpus)	Number of occurrences in a security context (*RTL-TVI* corpus)
Threat	*Identité* (identity)	0	1 (…) Muslims in their majority constitute a threat to the Christian identity of Europe. (03/09/2015)
	Culture*	1 This may provoke racism among citizens. This creates a culture of mistrust. (24/03/2015)	1 Main topics of concern for the evening: security and difficulties due to the cohabitation and cultural differences. (17/09/2015)
	Economi* (economics)	2 He considers that this blockage of the border is detrimental to the Serbian economy and has therefore taken retaliatory measures against Croatia. (24/09/2015)	2 (…) it is true that there are also many migrants who come only for economic reasons (…) (03/09/2015)
	Santé* Sanitair* (Health)	1 The sanitary conditions on site are deplorable. (04/09/2015)	2 A very complicated situation which complicates sanitary conditions. (16/09/2015)
	Total	4	6

security for refugees (September 22, 2015), and in a few cases in connection with refugees "being safe now" that they had entered Europe.

To be comprehensive, we studied separately the terms *identity, culture, economics,* and *health* when meaning 'threat' (Table 4.4).

As we can see in Table 4.4, very few references to identity, cultural, economic, or health threats are made explicitly with words directly related to the topic. Nevertheless, we looked further into our corpus and read each sequence carefully. We did not find any other references regarding identity, cultural, or economic threats. With respect to health threats we found two more references in *La Une*'s corpus (September 4, 2015: scabies cases and September 24, 2015: refugee children vaccination) but none on *RTL-TVI*. Neither did we find references to welfare or cultural enrichment on *RTL-TVI* and very few on *La Une*: two segments related to economic benefits due to the arrival of refugees (*In Germany, the Head of the Federation of German Industries explained that this wave of migration was an economic opportunity.*

September 5, 2015) and one referring to cultural enrichment (in a segment aired on September 3, 2015, Amir, a former Bosnian refugee in Belgium, states that cultural diversity enriches all).

From these results, we learn that the media coverage does not differ much from one channel to the other. While *La Une* makes more mentions of terms such as 'security', 'conflict', 'terrorism', and 'health threat', it does so in a more critical (*we recall it; opens Europe's eyes*) and balanced way, presenting divergent opinions, causes, and consequences. On the other hand, *La Une* makes three references to cultural or economic benefits while *RTL-TVI* shuns these aspects. *La Une* seems to adopt a more European perspective while *RTL-TVI* focuses on Belgium and the human/humanitarian aspect of the news. We conclude that our second hypothesis is partly rejected although it should be attenuated as *La Une* has more news items on security, conflict, and terrorism but fewer items regarding cultural and economic threats, while making more references to cultural and economic benefits. These results also illustrate how the same terms can have different meanings depending on their usage, fostering different conceptions of the refugee crisis. This is why it is helpful to undertake a qualitative analysis.

Conclusion

In this chapter we aimed to study the quantity and quality of the news items on immigration—with the emphasis on refugees—broadcast by Belgium's most popular French-language TV channels, *RTL-TVI* and *La Une*. As we supposed that market logic may guide both news selection and the way the public and commercial broadcasters produce the news, we focused on whether each channel's distinct logic was reflected in news on immigration. To test our hypothesis, we conducted a lexical analysis complemented by corpus linguistics tools on a corpus of 300 news items (101,851 words) spanning from March to September 2015.

At first sight divergences between the French-language public service and commercial broadcasters are negligible and match Van den Bulck and Broos's (2011: 2016) conclusion on the ways in which minority groups are stereotyped by Flemish commercial (VTM) and public (VRT) broadcasters alike. An in-depth qualitative analysis only partially confirmed our hypotheses.

Regarding the first hypothesis, although it is true that *La Une* offers longer newscasts, news items on immigration were less numerous than on *RTL-TVI*. This result contradicts De Bens's 2004 study which found that in general the RTBF broadcasts more news items than its commercial counterpart.

Nonetheless, even if the number of immigration segments is less significant on *La Une* for the period under study, the channel actually deals with a wider range of different topics and offers a wider view of the situation, including a greater number of different actors, while *RTL-TVI* mainly focuses on emotional events. Moreover, sequences documenting immigration contexts and legal tools are much more numerous on *La Une* than on *RTL-TVI*. In light of these results, we were not able to confirm H1 or H1a.

Our second hypothesis (H2 and H2a) was partially confirmed as *La Une* actually makes more references to threats, in an effort to achieve a wider variety of topics and to offer a more comprehensive understanding of the situation. While *RTL-TVI* never mentioned or referred to economic benefit or cultural enrichment, we found very few such instances in the corpus of *La Une*.

Although none of our hypotheses were fully confirmed, our qualitative analysis has shown the extent to which interpretation of specific terms may strongly vary depending on their usage.

Since the differences between the two channels are not significant, and knowing that the journalists' personal beliefs and experience inevitably color their approach to immigration topics (Van den Bulck & Broos, 2011), it is worth investigating whether any divergence should simply be ascribed to journalists' personal choices and/or beliefs, to their sensitivity as well as knowledge of the subject and/or whether her/his work was an assignment from an editor.

References

Baker, P., Gabrielatos, C., Khosravinik, M., Krzyzanowski, M., McEnery, T., & Wodak, R. (2008). A useful methodological synergy? Combining critical discourse analysis and corpus linguistics to examine discourses of refugees and asylum seekers in the UK press. *Discourse Society, 19*, 273–306.

Berry, M., Garcia-Blanco, I., & Moore, K. (2016). *Press coverage of the refugee and migrant crisis in the EU: A content analysis of five European countries*. [Project Report]. Geneva: United Nations High Commissioner for Refugees.

Bird, E.S. (2000). Audience demands in a murderous market: Tabloidization in U.S. television news. In C. Sparks, & J. Tulloch (Eds.), *Tabloid tales: Global debates over media standards* (pp. 213–228). New York: Rowman & Littlefield.

CIM (2018). *Top 20 programs of French-speaking TV in June 2018*. Retrieved July 30, 2018 from https://www.cim.be/fr/television/resultats-publics.

CIM TV – Sud (2017). *TV Audiences in French-speaking Belgium (2017)*. GfK Belgium NV.

Calabrese, L., & Mistiaen, V. (2018, forthcoming) Naming displaced people: new patterns in media discourse? *Diacrítica, 32*.

Chouliaraki, L., & Zaborowski, R. (2017). Voice and community in the 2015 refugee crisis: A content analysis of news coverage in eight European countries, *International Communication Gazette*, 79(6-7), 613–635.

Daclette, D. (2007). *Islam et violence dans les médias: dans quelle mesure les choix rédactionnels, les images et les propos choisis dans les JT de la RTBF et de RTL-TVI contribuent-ils à créer une association entre islam et violence?* Master's thesis. Université libre de Bruxelles.

De Bens, E. (2004). Belgium. In M. Kelly, G. Mazzoleni, & D. McQuail (eds.), *The Media in Europe. The Euromedia Research Group* (pp. 16–30). London: SAGE Publications.

De Cleen, B., Zienkowski, J., Smets, K., Dekie, A., & Vandevoordt, R. (2017). Constructing the 'refugee crisis' in Flanders: Continuities and adaptations of discourses on asylum and migration. In M. Barlai, B. Fähnrich, C. Griessler, & M. Rhomberg (Eds.), *The Migrant Crisis: European Perspectives and National Discourses* (pp. 59–78). Berlin: LIT Verlag.

d'Haenens, L., & Mattelart, T. (2011). Media and ethnic minorities. In J. Trappel, W.A. Meier, L. d'Haenens, J. Steemers, & B. Thomass (Eds.), *Media in Europe Today* (pp. 235–250). Bristol: Intellect Ltd.

Esser, F. (1999). Tabloidization' of news: A comparative analysis of Anglo-American and German press journalism. *European Journal of Communication*, 14(3), 291–324.

Gabrielatos, C., & Baker, P. (2008). Fleeing, sneaking, flooding. A corpus analysis of discursive constructions of refugees and asylum seekers in the UK press, 1996-2005. *Journal of English Linguistics*, 36(1), 5–38.

Georgiou, M., & Zaborowski, R. (2017). *Media coverage of the 'Refugee Crisis': A cross-European perspective*. Council of Europe.

Holmes, S., & Castañeda, H. (2016). Representing the 'European refugee crisis' in Germany and beyond: Deservingness and difference, life and death. *American Ethnologist*, 43(1), 12–24.

Jacobs, L., Meeusen, C., & d'Haenens, L. (2016). News coverage and attitudes on immigration: Public and commercial television news compared. *European Journal of Communication*, 31(6), 642–660.

Joris, W., De Cock, R., Mertens, S., Mistiaen, V., Sundin, E., Lams, L., & d'Haenens, L. (2018). Vluchtelingen in het nieuws: Een vergelijkende analyse van de berichtgeving in België en Zweden, *Vlaams Tijdschrift voor Overheidsmanagement*, 23(2), 37–49.

Kleemans, M. & Hendriks Vettehen, P. (2009). Sensationalism in television news. In R.P. Konig, P.W.M. Nelissen, & F.J.M. Huysmans (eds.), *Meaningful Media: Communication Research on the Social Construction of Reality* (pp. 226–243). Ubbergen: Tandem Felix.

Lecheler, S., Bos, L., & Vliegenthart, R. (2015). The mediating role of emotions: News framing effects on opinions about immigration, *Journalism & Mass Communication Quarterly*, 92(4), 812–838.

McManus, J. H. (1994). *Market-Driven Journalism: Let the Citizen Beware?* Thousand Oaks: Sage Publications.

Meeusen, C., & Jacobs, L. (2017). Television news content as a contextual predictor of differences between attitudes toward minority groups, *Mass Communication & Society*, 20(2), 213–240.

Mistiaen, V. (2017). *Essay N° 1: Les principaux résultats de l'analyse du journal L'Avenir*. Retrieved June 1, 2018 from https://kuleuven.be/soc/ims/immediate.essays.

Mistiaen, V. (2018). *Essay N° 3: Belgian French-language Channels adopt a Common Lens on the Migration Crisis*. Retrieved June 1, 2018 from https://kuleuven.be/soc/ims/immediate.essays.

Née, E. (2017). *Méthodes et outils informatiques pour l'analyse des discours*. Rennes: Presses Universitaires de Rennes.

Raeymaeckers, K., & Heinderyckx, F. (2018). Belgium: Divided along language lines. In T. Eberwein, S. Fengler, & M. Karmasin (Eds.), *The European Handbook of Media Accountability* (pp.14–23). London and New York: Routledge.

RTBF (2017). *Rapport annuel 2017*. Brussels: RTBF.

RTBF (2018a). *Our History*. Retrieved June 7, 2018 from https://www.rtbf.be/entreprise/a-propos/histoire.

RTBF (2018b). *Missions*. Retrieved June 7, 2018 from https://www.rtbf.be/entreprise/a-propos/nos-missions/detail_les-missions-de-la-rtbf?id=9302311.

RTL (2018). *RTL Belgium Missions*. Retrieved June 23, 2018 from https://www.rtlbelgium.be/a-propos/nos-missions/.

Thomass, B., & Kleinsteuber, H. J. (2011). Comparing media systems: the European dimension. In J. Trappel, W.A. Meier, L. d'Haenens, J. Steemers, & B. Thomass (Eds.), *Media in Europe Today* (pp. 235–250). Bristol: Intellect Ltd.

Tétu, J-F. (2004) L'émotion dans les médias: dispositifs, formes et figures, *Mots. Les langages du politique*, 75, 9–19.

Tink, J. (1998). *J.T. du midi, du soir et de la nuit sur la RTBF, RTL, TF1 et France 2: similitudes et différences*. Master's thesis. Université libre de Bruxelles.

Van den Bulck, H., & Broos, D. (2011). Can a charter of diversity make the difference in ethnic minority reporting? A comparative content and production analysis of two Flemish television newscasts. *Communications: The European Journal of Communication Research*, 36(2), 195–216.

Van Dijk, T. (1991). *Racism and the Press*. London/New York: Routledge.

Van Gorp, B. (2005). Where is the frame? Victims and intruders in the Belgian press coverage of the asylum issue. *European Journal of Communication*, 20(4), 484–507.

Vettehen, P.H., Nuijten, K., & Peeters, A. (2008). Explaining effects of sensationalism on liking of television news stories. The role of emotional arousal. *Communication Research*, 35(3), 319–338.

Appendices

Appendix 4.1

	RTBF	RTL-TVI
29-31/08/2015	- News item dealing with racism - Citizen initiatives - Germany will welcome 800,000 refugees - Meetings with asylum seekers queuing in front of the Foreign Office - European policies - Hungarian wall - Calais jungle	- Shipwrings - Tribute to the lorry's death people and statements of the police - Bart De Wever's declaration on a special status for refugees - News item dealing with integration in Germany - Pope declaration - Hungarian wall - Calais jungle
19-21/09/2015	- Tensions in Eastern Europe - Shipwrings - Migrants' uses of smartphones - Political ping-pong between Yvan Mayeur (Mayor of Brussels at that time, Socialist Parti) and Bart De Wever - Police controls at the Belgian borders - Hungary allows to open fire on refugees who pass illegally the border - The N-VA will to reduce family allowance for refugees - Visit of a Red-Cross center in Belgium	
7/09/2015		- Quotas repartition - 500 emergency beds set up in the center of Brussels - Fire in an asylum center in Germany - French president (François Hollande) declaration on a possible military intervention in Syria

	RTBF	RTL-TVI
10/09/2015		- Theo Francken's tweet and its consequences
- Belgian parliamentary decision on a possible military intervention in Syria
- UNIZO (De Unie van Zelfstandige Ondernemers – Union for self-employed and businessman)
- SB Overseas, non-profit organization that offers psychologist support to migrants
- Macedonia welcomes migrants with blows
- Denmark suspends train connections with Germany
- Merkel is welcomed in an asylum centre in Germany
16/09/2015		- Difficult situation in the Maximilian park
- Croatia opens its borders
- Marine Le Pen talk at the Dutch-speaking Parliament
18/09/2015		- Belgrade (Belgium) welcome 400 asylum seekers
- Documentary on a Syrian family settled in Estinnes (Belgium)
- Integration journey
- Croatia closes its borders
19/09/2015		- Calais manifestation
- Rescue operation in the Mediterranean Sea
- Tensions in Eastern Europe
- Munich beer party
23-26/09/2015		- 450 asylum seekers sleep in the WTC III
- Ministers council
- European summit
- King Philippe of Belgium visits asylum seekers
- Changes in the attribution of the refugee status in Belgium
- Death of a minor refugee in Calais
- Pope declaration
- Wallonia-Brussels Federation party

Appendix 4.2

		Number of occurrences in a security context (*La Une* corpus)	Number of occurrences in a security context (*RTL-TVI* corpus)
Security	***Mesure**** (*measure*)	21 (2 emergency measure – 1 safety measure – 3 retaliatory measure) (…), une mesure sécuritaire immédiatement critique par les organisations humanitaires. (31/08/15)	24 (3 emergency measure – 3 restrictive measures – 2 drastic measures) (…) les belges plébiscitent une mesure: plus de contrôles aux frontières (…). (27/08/15)
	Polic* (*police*)	49 (…) la police allemande a reçu l'ordre d'intensifier entre autres les fouilles. (14/09/15)	57 Des policiers les interpellent (…). (16/09/15)
	Problèm* (*problem, trouble, difficulty*)	40 Le problème c'est qu'ils sont aujourd'hui environ 1000 et qu'il n'y a place que pour 260 personnes dans la salle d'attente. (31/08/15)	23 Cela pose d'ailleurs un problème, la police vient de nous signaler qu'il y a énormément de pilleurs dans le camp (…).(05/09/15)
	Protection* (*protection*)	14 (…) le statut de réfugié est donc une protection qui n'est pas facile à obtenir. (23/09/15)	3 Celle-ci accorde aux réfugiés une protection sociale identique à celle des ressortissants du pays d'accueil. (22/09/15)
	Sécurit* and *sûreté* (*security* and *safety*)	26 La ville de Bruxelles doit-elle gérer l'afflux des demandeurs d'asile, avec toutes les questions liées à la sécurité, l'hygiène et le suivi social ? (11/09/15)	18 Les policiers sont venus en renfort au parc Maximilien. En cause: le manque de sécurité. (04/09/15)
	Urgence* (*emergency*)	18 C'est ici que la Croatie a installé en urgence un de ces centres d'enregistrement et de transit. (19/09/15)	18 Tous les leaders britanniques, français, allemands, affirment l'urgence d'intervenir. (03/09/15)
	Total	**168**	**143**

		Number of occurrences in a security context (*La Une* corpus)	Number of occurrences in a security context (*RTL-TVI* corpus)
	Arme* (*weapon, arms*)	13 (...), un garde côte sort son arme et tire plusieurs fois en l'air. (12/09/15)	19 Et on reste en Grèce ou de nombreux policiers et même l'armée ont été mobilisés (...). (06/09/15)
	Attentat* (*attack*)	8 De nombreux attentats suicides menacent en effet les citoyens tous les jours. (24/08/15)	2 Ils ont fui Bagdad parce qu'ils avaient été victimes d'un attentat (...). (09/09/15)
	Combat* (*fight*)	10 Un enfant qui, avec sa famille, n'a cessé de fuir les combats en Syrie. (03/09/15)	8 (...) elle raconte sa captivité aux côtés de cinq autres prisonnières dans une maison où défilent chaque jour des combattants. (03/09/15)
	Conflit* (*conflict*)	9 (...) les personnes qui fuient les conflits demandent l'asile (...) (23/09/15)	10 (...) l'Union européenne préfère miser sur l'accompagnement dans les pays voisins des zones de conflit. (24/09/15)
Conflict	*Danger** (*danger*)	17 Ce sont donc, on le rappelle, des personnes protégées, accueillies parce que leur vie est en danger dans leur pays. (23/09/15)	11 (...) un périple souvent très dangereux pour arriver en Europe (...)(08/09/15)
	Dram* (*drama*)	18 (...) ouvrir les yeux de l'Europe sur le drame humain qui se joue à ses portes. (03/09/15)	15 Un autre drame similaire une nouvelle fois en mer Méditerranée. (28/08/15)
	Guerre* (*war*)	42 (mostly references to wars in Middle Eastern countries) (...) ces migrants qui fuient guerres et conflits. (30/08/15)	41 (mostly references to wars in Middle Eastern countries) Dans cette crise humanitaire sans précédent depuis la seconde guerre mondiale, (...) (30/08/15)
	Mort* (*dead*)	24 L'OIM estime qu'on pourrait dépasser les 4000 morts en 2015. (01/09/15)	22 D'après l'Organisation Internationale pour les Migrations, depuis le début de l'année, plus de 2700 réfugiés sont morts en Méditerranée. (13/09/15)
	Total	141	128

		Number of occurrences in a security context (*La Une* corpus)	Number of occurrences in a security context (*RTL-TVI* corpus)
Terrorism	**Djihadiste*** (*jihad*)	9 *Alors, y a-t-il des djihadistes parmi les demandeurs d'asile ?* (10/09/15)	6 *Ils sont coincés entre deux feux: entre le régime et les djihadistes qui les persécutent.* (14/09/15)
	Islam* (*Islam*)	33 (among which 25 *Islamic State*) *(...), ce sont les dossiers à caractère islamophobe qui connaissent la plus forte hausse.* (29/08/15)	20 (among which 16 *Islamic State*) *(...) des organisations humanitaires islamistes, proches d'états du Golf, du Qatar, pour le citer, pousseraient les migrants, les refugies à rejoindre l'Europe.* (03/09/15)
	Menac* (*threat*)	15 *C'est une mesure provisoire qui est autorisée en cas de menace grave pour l'ordre publique ou la sécurité intérieure de l'État.* (14/09/15)	8 *Le premier ministre a terminé son discours en évoquant la question de la sécurité face à la menace terroriste.* (06/09/15)
	Terroris* (*terrorist – terrorism*)	8 (among which 3 ISIS terrorist organizations/groups) *(...) le démantèlement de la cellule terroriste de Verviers auraient contribué à la diffusion de propos racistes.* (29/08/15)	13 (among which 8 ISIS terrorist organizations/groups) *(...) enlevée et séquestrée en Irak par les terroristes du groupe État islamique.* (03/09/15)
	Total	65	47
TOTAL		374	318

Appendix 4.3

		Number of occurrences in a security context (*La Une* corpus)	Number of occurrences in a security context (*RTL-TVI* corpus)
Threat	*Identité* (identity)	0	1 (…) musulmans dans leur majorité constitue une menace pour l'identité chrétienne de l'Europe. (03/09/2015)
	Culture*	1 Cela peut provoquer chez les citoyens du racisme. Cela crée une culture de la méfiance. (24/03/2015)	1 Principaux sujets d'inquiétude de la soirée: la sécurité et les difficultés posées par la cohabitation et les différences culturelles. (17/09/2015)
	Economie* (economics)	2 Il estime que ce blocage de la frontière nuit à l'économie serbe et a donc pris des mesures de rétorsion contre la Croatie. (24/09/2015)	2 (…) c'est vrai qu'il y a aussi beaucoup de migrants qui viennent pour des raisons purement économiques (…) (03/09/2015)
	Santé* *Sanitair** (Health)	1 Les conditions sanitaires sur places sont déplorables. (04/09/2015)	2 Une situation très compliquée évidemment et qui complique les conditions sanitaires. (16/09/2015)
	Total	4	6

Chapter 5
Agency and Power in the Dutch-Language News Coverage of the Summer 2015 Refugee Situation in Europe: A Transitivity Analysis of Semantic Roles

Lutgard Lams

Introduction

Migration, as a global phenomenon, has a cyclical nature with ebbs and flows, depending on socioeconomic and political conditions in the migrants' home countries. Yet, over the last few decades the number of migrants has been rising steadily. Since summer 2015 Europe has witnessed an unprecedented growth of asylum seekers due to the Syrian war and the rise of terrorist activities in Afghanistan, Iraq and the wider Middle-East, and sub-Saharan Africa. Figures made available by the United Nations High Commissioner for Refugees (UNHCR, 2015) indicate a rise of 4.7 million people fleeing their home countries from late 2011, reaching 15.1 million in total by the end of 2015. Compared with the second quarter of 2015, the number of Syrian and Iraqi asylum seekers more than tripled between July and September 2015 (Eurostat, 2016). Since that period, the theme has featured at the top of the political agendas, and has been widely reported in most European media outlets.

Given the impact of media on shaping public opinion (McCombs & Shaw, 1972; Jacobs & Hooghe, 2015; Lecheler, Bos, & Vliegenthart, 2015), migration coverage in the media has attracted much scholarly attention. Our study inscribes itself in this vast literature on human mobility and presents a discourse-analytical perspective with an examination of the discursive positioning of the protagonist actors in the migration debate. While several cross-cultural studies have been conducted about immigration press coverage, most examine framing practices or conduct quantitative content analysis, probing variables such as mentioning of nationality and gender, or the extent to which refugees are treated as individuals and receive a voice. Others have focused on semiotic investigations of visual media data or used corpus-linguistic methods to analyze lexical choices and the type and connotation of words that keep company or collocate with the key term 'refugee(s).' Fewer studies examine the verbal processes associated with the refugees and hardly any project has analyzed the media portrayal of non-refugee actors, who receive considerably more media mileage than the refugees themselves. Hence, this chapter focuses on the representation practices of refugees and the most prominent participants (the EU, Germany, Hungary, and their leaders) in the migration debate in terms of agency and semantics of verbal processes.

The selected objects of investigation are accounts about the European refugee situation of late summer 2015 at the height of what was perceived as a crisis, in the Dutch-language progressive quality press *De Volkskrant* [VK] for the Netherlands and its equivalent in Belgium, *De Morgen* [DM]. The choice for the progressive press accounts facilitates comparison with an earlier study of the more conservative elite press of a number of countries, including the Netherlands and Belgium (Lams, 2018).[2] Findings in that study demonstrate that the refugee actor received hardly any agency. This begs the question whether the progressive press has been using similar representation patterns.

The Netherlands and Belgium are comparable, since both countries registered similar figures for asylum applications per 100,000 local citizens (266 and 397 respectively) in 2015 (BBC, 2016). The number of first-time asylum applicants in the third quarter of 2015 had jumped by 136 percent in the Netherlands and 191 percent in neighboring Belgium up from the preceding quarter (Eurostat, 2015). It concerned primarily refugees from Syria, Afghanistan, and Iraq, seeking international protection. Both the Netherlands and Belgium are also comparable in terms of real-world indicators, such as the Migrant Integration Policy Index (MIPEX), with Belgium indexing a slightly higher score on integration policy (67) than the Netherlands (60) and Germany (61).

---

2   This article is part of a larger project which analyses cultural and ideological convergences and divergences in a selection of British, French, Dutch, and Belgian media narratives about immigration. In a first phase, a cross-cultural discourse analysis examined the refugee coverage in what has been called the more conservative press, like the *Times* (UK), *Le Figaro* (France), *La Libre Belgique* (French-language part of Belgium), and *De Telegraaf* (the Netherlands) (Lams, 2018). The second, ongoing instalment compares the narratives of the more progressive press in the same countries (*The Guardian, Le Monde, Le Soir, De Morgen, De Volkskrant*) to eventually draw a comprehensive picture of the coverage across the ideological spectrum.

Dutch-language news coverage of refugees

We limit discussion of the extensive literature in the field to the research conducted on the Dutch-language press narratives, given our particular focus on the Netherlands and Flanders for this chapter. Yet, we first highlight recurrent scholarly conclusions about international (mainly Western) media coverage which deserve closer attention of media practitioners and politicians. The main findings relate to the high level of collectivization of the refugee actor (e.g., KhosraviNik, 2010; Thorbjørnsrud & Figenschou, 2016; Chouliaraki & Zaborowski, 2017), who is also deprived of a direct voice, since most forum space is given to the political elites, shifting the plight of the refugees and their personal histories to a focus on how the arrival of refugees creates a 'European crisis' (e.g., Philo, Briant, & Donald, 2013; Kaleda, 2014; Benson & Wood, 2015; Thorbjørnsrud & Figenschou, 2016; Sumuvuori et al, 2016; Chouliaraki & Zaborowski, 2017; De Cock et al., 2018; Lams, 2018). An additional highlight concerns the context-dependent fluctuations between themes of securitization ("narratives of security") and humanitarian themes ('narratives of care') (Benson, 2013; Caviedes, 2015) or between the 'intruder' and 'victim' frames for the refugees (Van Gorp, 2005; Thorbjørnsrud & Figenschou, 2016).

Studies about the power of language in public discursive representations of minorities were already being conducted in Flanders and the Netherlands in the early 1980s. In his analysis of national and regional Dutch newspapers of October 1981, Van Dijk (1983) concluded that news coverage reflects viewpoints of the political elites and government institutions, the police and the justice department, depriving minority groups of a voice. Most news coverage about the latter put the spotlight on sensational incidents, thus constructing a negative image of these minorities. Initiating research into elite discourses about immigration in Belgium, Blommaert and Verschueren (1998) drew attention to the discourse of (in)tolerance and hidden racism. d'Haenens and De Lange (2001) analyzed representation of asylum seekers and refugees in the Dutch national newspapers *De Telegraaf* and *De Volkskrant* as well as regional dailies in the early 1990s. The overall image of asylum seekers and refugees reportedly was largely negative, prompting d'Haenens and De Lange to conclude that there were erroneous generalizations, careless use of figures and other factual material, and suggestions of threat in the lexical choice of terms like 'flood' and 'stream' (2001: 849).

In the same decade, further research was conducted by Van Gorp (2005) and Roggeband and Vliegenthart (2007), looking into the Belgian and Dutch media coverage respectively. Roggeband and Vliegenthart (2007) discovered five frames in the Dutch media over a 10-year period from 1995 to 2004 with an overall dominance of the intruder frame (above all "Islam as threat"), except for the years 1998-2000, where the multicultural frame temporarily ranked first. Van Gorp (2005) analyzed migration coverage in eight Belgian newspapers from 2000 to 2003, concluding that while 50 per cent of the articles included both victim and intruder frames, in the articles with only one frame generally the intruder frame prevailed (26 percent) over the victim frame (21 percent), except in Christmas periods. Refugees were more often cast as intruders in the Flemish press, compared with the Francophone press. The popular press comprised more articles with a dominant intruder frame than the elite press, yet without any statistical significance. As for ideological differences between progressive and conservative papers, while the left-wing *De Morgen* used the victim frame slightly more often than the other Flemish newspapers, no statistical significance of this divergence was found (Van Gorp, 2005).

More recently, Masini and Van Aelst (2017) conducted a content analysis to examine the relation between actor diversity and viewpoint diversity on the one hand and ideological orientation on the other hand, in a sample of six Flemish newspapers, covering immigration between January 1, 2013 and April 30, 2014. Based on the person-positivity hypothesis (the presence or absence of key actors is significantly related to the positive/negative direction of the viewpoints), they concluded that the closure of the gates to the immigrants' voices resulted in a negative news representation in the Flemish press (Masini and Van Aelst, 2017).

Another analysis of the Dutch media coverage of immigration concerns the study by Krouwel (2008) about the ideological differences between the left- and right-wing newspapers. It was concluded that the left-of-center *De Volkskrant* and *NRC Handelsblad*, which had gradually changed its formerly liberal stance to a more leftist orientation (De Fijter, 2006), shared similar positions in the migration debate. *De Telegraaf* was said to harbor a clear right-wing ideology.

This brings us to the ideological orientation of the newspapers investigated in the present study. Both the Flemish *De Morgen* and the Dutch *De Volkskrant* are ideologically on the left of the political spectrum. The Flemish daily is generally considered to be a progressive paper, owned by a liberal press company, De Persgroep (De Bens & Raeymaeckers, 2010). With the circulation of its print and digital versions in 2015 standing at approximately 54,882 (CIM, 2018), it is the second most popular national quality paper in Flanders. Its older counterpart in the Netherlands, *De Volkskrant*, was established in 1919 and is currently the third largest newspaper in the Netherlands (Bakker, 2016). It originally catered to the Catholic labor movement. Since the 1960s it has profiled itself more as a progressive newspaper for the young generation. The newspaper is generally believed to hold a left ideological orientation (Van Zanten, 2006; Bakker & Vasteman, 2007; van Klingeren, Boomgaarden, Vliegenthart, & de Vreese, 2015).

Theory, method, and research questions

When engaging in cross-national media comparison, the analyst needs to consider journalistic systems and cultures. As for systems, both Belgium and the Netherlands belong to the same "democratic corporatist model" (Hallin & Mancini, 2004), in that the history of strong party newspapers coexisted with the commercial press throughout much of the twentieth century. Although opinion-oriented journalism has diminished in importance and journalists increasingly embrace neutral and information-oriented roles, opinionated reporting has not entirely disappeared. Since the early theories of Halllin and Mancini, new visions of the constituent parts of journalistic professionalism have emerged (Hanitzsch, 2007). Rather than thinking in terms of models, the Worlds of Journalism Project (WJP) advances the more flexible notion of 'journalistic culture,' which has been defined as "a particular set of ideas and practices by which journalists legitimate their role in society and render their work meaningful" (Hanitzsch, 2007: 369). The WJP country reports for Belgium and the Netherlands in the 2012-2016 period are comparable, although they show a slightly greater eagerness of journalists to promote tolerance and cultural diversity in Flanders (3.31/5) than in the Netherlands (2.77/5).[3]

The units of investigation were selected by singling out all articles published during the peak period of the asylum seekers' arrival in Belgium, starting from August 24, 2015 when long waiting queues for registration and a refugee camp in downtown Brussels attracted intense media attention up to September 20.[4] Search criteria were set at a minimum of 300 words for each article that featured refugees in Europe as the main theme. The key term for the LexisNexis and GoPress databanks search was 'refugees,' since the plural form yielded more articles than its singular equivalent. This key word was selected because the

---

3   The Worlds of Journalism Study's figure for Belgium, combining the perceptions of Flemish and French-language journalists, is 3.59. Separate scores for the latter are slightly higher for promoting tolerance and cultural diversity (3.93) than their Flemish counterparts (3.31) (See www.worldsofjournalism.org/country-reports).

4   Since 2015, similar scenarios have been playing out in the summers 2017 and 2018 at the same place in Brussels. Concerns by the spokesperson for the Federal Centre for Asylum Applications, Theo Francken, that this place might become a second [jungle of] 'Calais', if the mayor of Brussels who is in charge of security for that particular area, does not take decisive action, have been met with fierce opposition from this socialist and French-speaking mayor. The debate is one more element in the intricate political power games between conservative and progressive parties, aggravated by unclear divisions of competencies between the federal and the local levels and the long festering Belgian communitarian problems between the Dutch- and French-speaking political elites. All of this naturally fuels media attention and the refugees are caught up in the middle of this political polarization.

target actors were the people who, at that time, arrived in Europe in need of protection. The reference term 'refugee' used in this article does not adopt the judicial definition in terms of acquisition of legal 'refugee' status, but follows the dictionary definition of *transient people seeking refuge*, which appears to be the general reference for this actor in the Dutch-language media, often used interchangeably with the term '(im)migrant' or 'asylum seeker.'

The corpus selection yielded 137 articles for *De Morgen* and 146 for *De Volkskrant*. First, a content-analytical study was conducted on the full corpora to examine variables, such as the level of collectivization of the refugees, the voice allocated to them, the themes and the framing processes. In a second phase, both samples were halved for the in-depth discourse analysis of all predications about and descriptions of the main actors (the refugees, the EU as an institution, the German government with its Chancellor Angela Merkel, the Hungarian government and its Premier Victor Orban, the Dutch government with its Prime Minister Rutten, the Dutch Center for Asylum Applications (COA), the Belgian government and the Premier Charles Michel, the Belgian Federal Center for Asylum Applications (Fedasil) and its spokesperson Theo Francken. These were the most frequently mentioned actors in all the corpora. The present chapter discusses the actors common to both newspapers, i.e., the refugees, the EU institution, the German and Hungarian governments and their leaders.

Underpinning the epistemological premise in this study is the theoretical perspective in Critical Discourse Studies (e.g., Fairclough, 1989) that discourse is a powerful social practice in constructing meaning. This view goes hand in hand with the insights of Social Representations Theory (e.g., Moscovici, 2000), Social Identity Theory (e.g., Tajfel & Turner, 1979), and Framing Theory (e.g., Scheufele & Tewskbury, 2007), which are all concerned with ideological power involved in representations that shape social relations and identities or maintain the social status quo. In addition, Hallidayan Systemic-Functional Linguistics (Halliday & Matthiessen, 2014) supplied us with tools for transitivity analysis, which probes into the ways syntax and semantics jointly construct agency and power. These linguistic analytical instruments can help to lay bare power relations underlying media narratives. Research questions about this aspect of agency and power are as follows: *How are the protagonists in the immigration issue positioned syntactically in the sentences (as active agents or passive agents/beneficiaries)? With what type of verbal processes are these actors associated and what are the connotational values of these processes, leading to negative/positive/neutral semantic roles allocated to the actors involved?*

To determine the type of verbal processes and the semantic roles for all actors, a coding book was developed. Given the labor-intensive work of manually coding every single sentence component, the corpus was halved and one out of every other article was selected, yielding 73 articles for *De Volkskrant* and 69 for *De Morgen*. While it is hardly possible to taxonomize the kind of activities and predications ascribed to the refugee actor, categorization of the type of verbal processes that the actor was associated with was a more realistic venture. These include material/behavioral, relational, verbal, mental, affective and perception processes and a variety of modal auxiliary verbs. For the refugee actor, the most dominant processes were the material ones, which is the reason the current chapter focuses on this type. All processes, except for the relational descriptions, were first coded for the type of role bestowed on the person/group in terms of active or passive agency. This involved syntactical analysis of sentential composition (e.g., subject, (prepositional) object, passive or active mode, nominalization). Secondly, the semantics of the roles were coded by marking the connotation of the processes with positive/negative/neutral values. While coding the verbal processes, the co-text, essential in meaning generation, needs due consideration. This can include, for example, negations and any implicit meanings created by figurative language, like metaphors or irony. Figurative meaning took precedence over literal meaning at all times. This necessitated a manual coding process with training sessions and mutual consultations. Intercoder reliability was measured on a sample of the corpora and rendered a figure for Krippendorff's Alpha's, varying from .611 to 1 (full agreement) for 24 variables. It is some of these variables that will be discussed in the empirical section of this chapter.

Patient or agentive roles were determined on the basis of dominance per article, excluding any ex aequos. Dominance was established upon the majority principle. All 'winning' codes per text were then aggregated over the entire corpus, delivering a total picture of the absolute and relative number of articles featuring the actors in a majority (positive/negative) active or (positive/negative) passive role. Portraying the refugee as primarily undergoing negative processes contributes to a victim frame. By contrast, a depiction of the refugees engaging in negative actions could generate the moral panic or intruder frame. Here are some examples of the semantic roles for the refugee:

– neutral agentive role:

"Hij laat een foto zien op zijn smartphone" [He is showing a picture on his smartphone], *De Volkskrant*, 19 September 2015

- positive agentive role:

    "Deze vluchtelingen zijn dan misschien de eersten die in hun thuisland aan de wederopbouw zullen bijdragen" [These refugees will perhaps be the first ones to contribute to the reconstruction of their homeland], *De Volkskrant*, 17 September 2015

- negative agentive role:

    "Het station was gisteren urenlang gesloten, nadat de asielzoekers voor chaos op perrons en bomvolle treinen zorgden" [the station was closed for hours yesterday, after the asylum seekers created chaos on the platforms and caused trains to be crowded], *De Morgen*, 2 Sept 2015

- positive patient role:

    "Bezorgde burgers bieden de vluchtelingen hulp, maar niemand lijkt goed te weten wat er waar precies nodig is" [concerned citizens offer help to the refugees, but nobody seems to know what exactly is necessary and where], *De Morgen*, 3 Sept 2015

- negative patient role:

    "Het cabinet bouwt een hek om Europa en keert vluchtelingen de rug toe" [The cabinet is building a fence around Europe and turning its back on the refugees], *De Volkskrant*, 9 Sept 2015

Results of the empirical analysis: *De Volkskrant* and *De Morgen*

The bulk of the study contained the transitivity analysis of semantic roles and verbal processes associated with the main actors. Only the findings of the material action processes are discussed since they represented the largest category. Although the study also yielded interesting results about the media's position toward the *local* Dutch/Belgian political elites, for practical reasons of space we zoom in on only the refugees and the most prominent common actors to both corpora (EU, Germany, Hungary). Germany and Hungary are the two countries that registered the highest numbers of new asylum applications in 2015, over 47,000 and 177,130 applications respectively (BBC,

2016).[5] This can explain why their leaders' voices ranked among the top five prominent actors in the media coverage of that period.

Agency and power: semantic roles of the refugee actor

As is clear from Table 5.1, in the Flemish corpus of *De Morgen* the refugee is depicted unambiguously in a passive position, since the majority of articles reveal a dominant patient role (75.4 percent or 52 out of 69 articles). Only 31.9 percent (22/69) of the articles give the actor a leading agentive role. As for semantics of agency, most articles with a dominantly agentive role adopt a neutral stance (86.4 percent or 19/22). The percentage difference between 4.5 percent and 9.1 percent for the refugee's positive and negative actions is negligible since this concerns only one and two articles respectively. Most articles with dominantly patient processes have a positive tenor (53.8 percent or 28/52 articles), followed by 21.2 percent (11/52) negative and 15.4 percent (8/52) neutral connotation.

As in *De Morgen*, more articles in *De Volkskrant* position the refugee in a dominant patient role as receiver of an action (54.8 percent or 40/73) than as an agent (42.5 percent or 31/73).[6] Yet, the distance between active and passive roles is smaller than in *De Morgen*. Concerning semantics, the results are very similar to the findings in *De Morgen*. The majority of the dominant active processes have a neutral tenor (87.1 percent or 27 out of the 31 articles with a dominant agent role), with only 3.2 percent (1/31) and 0 percent reserved for a positive and negative orientation respectively.[7] As for the passive processes associated with this actor, 60 percent (or 10/40) are positive, 25 percent (or 10/40) are negative and 10 percent (or 4/40) are neutral, leading to a beneficiary frame and, to a lesser extent, a victim frame.

Clearly, in both newspapers the refugee is cast as a beneficiary of help, to a lesser extent as a victim of negative processes, but not as an agent of doom. Hence, no intruder or moral panic frame can be found in the data. The high level of neutrality in the active material processes indicates how the journalists and the editors strive for objectivity in this hotly debated migration issue. On the other hand, rarely does one find discussions about the positive contributions refugees can actively make to the local host communities.

5   While the EU average of asylum applications per 100,000 of a country's local population was 260, nearly 1800 refugees per 100,000 of Hungary's local population claimed asylum in 2015. The figure for Germany stood at 587 (BBC, 2016).
6   Further research is necessary to determine statistical significance of these relative differences.
7   The aggregate percentages do not always amount to 100, since the few ex aequos are not taken up in the calculation.

Table 5.1: Semantic roles of the refugee actor by newspaper

	Articles with majority agent role	Positive agency	Negative agency	Neutral agency	Articles with majority affected role	Beneficiary	Patient	Neutral
VK	31/73 (42.5%)	1/31 (3.2%)	0/31 (0%)	27/31 (87.1%)	40/73 (54.8%)	24/40 (60.0%)	10/40 (25.0%)	4/10 (10.0%)
DM	22/69 (31.9%)	1/22 (4.5%)	2/22 (9.1%)	19/22 (86.4%)	52/69 (75.4%)	28/52 (53.8%)	11/52 (21.2%)	8/52 (15.4%)

Agency and power: semantic roles of the EU, Germany, and Hungary

The most salient gap between the Dutch and the Flemish papers lies in the semantic role allocated to Europe as an institution. As can be seen in table 5.2, the EU agency role dominates in both newspapers (67.1 percent or 29/43 [DM] and 65.4 percent or 17/26 [VK]). However, while the neutral tone of the agentive processes takes the lead in both papers (34.5 percent (or 10/29) for DM and 52.9 percent (or 9/17) for the VK), the second position is taken up by negative EU actions in the Flemish paper (24 percent or 7/29) and by positive EU actions in the Dutch paper (29.4 percent or 5/17). The Belgian daily with its headquarters in Brussels, the heart of the EU, is clearly more critical of EU actions than the Dutch paper. Yet, the Belgian paper also allocates positive agency to the EU with 17.2 percent (or 5/29) of the articles, but these rank only third after the negative and neutral accounts. Within the minority category of passive processes, a negative tenor prevails in both papers, with

Table 5.2: Semantic roles of Europe as an institution

	Articles with majority agent role	Positive agency	Negative agency	Neutral agency	Articles with majority affected role	Beneficiary	Patient	Neutral
VK	17/26 (65.4%)	5/17 (29.4%)	**1/17 (5.9%)**	9/17 (52.9%)	5/26 (19.2%)	1/5 (20.0%)	2/5 (40.0%)	1/5 (20.0%)
DM	29/43 (67.4%)	5/29 (17.2%)	**7/29 (24.1%)**	10/29 (34.5%)	6/43 (14%)	0/6 (0%)	5/6 (83.3%)	0/6 (0%)

a higher percentage (83.3 percent or 5/6) in DM than in the VK (40 percent or 2/5). The EU is thus presented in both papers as being affected negatively by the sudden rise of immigration, with a stronger focus on this crisis for the EU in the Belgian than in the Dutch newspaper.

The German government, in the spotlight because of its Chancellor's widely reported phrase "Wir schaffen das" at the end of August, is credited with an overall active role in both papers, as table 5.3 demonstrates (72 percent or 18/25 for DM and 63.2 percent or 12/19 for the VK). In *De Morgen*, we note an equal number of articles with a leading neutral and positive tone to the action verbs (38.9 percent or 7/18), whilst the neutral actions dominate in the VK (41.7 percent or 5/12), followed by the positive processes (16.7 percent with only 2 out of 12 articles associating Germany with positive active processes), in a distant second position. It seems that the Dutch accounts are somewhat less enthusiastic about Germany's actions than the Flemish narratives. The articles with predominantly negative actions for Germany account for 5.6 percent (or 1/18) and 8.3 percent (or 1/12) in DM and the VK respectively. When examining the roles for Chancellor Angela Merkel, a similar pattern emerges. DM allocates more positive agency to her (57 percent or four out of the seven articles with a dominant agency role), while the Chancellor receives only 16.7 percent (or 1/6) of the articles with a dominant positive agency in the VK.

Table 5.3: Semantic roles of the German government, including its leader Angela Merkel, and of Merkel alone

	Articles with majority agent role	Positive Agency	Negative agency	Neutral agency	Articles with majority affected role	Beneficiary	Patient	Neutral
Germany (incl. Merkel)								
VK	12/19 (63.2%)	2/12 (16.7%)	1/12 (8.3%)	5/12 (41.7%)	5/19 (26.3%)	0/5 (0%)	2/5 (40.0%)	3/5 (60.0%)
DM	18/25 (72.0%)	7/18 (38.9%)	1/18 (5.6%)	7/18 (38.9%)	4/25 (16.0%)	1/4 (25.0%)	2/4 (50.0%)	1/4 (25.0%)
Merkel								
VK	6/10 (60.0%)	1/6 (16.7%)	0/6 (0%)	4/6 (66.7%)	1/10 (10.0%)	1/10 (100%)	0/10 (0%)	0/10 (0%)
DM	7/13 (53.8%)	4/7 (57.1%)	0/7 (0%)	2/7 (28.6%)	0/13 (0%)	0/0 (0%)	0/0 (0%)	0/0 (0%)

As for the Hungarian government with the conservative Premier Victor Orban, articulating the ideologically opposite stance of Angela Merkel's welcoming position, the agentive roles are also dominant in both papers (85.7 percent or 18/21 for DM and 75 percent or 9/12 for the VK), as is obvious in table 5.4. The VK gives this actor negative agency with a prevalence of negatively connotated verbal processes (55.6 percent or 5/9), followed by 33.3 percent (3/9) of the articles with a neutral tenor. For *De Morgen*, the ranking order is just the opposite with the neutral articles coming first (44.4 percent or 8/18) and the negative ones next (27.8 percent or 5/18), thus demonstrating a higher level of neutrality toward Hungary than the Dutch newspaper. Not a single article featuring dominant positive actions by the Hungarian government appears in both newspapers. When zooming in on the roles for Premier Orban, the same pattern becomes apparent with dominance of agentive roles at 60 percent (3/5) for *De Volkskrant* and 57.2 percent (4/7) for *De Morgen*, and negative agency ranking on top at 66.7 percent (2/3) for *De Volkskrant*, while it comes only second with 25 percent (1/4) after neutral agency for 75 percent or three out of four articles with dominant agency position in *De Morgen*.

Table 5.4: Semantic roles of Hungarian government, including its Premier Victor Orban, and Orban alone

	Articles with majority agent role	Positive agency	Negative agency	Neutral agency	Articles with majority affected role	Beneficiary	Patient	Neutral
Hungary (incl. Orban)								
VK	9/12 (75.0%)	0/9 (0%)	5/9 (55.6%)	3/9 (33.3%)	1/12 (8.3%)	0/1 (0%)	0/1 (0%)	1/1 (100%)
DM	18/21 (85.7%)	0/18 (0%)	5/18 (27.8%)	8/18 (44.4%)	1/21 (4.8%)	1/1 (100%)	0/1 (0%)	0/1 (0%)
Orban								
VK	3/5 (60.0%)	0/3 (0%)	2/3 (66.7%)	0/3 (0%)	0/5 (0%)	0/0	0/0	0/0
DM	4/7 (57.2%)	0/4 (0%)	1.4 (25.0%)	3/4 (75.0%)	1/7 (14.3%)	1/1 (100%)	0/1 (0%)	0/1 (0%)

Discussion

In both newspapers, the EU, Germany, Hungary, and local political institutions and elites receive impressive media attention and are predominantly presented as active participants in the debate. They can thus advance their immigration views, which increasingly become central on their electoral platforms. This way, the refugees' plight gets politicized and also domesticated, which is also evident in the prevalence of local elites' political response and policy themes in both newspapers. Evidence of this is the renewed heated debate in summer 2018 among Belgian political elites concerning the situation with the newly arrived refugees in Brussels and the protracted Belgian federal government impasse in December 2018 about signing up to the UN global pact, the first ever international deal on the migration situation, approved by delegates from 164 countries in Marrakesh. Similar to the findings by Parker, Naper, and Goodman (2018) and Sumuvuori et al. (2016), the discourse in both newspapers centers on Europe as the focus of the crisis, thus shifting attention away from the crisis for the refugees, escaping the dismal circumstances in their home countries and having to face critical and life-threatening conditions on their journey to safer havens.

When it comes to semantics of the processes which these political players are associated with, we note subtle differences in attitude between the Dutch and the Belgian/Flemish corpora under investigation, which can by no means be generalized without further research into larger corpora. The EU receives a more positive coverage in *De Volkskrant* than in *De Morgen*. Several articles in *De Morgen* criticize the EU for its internal divisions, resulting in a Hamlet-like hesitation to efficiently handle the situation. As for the semantic positioning of the German government and its Chancellor Merkel, the Flemish paper appears to give them more credit than is the case in its Dutch counterpart. It also prints more articles with Hungarian neutral active processes than *De Volkskrant*. Yet, both papers are aligned in not publishing any positive articles about the Hungarian government and its leader's actions.

In contrast to the active roles bestowed on the EU's political institutions and leaders, refugees are presented by both papers in primarily nonagentive roles, and are deprived of power by being muted in not getting access to the public forum to tell their own stories as political and social subjects, situated against a troubled historical background in their home countries. However, in the Dutch newspaper the difference between active and passive roles for the refugee is smaller than in the Flemish daily, where the articles with a leading passive role far outnumber those which offer the refugee some agency. In other words, *De Volkskrant* offers the refugee a more active function than *De*

Morgen, although this agency is still overshadowed by the larger percentage of processes the refugees undergo.

The lack of voice and agency for the refugees is generated not only in the absence of direct or indirect quotation, but also in the syntactic and semantic positioning of the refugees in passive roles without agentive power. As for semantics, whenever agency is allocated to the refugees, it is associated with *neutral* material action verbs, thus giving an overall impression of a neutral tenor and objective reporting. A brief digression on methodological approach is in order here. This result underscores the importance of adjudging not only positive and negative, but also neutral evaluation to all processes examined. It is essential to factor in *all* material processes, including the neutral action verbs, instead of merely focusing on the minority of colored lexical items in the texts, which often blinds the eye of the researcher examining framing processes. This rigorous approach complicates the research and is, above all, a time-consuming exercise if it is to be carried out manually. But judging from the many cases where the figurative meaning prevailed over the literal one, we argue that, so far, computer-aided linguistic analysis cannot replace the human interpretative capacities to distinguish connotation, even denotation, of certain verbs for categorization into the various verbal processes.

It says a lot for the journalists and authors of these particular corpora that in the majority of the verbal processes associated with refugees a neutral stance was adopted, and a high level of editorial objectivity was reached, at least as far as material action verbs are concerned. This echoes earlier findings published in the Finnish report about the migration coverage in a selection of European media outlets, including *De Morgen*, six months later (Sumuvuori et al., 2016). Yet, this dominant neutrality does not preclude an additional examination of the ratio between positive and negative actions allocated to the refugees. As for the material action verbs, negative actions appear twice as much as positive action processes, but their numbers are still negligible in comparison with the neutral action verbs and the passive processes in general. Therefore, just like the findings about the center-right newspapers' coverage of the refugee situation in that same crisis period (Lams, 2018), no moral panic or threat frames underlie the narratives of these center-left newspapers.

On the basis of this semantic role analysis, it can be concluded that, unlike earlier findings by Van Gorp (2005) and Roggeband and Vliegenthart (2007) about the contribution of the negative frames for the migrants and refugees to a dominant securitization sphere in the previous decade, the current corpora do not cast the refugee in such a dominant position of intruder. The ascription of maliciousness, as discussed in Chouliaraki and Zaborowski (2017), which "narrows down the refugee's agency to the capacity to harm"

(2017: 268) is largely absent in this emotional period of a crisis atmosphere in which the sufferer is portrayed as in dire need of help. If maliciousness surfaces at all, it often originates through quotations from frame sponsors, like right-wing political leaders. Moreover, when it comes to the passive role of the refugees, the negative victim position is only secondary to the more dominant positive image of refugees as beneficiaries. This representational shift from intruder to victim and beneficiary demonstrates the importance of political context and the transient nature of events for discursive change and frame dominance (Benson, 2013). More negative images can easily return after single incidents involving refugees, and confirms the need for periodical revisits of previous research, as called for by Caviedes (2015). As for the active role of the refugees, articles about the positive impact the newcomers could have on the local communities unfortunately remain largely absent. Yet again, this can, to some extent, be attributed to the historical and situational context of that time period, with all focus on the European authorities, unprepared to welcome a sudden surge of newcomers in dire need of humanitarian assistance.

Acknowledgments

Much gratitude goes to my two students, Katrien Hertogs and Birthe Van der Veken, for collecting the data and coding the corpora after several training sessions and intensive consultation rounds.

References

Bakker, P., & Vasterman, P. (2007). The Dutch media landscape. In G. Terzis (ed.), *European Media Governance: National and Regional Dimensions* (pp.145–156). Bristol: Intellect books.
BBC (2016). *Migrant crisis: migration to Europe explained in seven charts*, Retrieved March 8, 2016, from http://www.bbc.com/news/worl-europe-34131911.
Benson, R. (2013) *Shaping Immigration News: A French-American Comparison*, New York: Cambridge University Press.
Benson, R., & Wood, T. (2015). Who says what or nothing at all? Speakers, frames and frameless quotes in unauthorized immigration news in the UK, Norway and France. *American Behavioural Scientist*, 59(7), 802–821.
Blommaert, J., & Verschueren, J. (1998). *Debating diversity: Analysing the discourse of tolerance*. London: Routledge.
Caviedes, A. (2015). An emerging European news portrayal of immigration? *Journal of Ethnic and Migration Studies*, 42(6), 897–917.

Chouliaraki, L., & Zaborowski, R. (2017). Voice and Community in the 2015 Refugee crisis: A content analysis of news coverage in eight European countries. *International Communication Gazette*, 79(6-7), 613–635.

CIM, Information Center for Media (2018). CIM-figures, Retrieved July 15, 2018, from http://www.cim.be/nl/pers/echtverklaring-resultaten.

De Bens, E., & Raeymaeckers, K. (2010). *De Pers in België: het Verhaal van de Belgische Dagbladpers: Gisteren, Vandaag en Morgen* [The Press in Belgium: The Story of the Belgian Newspaper Press: Yesterday, Today and Tomorrow] (4th revised version). Leuven: Lannoo.

De Cock, R., Mertens, S., Sundin, E., Lams, L., Mistiaen, V., Joris, W., & d'Haenens, L. (2018). Refugees in the news: Comparing Belgian and Swedish newspaper coverage of the European refugee situation during summer 2015. *Communications: The European Journal of Communication Research*, 43(3), 301–323.

De Fijter, N. (2006, December 13). Vrouw als hoofdredacteur [Woman as editor-in-chief]. *Trouw*. Retrieved July 21, 2018 from http://www.trouw.nl/tr/nl/4324/NIeuws/article/details/1704882/2006/12/13/Vrouw-als-hoofredacteur.dhtml.

d'Haenens, L., & De Lange, M. (2001). Framing of asylum seekers in Dutch regional newspapers. *Media, Culture & Society*, 23, 847–860.

Eurostat (2015). *Asylum in the EU Member States. More than 410 000 first time asylum seekers registered in the third quarter of 2015*. Retrieved April 15, 2016, from https://ec.europa.eu/eurostat/documents/2995521/7105334/3-10122015-AP-EN.pdf

Eurostat (2016). *Asylum in the EU Member States. Record number of over 1.2 million first time asylum seekers registered in 2015*. Retrieved November 10, 2017, from http://ec.europa.eu/eurostat/web/products-press-releases/-/3-04032016-AP.

Fairclough, N. (1989). *Language and Power*. London: Longman.

Halliday, M.A.K., & Matthiessen, C.M. (2014). *Halliday's Introduction to Functional Grammar*, 4th edition. Abingdon, NY: Routledge.

Hallin, D.C., & Mancini, P. (2004). *Comparing Media Systems: Three Models of Media and Politics*. New York: Cambridge University Press.

Hanitzsch, T. (2007). Deconstructing journalism culture: towards a universal theory. *Communication Theory*, 17(4), 367–385.

Jacobs, L., & Hooghe, M. (2015). *Worden we overspoeld door immigratie(nieuws)? Een onderzoek naar de berichtgeving over immigratie in de Vlaamse televisiejournaals*. [Are we being flooded by immigration (news)? A study on the news coverage of immigration in Flemish television news]. Newsletter Steunpunt Media.

Kaleda, C. (2014). Media perceptions: Mainstream and grassroots media coverage of refugees in Kenya and the effects of global refugee policy. *Refugee Survey Quarterly*, 33(1), 94–111.

KhosraviNik, M. (2010). The representation of refugees, asylum seekers and immigrants in British newspapers: A critical discourse analysis. *Journal of Language and Politics*, 9(1), 1–28.

Krouwel, A. (2008). *Links en rechts in de nieuws. Aandacht voor politieke partijen en politici in de Nederlandse media* [Left and right in the news. Attention to political parties and politicians in the Dutch media]. Amsterdam: Free University of Amsterdam, Centre for Applied Political Science.

Lams, L. (2018). Discursive constructions of the summer 2015 refugee crisis: a comparative analysis of French, Dutch, Belgian Francophone and British centre-of-right narratives. *Journal of Applied Journalism and Media Studies*, 7(1), 103–127.

Lecheler, S., Bos, L., & Vliegenthart, R. (2015). The mediating role of emotions: news framing effects on opinions about immigration. *Journalism & Mass Communication Quarterly*, 92(4), 812–838.

Masini, A., & Van Aelst, P. (2017) Actor diversity and viewpoint diversity: Two of a kind. *Communications: The European Journal of Communication Research*, 42(2), 107–126.

McCombs, M.E., & Shaw, D.L. (1972). The agenda-setting functions of mass media. *Public Opinion Quarterly*, 36(2), 176–187.

Moscovici, C. (2000). *Social Representations. Explorations in Social Psychology*. Cambridge, UK: Polity Press.

Parker, S., Naper, A.A., & Goodman, S. (2018). How a photograph of a drowned refugee child turned a migrant crisis into a refugee crisis: a comparative discourse analysis. *For(e)dialogue*, 2(1), 12–28.

Philo, G., Briant, E., & Donald, P. (2013). *Bad News for Refugees*. London: Pluto Press.

Roggeband, C., & Vliegenthart, R. (2007). Divergent framing: the public debate on migration in the Dutch parliament and media, 1995-2004. *West European Politics*, 30(3), 524–548.

Scheufele, D.A., & Tewksbury, D. (2007). Framing, agenda setting, and priming: the evolution of three media effects models. *Journal of Communication*, 57, 9–20.

Sumuvuori, J., Vähäsöyrinki, A., Eerolainen, T., Lindvall, J., Pasternak, R., Syrjälä, M., & Talvela, A. (2016). *Refugees and asylum seekers in press coverage. A comparative content analysis of texts published in Helsingin Sanomat and Aamulehti (FI), The Guardian and The Times (UK) and Le Soir and De Morgen (BE) newspapers in the time period from 1 January to 31 January 2016*. London: The Finnish Institute in London.

Thorbjørnsrud, K., & Figenschou, T.U. (2016). Do marginalized sources matter? A comparative analysis of irregular migrant voice in western media. *Journalism Studies*, 17(3), 337–355.

UNHCR (2015). *Mid-Year Trends 2015*, 4. Retrieved July 15, 2016 from http://www.unhcr.org/56701b969.html.

Van Dijk, T. (1983). *Minderheden in de media: een analyse van de berichtgeving over etnische minderheden in de dagbladenpers* [Minorities in the media: an analysis of news reporting on ethnic minorities in the press]. Amsterdam: SUA.

Van Gorp, B. (2005). Where is the frame? Victims and intruders in the Belgian press coverage of the asylum issue. *European Journal of Communication*, 20(4), 484–507.

Van Klingeren, M., Boomgaarden, H.G., Vliegenthart, R., & de Vreese, C.H. (2015). Real world is not enough: the media as an additional source of negative attitudes toward immigration, comparing Denmark and the Netherlands, *European Sociological Review*, 31(3), 268–283.

Van Zanten, C. (2006, November 23). *Redactie Volkskrant stemt massaal links*. [Editorial team Volkskrant massively votes left], Elsevier. Retrieved July 21, 2016, from http://www.elsevier/nl/Nederland/nieuws/2006/11/Redactie-Volkskrant-stemt-massaal-links-ELSEVIER101901W.

Worlds of Journalism Studies (WJS) (2017). *The WJS 2012-2015 Study: Conceptual Framework* [online]. Retrieved November 23, 2017, from http://www.worldsofjournalism.org/research/2012-2016-study/conceptual-framework/.

Chapter 6
A Diverse View on the Promotion of Tolerance and Cultural Diversity through the Eyes of Journalists: Focus on Belgium and Sweden

Stefan Mertens, Leen d'Haenens, Rozane De Cock, and Olivier Standaert

Cultural values, migrant integration policy, and journalistic role perceptions: Collusion or Collision?

For several years now, immigration has steered the policy debate in Europe and it continues to do so as new urgent matters keep on setting the agenda. Integration of immigrants and immigration as a whole is a major political issue, not only in the realm of policy, but also in those of public opinion and journalism, (e.g., Watson & Riffe, 2013). A country's cultural values can also stimulate or reject immigration (Leong & Ward, 2006). This chapter explores the interrelationships between data on policy, public opinion, cultural values, and journalistic cultures in an effort to integrate databases that were hitherto only studied separately, and we do so with an emphasis on journalistic cultures. The databases used are the Migrant Integration Policy Index (MIPEX), the World Values Survey (WVS), and the Worlds of Journalism Study (WJS).

The MIPEX classification is in fact a normative evaluation of countries whereby experts attribute scores of between 0 and 100 to the list of countries, assuming at least implicitly that 'less' developed policy contexts should be adjusted based on the better-developed migration policies of the 'more' developed countries. 'Policy' does not operate in a cultural vacuum, so it comes as no surprise that researchers have sought and found (Callens, 2015; Hooghe & De Vroome, 2015; Schroyens, Meuleman, & Galle, 2015) links between the public opinion of nation states on the one hand and the latter's migration and integration policies on the other. The aforementioned researchers have weighed the importance of two conflicting hypotheses. The first hypothesis states that liberal immigration policies foster competition, and hence public attitudes that oppose increased immigration. The second hypothesis that was already vindicated in research prior to ours stresses a positive correlation between a more welcoming public opinion and policies in migrant-friendly countries.

Welzel (2013)—a key specialist of the World Values Survey—developed a theory of human development according to which social-economic development, emancipative cultural change, and democratization constitute a coherent entity of social progress. The author classifies countries according to their cultural values and the extent to which opportunities for emancipative values are on offer.

Communication scientists (see e.g., Vliegenthart, 2015) have stressed the importance of a third sphere alongside cultural attitudes and policy orientations, where political issues get constructed: the media sphere. There are important agenda interactions between political actors, the general public, and the media. McCombs (2011: 1) argued that: "The power of the news media to set a nation's agenda, to focus public attention on a few key public issues, is an immense and well-documented influence." Nevertheless, the impact of the media on the public is currently assessed as important, but not as unilaterally and predominantly as has been suggested by early communication scholars.

When it comes to the influence of the media on politics, most of the relevant literature confirms the existence of media effects on the political agenda (Walgrave & Van Aelst, 2016), although contingency—depending on specific circumstances—has also been observed. What works for agendas might also work for values. The emancipative values in national public opinion cultures and political cultures may very well go together with similar journalistic values. Investigating the extent to which this holds true is the goal of our study.

We studied the relationship between the media and other spheres based on data from the Worlds of Journalism international research study. These data contain information about the way journalists in 67 countries view their professional roles. The empirical goal of this chapter is to compare the degree to which emancipative values in the Worlds Value Survey coexist with MIPEX policies (as reflected in prior research results) as well with journalistic role perceptions (a less explored domain so far). Our analysis will focus on countries for which data on three research dimensions are available: the MIPEX policy index, the international World Values survey and the Worlds of Journalism international journalists' study, that is a set of 24 countries.

The three databases

MIPEX shows an integrated score on eight policy areas in 40 western countries. The eight domains are *labor market mobility, family reunion, education* (since 2010), *political participation, long-term residence, health, access to nationality,* and *anti-discrimination*. An integrated score is calculated based on assessments of experts involved in a peer-review process. Although theoretically each domain has independent index scores (from 1 to 100), we refer to the integrated score, leading to an overall score out of 100. The experts who score the different dimensions are independent legal scholars and practitioners within the domain of migration law (Niessen, 2009: 7). The consulted experts rely on in-depth knowledge of the national legal and regulatory provisions on legal policy within their own country, and are also able to assess the regulatory frameworks of other countries from a comparative perspective. In order to achieve optimal objectivity in scoring, a second opinion of an extra expert is always requested to peer-review the scores of the individual expert assessments.

The MIPEX database is the only database used in this study that is derived from judgments by experts. The other two databases are based on survey research input. Current World Values Survey data (WVS, 6th wave, 2010-2014) gathered in 60 countries made it possible to put together a number of different scales (http://www.worldvaluessurvey.org). The WVS targets a representative adult population sample (at least 1,200 respondents per country) in different countries with the same survey questionnaire, aimed at providing essential insights into political and social-cultural change.

Especially relevant for research on immigration opinions is the Emancipative Values Index. Emancipative values emphasize freedom for everyone. Based on these values a scale is constituted ranging from 0 to 1. The Emancipative Values Index is based on four sub-indices: *autonomy, equality, choice,* and *voice*. The institutional spheres from which these four indices are derived are widely different. Autonomy mainly points to the autonomy of children in the family context. Equality refers to gender equality, whereas choice is an indicator of ethical matters such as homosexuality, abortion, and divorce. The last index, voice, refers to political participation. Previous research has shown that these core values (Welzer, 2013) are related to important concepts such as well-being, democracy, and environmental sustainability. Our study thus wants to advance the scientific knowledge of the interrelational connections between values in policy (MIPEX), public opinion (WVS), and journalism (Worlds of Journalism Study).

The third used database is on journalism. Journalism (Deuze, 2005) is among other professions known to have an ideology of its own; this ideology has been interpreted in many different ways across the globe. The *Worlds of Journalism* study brought together researchers from 67 countries. In an unprecedented collaborative effort, more than 27,500 journalists were interviewed between 2012 and 2016, based on a common methodological framework (http://www.worldsofjournalism.org). The Worlds of Journalism questionnaire deals with many dimensions of the occupational ideology. One of the questions raised was the degree to which journalists see it as their professional role to promote tolerance and cultural diversity in the countries where they work, although this conception conflicts somewhat with the universal ideal of 'objectivity' (e.g., Broersma, 2015), which implies that journalists should not take sides in public debates, even when ideals such as cultural diversity are at stake. Since immigration issues policy and public opinion are interrelated (Callens, 2015), we will study whether journalistic culture has been following this trend.

The question about journalistic roles relates to a wider set of questions regarding journalists' perceptions of professional roles. The items in question can be grouped under four headings: the *monitoring* role, the *interventionist* role, the *collaborative* role, and, finally, the *accommodating* role of journalism. The monitoring role implies that journalists want to provide political information, monitor and scrutinize political and business actors, and motivate people to participate in politics. The interventionist role refers to journalists' advocating for social change, influencing public opinion, setting the political agenda, and supporting national development. The collaborative role of journalism concentrates on supporting government policy and conveying a positive image of political leadership. Finally, the accommodating role of journalism refers to the provision of entertainment, news that attracts the largest audience possible, and offers advice for daily life. In our study, we will investigate how the role promoting tolerance and cultural diversity relates to the other perceived roles.

Obviously, this analysis cannot answer questions on causality. It is most likely that journalism, cultural values, and policy will influence each other in a constant intermingling of causes and effects. Each one of these databases has had a large influence on research, so that it is interesting to see whether their items correlate, although the databases are based on different theoretical frameworks. A large-scale multi-country study of values, policy, and journalism measured with a unified theoretical background is lacking, and is practically unfeasible. Therefore, it is most necessary to compare these existing databases with different backgrounds to get a grasp of how culture, policy, and journalism are intertwined.

After having provided a general overview of the databases and pointed at the interaction between them, we specifically focus on the similarities and differences between Belgium (both French- and Dutch-speaking) and Sweden, as this is a central dimension of the IM²MEDIATE project on which this book reports.

Although an integration of the databases mentioned here (MIPEX, World Values Survey, and Worlds of Journalism) was not undertaken in previous research, it has to be noted that in their classic work on comparing media systems, Hallin and Mancini (2004) have made an international comparison including Sweden and Belgium and classified both Belgium and Sweden as democratic corporatist media systems. The democratic corporatist model (Hallin & Mancini, 2004: 298) is characterized by a strong emphasis on the role of organized social groups in society, but simultaneously a strong adherence to the 'common good'. The free flow of information is deemed important, but the state has a positive obligation to sustain that free flow.

Despite this similar background in both Sweden and Belgium, there are some peculiarities that need to be pointed out. Van Aelst and Aalberg (2011) compared the degree of formality of relations between politicians and journalists in three countries, i.e., Sweden, Norway, and Belgium. The study found that the relations between members of both professions were most formal in Sweden and least formal in Belgium, with Norway occupying an in-between position. This higher degree of formality might go together with a strong emphasis on the monitoring role of journalism in Sweden, when compared to Belgium. Indeed, Swedish journalism has been said to be influenced strongly by the 'Granskningsidealet' (i.e., the Watchdog Ideal) of journalism (Wiik, 2007). This watchdog ideal might also imply that the collaborative role of journalists (such as journalists supporting government policy) might be more outspokenly sustained in Belgium when compared with Sweden.

The supposed detachment of Swedish journalism is however ambiguous. Another dimension of Swedish journalism is its preoccupation with diversity. Comparing Swedish journalism with German journalism, Graf and Jönhill (2011: 10) remark that Sweden has a long history of being occupied with diversity in journalism and making plans sustaining diversity in journalism. Journalists might not only be critical toward authorities, but also engaged to change society according to the ideals of multiculturalism. This orientation might imply that Swedish journalists more often see it as their role to promote tolerance and cultural diversity in society, when compared with Belgian journalists. This might go together with other more interventionist role perceptions in Sweden when compared to Belgium.

Strömbäck, Nord, and Shehata (2012) remark that journalism in Sweden is nowadays caught between professionalization and commercialization. Commercialization might imply that increasingly role perceptions are oriented toward pleasing the audience, rather than controlling politics. Also in Belgium (Raeymaekers, Paulussen, & De Keyser, 2012: 152) journalists worry that the impact of sensationalism is increasing. Although both Swedish and Belgian journalism are probably influenced by the evolution toward commercialism, we might suspect that as a corroboration of the more pronounced watchdog role of journalism in Sweden the accommodative role of journalism is less developed compared to Belgium as well.

It must furthermore be noted that a comparison between Belgian and Swedish journalism also has to take into account that journalism in Belgium is far from homogenous. Belgian journalism includes both French-language and Dutch-language journalism. French-speaking journalism (Bonin et al., 2017) is more influenced by what Hallin and Mancini (2004) call the polarized pluralist model. This Mediterranean oriented cluster of media systems historically has a greater degree of political parallelism than the democratic corporatist model. This might result in a higher degree of monitoring journalism, interventionism, and collaborative journalism in French-speaking Belgian journalism. Promoting tolerance and cultural diversity by journalists might be a more prominent role in French-speaking Belgium as well, because historically (Billiet, Maddens, & Beerten, 2003) this region is associated with a greater openness toward migration and multiculturalism than Flanders. As the degree of market orientation is also lower in polarized pluralist media systems, we might also expect to have a lower accommodative role of journalism in French-speaking journalism.

Hypotheses and research questions

The links between MIPEX and public opinion (as expressed in the WVS) have been explored in earlier research. The links with journalism culture have not yet been extensively investigated. Nevertheless, it is logically consistent to assume that the degree to which journalists see it as their professional role to promote tolerance and cultural diversity is connected with integration-friendly options in policy and public opinion. This leads us to the following hypotheses:

H1: In countries with high MIPEX values, journalists will view promoting tolerance and cultural diversity as an important professional role.

H2: In countries with high emancipative values, journalists will view promoting tolerance and cultural diversity as an important professional role.
Furthermore, logical assumptions on the resonance between policy, public opinion dimensions, and other dimensions of journalism culture are less derivable from earlier research. Therefore, we formulated open research questions here rather than hypotheses.
RQ1: Is there a correlation between MIPEX and the role perception on promoting tolerance and cultural diversity and the four other journalistic role perceptions (i.e., monitoring, interventionist, collaborative, accommodating roles)?
RQ2: Is there a correlation between emancipative values and the role perception on promoting tolerance and cultural diversity and the four other journalistic role perceptions?
To test these research questions, a database of countries was compiled that consisted of all the 24 countries that were included in all three central databases. The countries for which data are available are all Western countries, except for South Korea, the only non-Western country that met the criteria for inclusion in this study.

Table 6.1: Countries under study

Australia	Estonia	Ireland	Spain
Austria	Finland	Latvia	Sweden
Belgium	Germany	The Netherlands	Switzerland
Bulgaria	Greece	Portugal	Turkey
Canada	Hungary	Romania	UK
Czech Republic	Iceland	South Korea	USA

In addition to the study of the interrelations, we aimed to examine whether these countries group together on the dimensions specified in these three databases. Focusing specifically on the role perception that journalists would like to promote tolerance and cultural diversity, we ran analyses of the clustering of countries on three dimensions, combining each dimension with this particular role perception. These three dimensions are the MIPEX data, the World Values Survey, and the four other role perceptions borrowed from the Worlds of Journalism Study.
RQ3: How do Western countries cluster together when it comes to the role perception that journalists should promote tolerance and cultural diversity in correlation

with data on integration policy, emancipative values, and other journalistic role perceptions?

Finally, we test hypotheses comparing Belgian with Swedish journalism cultures and Francophone Belgian journalism with Dutch-speaking Belgian journalism.

H3: *Journalistic role perceptions will be different in Belgium and Sweden.*

H3a: *The role perception that journalism needs to promote tolerance and cultural diversity is more important for Swedish journalism when compared to Belgian journalism.*

H3b: *The monitoring role of journalism is more important for Swedish journalists when compared to Belgian journalists.*

H3c: *The collaborative role of journalism is more important for Belgian journalists when compared to Swedish journalists.*

H3d: *The interventionist role of journalism is more important for Swedish journalists when compared to Belgian journalists.*

H3e: *The accommodative role of journalism is more important for Belgian journalists when compared to Swedish journalists.*

H4: *Journalistic role perceptions will be different in French-speaking and Dutch-speaking Belgian journalism.*

H4a: *The role perception that journalism needs to promote tolerance and cultural diversity is more important for French-speaking journalism when compared to Dutch-speaking Belgian journalism.*

H4b: *The monitoring role of journalism is more important for French-speaking Belgian journalists when compared to Dutch-speaking Belgian journalists.*

H4c: *The collaborative role of journalism is more important for French-speaking Belgian journalists when compared to Dutch-speaking Belgian journalists.*

H4d: *The interventionist role of journalism is more important for French-speaking Belgian journalists when compared to Dutch-speaking Belgian journalists.*

H4e: *The accommodative role of journalism is more important for Dutch-speaking Belgian journalists when compared to French-speaking Belgian journalists.*

Methods and analysis techniques

Technique 1: Correlation analysis

We used a data set of 24 countries that met the abovementioned inclusion criteria. Each country was entered as a case, and each dimension from the chosen databases was entered as a variable. These scores have a value of between 0 and 100 for each country on each dimension. These values are percentage scores in the case of the WVS and the Worlds of Journalism Study, and Evaluation by Experts scores in the case of MIPEX. This dataset is available upon request from the authors of this study. Pearson's correlations were calculated. Tables are presented with the dimensions from the four databases used on the horizontal and the vertical axis, indicating their interrelations. The cells of the tables are Pearson's correlation coefficients, representing the degree to which the different dimensions are intertwined. We calculated significance at the .01, .05, and .10 levels. The higher (.10) level of significance is included because we are dealing with a statistically small sample of European countries ($N = 24$).[8]

Technique 2: Cluster analysis

We ran a cluster analysis with four clusters to identify countries with similar or dissimilar profiles, while focusing on the role of journalism to promote tolerance and cultural diversity and combining each of the four databases with this role perception. We went through several exercises in dividing the map of Europe (plus some non-European countries) to come up with "four clusters of the press" when it comes to promoting tolerance and diversity, paraphrasing the seminal work of Siebert, Peterson, and Schramm (1956) on media models across the globe.

This allowed us to didactically evaluate the impact of each database on the specific role perception we focused on. The clustering method used is the furthest neighbor method, which tends to produce compact clusters of similar size. This method allows us to explain differences and similarities between groups of countries more didactically, compared to other methods that create a large center cluster and a few smaller clusters containing a few countries or containing only one. Graphically the clusters are presented using dendrograms, i.e., tree-like structures to visually present how countries group together.

Technique 3: t-tests

The questions about role perceptions of journalism in the Worlds of Journalism Study used a five-point Likert scale. These ordinal data are used quantitatively with a comparison of means using t-tests. The t-tests allow two by two comparisons between Belgian journalists and Swedish journalists and between Dutch-speaking Belgian journalists and French-speaking Belgian journalists.

---

8   This results in a slightly different reporting of significance levels in this chapter of the book.

Results

Correlation analysis

Emphasis (see Table 6.2) on the importance of promoting tolerance does not significantly correlate with the MIPEX scores ($r = -0.133, p = .534$), nor does this role perception significantly correlate with emancipative values ($r = -0.331, p = .114$). In other words, the hypotheses on MIPEX (H1) and emancipative values (H2) are not confirmed.

Table 6.2: Correlations between journalistic role perceptions and MIPEX and emancipative values and Hofstedian dimensions

	MIPEX	Emancipative values
Tolerance	-0.133	-0.331
Monitoring	0.217	-0.126
Interventionism	-0.479**	-0.714***
Collaboration	-0.402*	-0.590**
Accommodation	-0.355*	-0.034

Note: * = $p < .1$, ** = $p < .05$, *** = $p < .01$

Additional research questions (RQ 1 and 2) deal with the link between MIPEX and emancipative values on the one hand, and other role perceptions of journalists on the other hand.

The journalistic role perceptions that correlate most strongly with the other databases are interventionism and collaboration. Both these journalistic role perceptions tend to be associated with lower MIPEX values and lower emancipative values. The correlations are more blatant in the case of interventionism (i.e., MIPEX: $r = -0.479, p = .018$; emancipative values, $r = -0.714, p = .000$). The correlations with collaboration, while somewhat lower, follow the same trend (i.e., MIPEX: $r = -0.402, p = .052$; emancipative values, $r = -0.590, p = .002$).

The perception that journalists should promote tolerance and cultural diversity throughout their work co-occurs with the perception that they should monitor society ($r = 0.538, p = .007$) as well as with interventionism ($r = 0.691, p = .000$) (see Table 6.3). Interventionism itself is tied up with collaboration in a high correlation ($r = 0.752, p = .000$). A last significant correlation to be noted in table 3 indicates that monitoring and accommodating forms of journalism clearly do not go together, as indicated by a strong negative correlation ($r = -0.532, p = .007$).

Table 6.3: Intercorrelations among journalistic role perceptions

	Monitoring	Interventionism	Collaboration	Accommodation
Tolerance	0.538***	0.691***	0.305	-0.009
Monitoring		0.367*	0.260	-0.532***
Interventionism			0.752***	0.073
Collaboration				0.161

Note: * = $p < .1$, ** = $p < .05$, *** = $p < .01$

Cluster Analysis

Only two countries have both a strong integration policy (high MIPEX) and a strong emphasis on tolerance among journalists These two countries are Portugal and Sweden. Another small cluster consists of Latvia and Turkey: both on the outside of Europe, these two countries exhibit a strong emphasis on tolerance among journalists, but also a weak integration policy, based on the MIPEX score.

Next to these two small clusters, we identified two larger clusters, which are clearly different regions. The first one consists of Western European countries. These countries have highly developed integration policies, but their journalists do not seem too concerned with promoting tolerance and cultural diversity. Next to the Western European countries, English-speaking Western countries outside Europe join this cluster: Australia, Canada, and the United States.

The second large cluster includes only one English-speaking country: Ireland. Iceland is also included in this cluster. In addition to Iceland and Ireland, a large group of Central and Eastern European countries are part of the cluster as well. South Korea also joins this cluster.

The second clustering exercise is a further attempt to classify the data with four clusters using other variables. It resulted in four clusters of the press based on emancipative values measured in the World Values Survey and the journalists' perception of their role as promoting tolerance and cultural diversity (Figure 6.2). This cluster solution also includes two small clusters and two large clusters. Two countries that already stood out in the first clustering exercise once again confirm their uniqueness. Sweden, high on MIPEX, is

Figure 6.1: Four clusters of the press based on MIPEX and the role perception that journalists should promote tolerance and cultural diversity

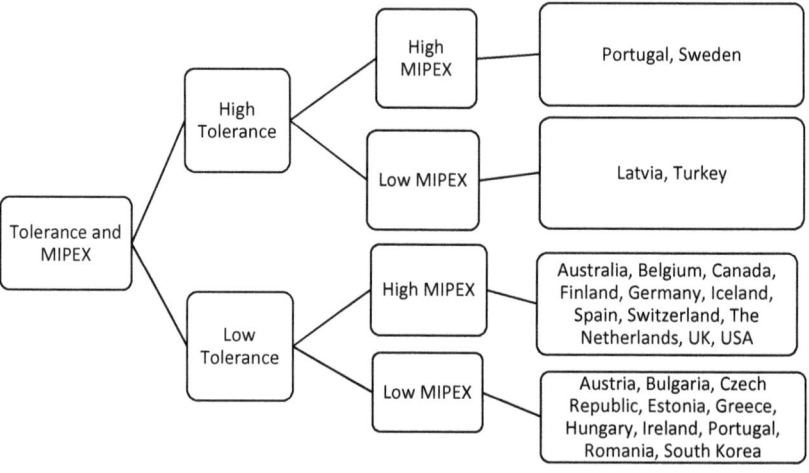

Figure 6.2: Four clusters of the press based on emancipative values and journalists' perception of their role as promoting tolerance and cultural diversity

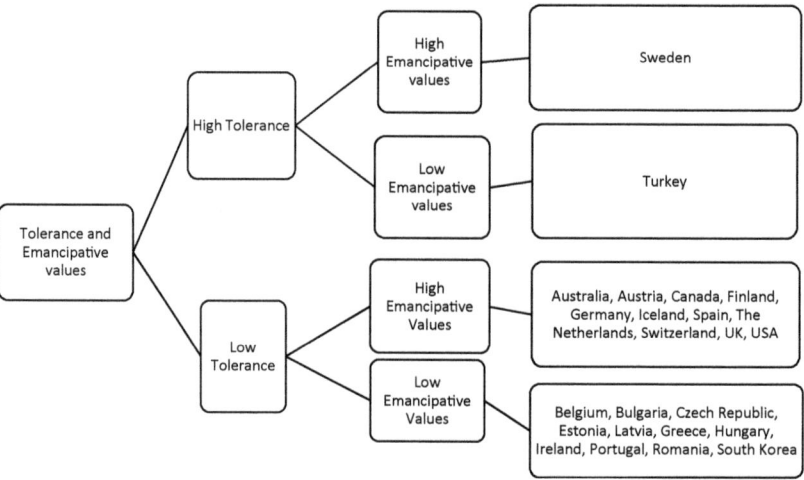

also scoring very high on the emancipative values. On the other hand, Turkey is scoring low on emancipative values as well as on MIPEX. Although the clustering method we used does not tend to form small clusters the uniqueness of Sweden and Turkey makes them one-country clusters anyhow.

Figure 6.3: Four clusters of the press based on interventionism and journalists' perception of their role as promoting tolerance and cultural diversity

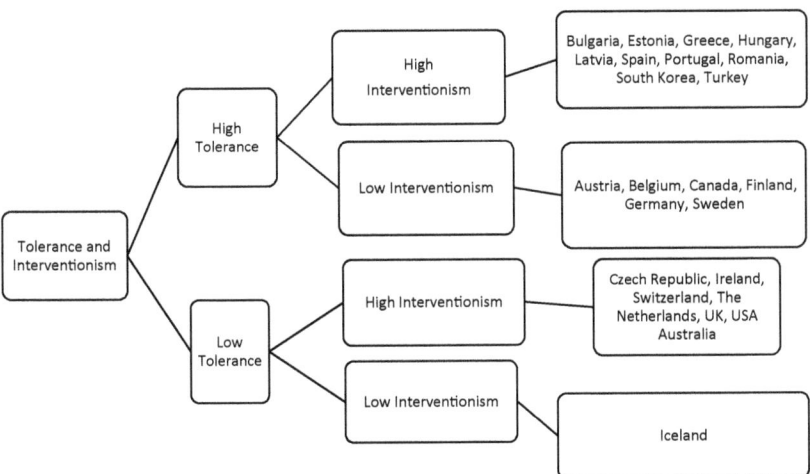

The two other countries—Portugal and Latvia—that belong to the first cluster's small groups join another, larger cluster. This cluster includes the bulk of countries that were grouped together in the 'low MIPEX-low tolerance' cluster. There is once again similarity between the large group of countries in the 'high emancipative values and low tolerance' cluster and the 'high MIPEX-low tolerance' cluster.

Finally, we produced clusters using interventionism and the journalistic focus on tolerance as input. Iceland, a country appearing together with very different countries in the earlier cluster analyses, has its very own place in this cluster analysis, characterized by low interventionism and a low focus on promoting tolerance among journalists.

The combination of high interventionism with a high focus on tolerance among journalists has a clear regional Southern identity in this cluster analysis. Journalism in the Baltic countries has the features found in Southern countries, making these countries also a part of this cluster.

In this cluster analysis the countries that are in the 'high-high' and 'low-low' clusters are easily identified from a geographic point of view. In the 'high-low' and 'low-high' groups, however, we find all the Germanic language-speaking countries, as well as Finland and the Czech Republic, two countries that are geographically close to these Germanic countries. It is however difficult to make a clear distinction between the two groups since the countries mentioned are scattered throughout these two clusters.

Comparing Belgium and Sweden

The results comparing Belgium and Sweden confirm most hypotheses on differences between Belgium and Sweden very clearly. All tested role perceptions differ statistically significantly from each other in the two countries, although not always in the predicted direction.

Indeed, as hypothesized, Swedish journalists pay more attention to promoting tolerance and cultural diversity (4.06 versus 3.59 on a five-point scale, 4.06 versus 3.59, $t = -7.234, p < .001$). The Swedish journalists also score higher on the four role perceptions associated with the monitoring role, i.e., to provide analysis of current affairs (4.06 versus 3.59, $t = -7.234, p < .001$), to monitor and scrutinize political leaders (4.35 versus 3.38, $t = -4.732, p < .001$), to monitor and scrutinize business (4.20 versus 3.25, $t = -14.446, p < .001$), and to motivate people to participate in political activity (2.92 versus 2.52, $t = -5.482, p < .01$).

The role of promoting tolerance and the monitoring roles generally score higher on the five-point scale compared with the interventionist and collaborative role perceptions, both in Sweden and Belgium. Nevertheless the results from Belgium and Sweden are different. In four of the five cases this confirms our hypotheses. Indeed, as to interventionism, Swedish journalists are more motivated to influence public opinion (2.62 versus 2.48, $t = -2.048, p < .05$), to advocate for social change (2.98 versus 2.58, $t = -5.559, p < .001$), and to support national development (2.38 versus 2.10, $t = 3.896, p < .001$). The only interventionist role perception that is more prominent in Belgium is the urge to set the political agenda (2.50 versus 2.76, $t = 3.840, p < .001$). Belgian journalists also score higher on the will to support government policy (1.03 versus 1.49, $t = 13.913, p < .001$) and the need to convey a positive image of political leadership (1.37 versus 1.50, $t = 3.082, p < .001$), but the higher preference for these last-mentioned two roles confirm our hypothesis, as we hypothesized a more outspoken collaborative role in Belgium.

The final three role perceptions documented in the table deal with the accommodating role of journalism. The two role perceptions that link most clearly to entertainment are most supported in Belgium, i.e., to provide entertainment and relaxation (2.54 versus 2.78, $t = 3.758, p < .001$) and to provide the kind of news that attracts the largest audience (2.0 versus 2.90, $t = 14.197, p < 001$). The more ambiguous role perception related to the accommodating role, because it could also be interpreted as leaning a bit toward the monitoring role is more prominently supported in Sweden and not so much in Belgium, i.e., the will to provide advice, orientation, and direction for everyday life (3.23 versus 2.96, $t = -4.446, p < .05$). It needs nevertheless

Table 6.4: Role perceptions of journalists in Belgium and Sweden

Role	Sweden	Belgium	t-value	p-value
Promote tolerance and cultural diversity	4.06	3.59	-7.234	.000***
Provide analysis of current affairs	4.05	3.85	-3.676	.000***
Monitor and scrutinize political leaders	4.35	3.38	-14.732	.000***
Monitor and scrutinize business	4.20	3.25	-14.446	.000***
Motivate people to participate in political activity	2.92	2.52	-5.482	.050*
Influence public opinion	2.62	2.48	-2.048	.041*
Advocate for social change	2.98	2.58	-5.559	.000***
Set the political agenda	2.50	2.76	3.840	.000***
Support national development	2.38	2.10	3.896	.000***
Support government policy	1.03	1.49	13.913	.000***
Convey a positive image of political leadership	1.37	1.50	3.082	.000***
Provide entertainment and relaxation	2.54	2.78	3.758	.000***
Provide the kind of news that attracts the largest audience	2.00	2.90	14.197	.000***
Provide advice, orientation, and direction for daily life	3.23	2.96	-4.446	.040*

Note: *= $p < .01$, **= $p < .05$, ***= $p < .001$

to be added that whatever the differences between Sweden and Belgium may be on the accommodating role perceptions, these role perceptions are always deemed less important than the monitoring role perceptions and the need to promote tolerance and cultural diversity.

Differences on role perceptions within Belgium

The role perception that journalism should promote tolerance and cultural diversity is more popular for French-speaking Belgian as compared to Dutch-speaking Belgian journalists. This confirms our hypothesis (3.31 versus 3.93, $t = -6.554$, $p < .001$). This is an important difference, but on the monitoring, interventionist, collaborating, and accommodating roles we perceive that often the differences between Flemish and Francophone journalists are statistically insignificant, confirming a great similarity in journalism in both Belgian language communities.

Table 6.5: Role perceptions of journalists in Flanders and French-speaking Belgium

Role	Flanders	French-speaking Belgium	t-value	p-value
Promote tolerance and cultural diversity	3.31	3.93	-6.554	.000***
Provide analysis of current affairs	3.80	3.90	-1.377	.169
Monitor and scrutinize political leaders	3.31	3.46	-1.355	.176
Monitor and scrutinize business	3.19	3.33	-1.393	.164
Motivate people to participate in political activity	2.09	3.01	-9.436	.000***
Influence public opinion	2.61	2.33	3.138	.002**
Advocate for social change	2.55	2.63	-0.799	.425
Set the political agenda	2.46	3.12	-6.888	.000***
Support national development	2.31	2.46	-1.473	.146
Support government policy	1.47	1.50	-0.367	.714
Convey a positive image of political leadership	1.68	1.29	6.559	.000***
Provide entertainment and relaxation	2.90	2.66	2.480	.051
Provide the kind of news that attracts the largest audience	3.05	2.72	3.299	.000***
Provide advice, orientation, and direction for daily life	2.94	2.99	-0.549	.583

Note: *= $p < 0.1$, **= $p < .05$, ***= $p < .01$

Nevertheless, some hypothesis confirming differences between the two Belgian regions exist. Francophone journalists urge their audience more to participate in political activity (2.09 versus 3.01, $t = -9.436, p < .001$), confirming a stronger monitorial role in French-speaking Belgium. The Francophone journalists also want to set the political agenda more explicitly (2.46 versus 3.12, $t = -6.888, p < .001$). A role perception that contradicts the hypothetical difference between Flemish and Francophone journalism is the stronger will to influence public opinion in Flanders (2.61 versus 2.33, $t = 3.138, p < .05$). This role perception pertains to the interventionist role, but as it is also an audience-oriented role perception it might be seen as leaning toward the accommodating role. A difference between Flanders and French-speaking Belgium also exists in the more clearly accommodating role perception to provide the kind of news that attracts the largest audience (3.05 versus 2.72, $t = 3.299, p < .001$). A final hypothesis confirming difference between the two parts of the country lies in the higher will to convey a positive image of political leadership in Flanders (1.68 versus 1.29, $t = 6.559$, $p < .001$), confirming the hypothesis on a more outspoken collaborative role taking in Flemish journalism.

Conclusion

Our main conclusion is that, contrary to what we expected, countries with a higher focus on promoting tolerance in journalism cultures have less emancipative values and migrant-friendly policies (hence falsifying hypothesis 1 and 2). Promoting tolerance is a value in countries where journalistic culture is interventionist, and hence opposed to the values in policy (as measured by MIPEX, cfr. Research question 1) and society (as measured by the WVS, cfr. Research question 2). Our results indicate that journalism professionals in countries without a clear migrant integration policy seem to consider it as their explicit task to counterbalance the main policy line set out in their home country when it comes to immigration and openness.

Interventionism—often seen through its political dimension—can also be viewed as a will to actively promote some civic values among public opinion. This refers to the 'opinion guide' role that journalists take on when political or social issues are being strongly debated. During the 2015 migration crisis certain media outlets adopted a welcoming tone toward refugees and tried to counter negative perceptions and stereotypes. Recent research shows that this is far from clear: The UNHCR report on press coverage of the refugee crisis in Europe shows that in many countries refugees have been presented in a negative light, primarily as a problem, and not as a resource that could benefit the receiving country (Finnish Institute, 2016; Berry, Garcia-Blanco, & Moore, 2016). Also our content analysis (chapter 3 in this book) proved these negative orientations in both national contexts investigated in the IM²MEDIATE project, i.e., Sweden and Belgium, with an equal emphasis on collectivization, although Swedish newspapers do attach more importance to the topic if we take the amount of coverage as an indicator.

Moving on to the results of our cluster analyses (Research question 3), Sweden—one of the most welcoming countries during the recent refugee crisis—typifies countries with both a tolerance-oriented journalism culture and strongly tolerance-oriented policies and public opinion. Nevertheless Sweden has a journalistic workforce that does not adhere to interventionist ideals. This means that Sweden has a more positive approach toward refugees than Belgium, as was pointed out in Chapter 3 of this book.

Our exercise identified different clusters of Southern countries, always including Turkey. Promoting tolerance in these countries is an important journalistic value, and this echoes interventionism in journalism culture, so as to remedy the lack of a tolerance-oriented policy and public opinion.

Clusters including other Northern and Southern countries are less straightforward. Eastern Europe occasionally joins the Southern cluster, but it also stands out of the latter because it has a lower focus on promoting tolerance and cultural diversity in journalism.

Some Western European countries join the cluster which includes Sweden, but not always. They are characterized by a noninterventionist journalism culture and adhere to migrant-friendly values (emancipative values index and MIPEX). However, promoting tolerance and cultural diversity is less important in their journalistic culture.

The Iberian countries, Spain and Portugal, are special in that they share similarities with Western European countries, especially in developing migrant-friendly policies, but they are also more interventionist in their journalism cultures.

When making a two-by-two comparison of Belgium and Sweden, the differences already set out in the cluster analysis were clearly confirmed. Swedish journalism is more tolerance oriented (Hypothesis 3a), monitorial (Hypothesis 3b), and interventionist (Hypothesis 3d), but less collaborative (Hypothesis 3c) and accommodating (Hypothesis 3e) than Belgian journalism. Belgian journalism itself consists of a merging of two language cultures that also are somewhat different, with more tolerance oriented (Hypothesis 4a), monitorial (Hypothesis 4b) and interventionist (Hypothesis 4d) accents in Francophone Belgium and more collaborative (Hypothesis 4c) and accommodating (Hypothesis 4e) accents in Flanders. Hence, Francophone role perceptions of journalists are closer to their Swedish counterparts than the Flemish ones.

These results raise the question of the specific values and discourses shared by journalism as a distinct field in societies. We see that journalists often claim to defend and promote tolerance and diversity, even in countries where the data point at a weaker culture of tolerance. Cultural and political causes of this particular discourse warrant further study. We must keep in mind that journalists' discourses ought to be considered in their normative dimension. Discourses about core values of journalists often embrace broad notions such as freedom of speech, respect, and tolerance. They are well developed in journalistic cultures and play an identity role that anchor journalism's autonomy in society (Hanitzsch & Vos, 2018), even if those values and roles are not followed in day-to-day practices. The promotion of tolerance and diversity—just like other traditional values that underscore the links between western journalism and democratic systems—is thus a complex issue that requires a distinction between its declarative dimension (seen in databases such as the WJS Study) and its concrete expression in news stories and editorial lines.

References

Berry, M., Garcia-Blanco, I., & Moore, K. (2016). *Press coverage of the refugee and migrant crisis in the EU: A content analysis of five European countries*. Geneva: United Nations High Commissioner for Refugees.

Billiet, J., Maddens, B., & Beerten, R. (2003). National identity and attitude toward foreigners in a multinational state: a replication. *Political Psychology*, 24(2), 241–257.

Bonin, G., Dingerkus, F., Dubied, A., Mertens, S., Rollwagen, H. Sacco, V., Shapiro, I., Standaert, O., & Wyss, V. (2017). Quelle différence? Language, culture and nationality as influences on francophone journalists' identity. *Journalism Studies*, 18(5), 536–554.

Broersma, M. (2015). Objectiviteit als professionele strategie. Nut en functie van een omstreden begrip. [Objectivity as a professional strategy. Utility and function of a contested concept]. In J. Bardoel & H. Wijfjes (Eds.), *Journalistieke cultuur in Nederland [Journalism culture in the Netherlands]*, (pp.163–182). Amsterdam: Amsterdam University Press.

Callens, M. (2015). *Integration policies and public opinion: In conflict or in harmony? LISER Working Paper no 2*. Luxemburg Institute of Socio-economic Research. Retrieved from mipex.eu/sites/default/files/downloads/files/mipexpublicopinioninconflictorinharmony.pdf December 2017.

Deuze, M. (2005). What is journalism? Professional identity and ideology of journalists reconsidered. *Journalism Theory Practice & Criticism*, 6(4), 443–465.

Finnish Institute (2016). *Refugees and Asylum Seekers in Press Coverage. A comparative content analysis of texts published in Helsingin Sanomat and Aamulehti (FI), The Guardian and The Times (UK) and Le Soir and De Morgen (BE) newspapers in the time period from 1 January to 31 January 2016*. London: The Finnish Institute.

Graf, H., & Jönhill, J. I. (2011). Introduction. In H. Graf (Ed.), *Diversity in Theory and Practice: News journalists in Sweden and Germany* (pp. 9–21). Göteborg: Nordicom.

Hallin, D.C., & Mancini, P. (2004). *Comparing Media Systems: Three Models of Media and Politics*. New York: Cambridge University Press.

Hanitzsch, T., & Vos, T. (2018). Journalism beyond democracy: A new look into journalistic roles in political and everyday life. *Journalism*, 19(2), 146–164.

Hooghe, M., & De Vroome, T. (2015). How does the majority public react to multicultural policies? A comparative analysis of European countries. *American Behavioral Scientist*, 59(6), 747–768.

Leong, C.H. & Ward, C. (2006). Cultural values and attitudes towards immigrants and multiculturalism: The case of the Eurobarometer survey on racism and xenophobia. *International Journal of Intercultural Relations*, 30, 799–810.

McCombs, M. (2011). *The Agenda-Setting Role of the Mass Media in the Shaping of Public Opinion*. Retrieved December 15, 2017 from https://www.researchgate.net/publication/237394610_The_Agenda-Setting_Role_of_the_Mass_Media_in_the_Shaping_of_Public_Opinion.

Niessen, J. (Ed.) (2009). *Legal Frameworks for The Integration of Third Country Nationals*. Leiden: Martinus Nijhoff Publishers.

Raeymaeckers, K., Paulussen, S., & De Keyser, J. (2012). A survey of professional journalists in Flanders (Belgium). In D. Weaver, & L. Willnat (Eds.), *The global journalist in the 21st century* (pp. 141–154). (Routledge Communication Series). London: Routledge.

Schroyens M., Meuleman B., & Galle J. (2015). Welcome to the club? Een comparatieve studie naar het verband tussen integratiebeleid en welvaartschauvinisme [Welcome to the club? A comparative study on the relationship between integration policy and welfare chauvinism]. *Mens en Maatschappij [M&M]*, *90*(2), 117–142.

Siebert, F.S., Peterson, T., & Schramm, W. (1956). *Four Theories of the Press*. Urbana: University of Illinois Press.

Strömbäck, J., Nord, L., & Shehata, A. (2012). Swedish journalists: Between professionalization and commercialization. In D. Weaver, & L. Willnat (eds.), *The Global Journalist in the 21st Century* (pp. 306–319). (Routledge Communication Series). London: Routledge.

Van Aelst, P., & Aalberg, T. (2011). Between trust and suspicion. *Javnost – The Public*, *18*(4), 73–88.

Vliegenthart, R. (2015). Mediamacht. De interactie tussen media, publiek en politiek. [Media Power. The interaction between media, the audience and politics.] In J. Bardoel & H. Wijfjes (Eds.), *Journalistieke cultuur in Nederland [Journalism Culture in the Netherlands]*. (pp.221–236). Amsterdam: Amsterdam University Press.

Watson, B.R., & Riffe, D. (2013). Perceived threat, immigration policy support, and media coverage: Hostile media and presumed influence. *International Journal of Public Opinion Research*, *25*(4), 459–479.

Walgrave, S., & Van Aelst, P. (2016). Political agenda setting and the mass media. In W.R. Thompson (ed.), *Oxford Research Encyclopedia of Politics* (pp.1–26), https://doi.org/10.1093/ACREFORE/9780190228637.013.46.

Welzel, C. (2013). *Freedom Rising Human Empowerment and the Quest for Emancipation*. Cambridge: Cambridge University Press.

Wiik, J. (2007). Granskningsidealet [The Watchdog Ideal]. In K. Asp (Ed.), *Den svenska journalistkåren [Swedish Journalists]* (pp. 79–86). Göteborg: JMG.

Worlds of Journalism Project. Retrieved December 15, 2017, from http://www.worldsofjournalism.org.

World Values Survey. Retrieved December 15, 2017, from http://www.worldvaluessurvey.org.

PART III

PUBLIC OPINION

Chapter 7
Discordance between Public Opinion and News Media Representations of Immigrants and Refugees in Belgium and Sweden

David De Coninck, Hanne Vandenberghe, and Koen Matthijs

Introduction

Currently, the migration issue is high on the agenda of European policy, news, and public. On June 29, 2018, EU leaders announced that they had reached a long-awaited agreement on aspects of (re)settlement of refugees and asylum seekers. Member states agree to send rescued refugees on EU territory to 'check centers' across the EU. This agreement was the result of an EU summit, dominated by the political crisis on how to handle irregular immigration into Europe. This summit is seen as a delayed political reaction to Europe's 2015 refugee crisis. Although refugee numbers have been decreasing since 2015 (UNCHR, 2018), the migration issue has swayed elections in France, Germany, Austria, Italy, and Hungary. For instance, the Hungarian Parliament has recently voted on the so-called 'Stop Soros' law, which criminalizes helping illegal asylum seekers both as individuals or groups, defying both the European Union and human rights groups.

Migration is also a dominant issue in the public debate in the two countries under study, Belgium and Sweden. In May 2018, the Belgian Federal Finance Minister Van Overtveldt asked the National Bank of Belgium to calculate the economic impact of migration in order to bring some 'objectivity' into the debate on this issue. A Swedish report published in June 2018 from the Expert Group for Economic Studies (ESO), operating under the Swedish Finance Ministry, states that an average immigrant costs the Swedish tax payer about SEK 74,000 per year (€7,200). However, these figures are in contrast with the general discourse in Swedish media that immigration is economically beneficial.

This chapter will focus on how news media consumption and trust have an impact on attitudes about immigrants and refugees both in Belgium and Sweden. Moreover, we will analyze if and to what extent the level of importance of the migration issue and the presence of intergroup contact are mediators of news consumption. Generally, in Belgium the debate is more negative than in Sweden (De Cock et al., 2018). This study will also analyze whether there are any differences between Belgians and Swedes on attitudes about immigrants and refugees. We begin our research by outlining the theoretical frame, focusing on how news media and attitudes toward minority groups are linked. Subsequently, we outline the three research questions which ask whether or not there are any attitude differences between Belgium and Sweden, to what extent media consumption and media trust play a role in the formation of these attitudes, and how direct intergroup contact and the subjective importance of the migration issue relate to attitudes. In the section on data and methodology, we describe how our sample of 3,000 respondents was collected and how we operationalized concepts such as media trust, news consumption, and the importance of the migration issue. Finally, we will present and discuss the results of the analyses, to end with a brief conclusion.

Literature review

News media play a major role in the attitude formation of the audience with regard to the migration issue (Jacobs, Hooghe, & de Vroome, 2017). By selecting certain perspectives from which to report news, they can contribute to or prevent the stereotyping of (sub)groups in the population (De Cock et al., 2018; Leavitt, Covarrubias, Perez, & Fryberg, 2015; Segijn, Bartholomé, Pennekamp, & Timmers, 2014). This influence of news media is embedded in two communication science theories that take a central position in this chapter: agenda-setting theory and framing theory. Agenda-setting theory suggests that news media can influence the public agenda by prioritizing certain topics in their reporting (McCombs & Shaw, 1972). For example, the increasing attention of the news media to the migration issue could raise awareness amongst the audience. The salience of media coverage on immigration is therefore not necessarily related to actual migration numbers (Jacobs, Claes, & Hooghe, 2015; Vliegenthart & Boomgaarden, 2007), which often misleads the audience and causes them to under- or overestimate the influx of migrants (Alba, Rumbaut, & Marotz, 2005; Semyonov, Gorodzeisky, & Glikman, 2012; Sides & Citrin, 2007; Strabac, 2011). Moreover, framing theory, or second-level agenda-setting, suggests that emphasizing specific aspects of reality in a news story such as a specific problem definition or a causal interpretation, can systematically affect how the news users interpret news events (Entman, 1993; Scheufele, 1999).

The reason news media representations have such an impact on attitudes can be explained by the social identity theory (Van Klingeren, Boomgaarden, Vliegenthart, & De Vreese, 2014), which constitutes the third theory around which we build this chapter. This theory states that people's self-concept is dependent on the social groups they belong to (Tajfel & Turner, 1979). People tend to categorize individuals into groups and assign positive characteristics to members of the social groups they belong to (in-group favoritism), and negative characteristics to members of social groups they do not belong to (outgroup discrimination) (Tajfel & Turner, 1979; Van Klingeren et al., 2014). Stereotypes that are disseminated through news media can lead to prejudices about outgroups in question, causing members of the ingroup to attribute the negative characteristics which are presented in the news to every member of a given outgroup (Allport, 1954; Fishbein & Ajzen, 1977; Jacobs et al., 2017).

The plurality of cultural and ethnic identities is inherent in current Western multicultural societies, such as Belgium and Sweden. Following social identity theory, to stimulate integration it is crucial to embrace the different identities within multicultural society instead of emphasizing the differences between 'us' and 'them' (Hogg, 2016). Consequently, European media policy stipulates that media build bridges within societies and between subpopulations to ease tensions by promoting inter-ethnic understanding rather than using stereotypes and misrepresentations (Campion, 2005; Mattelart & d'Haenens, 2014). However, previous research on the representation of refugees and immigrants in news media has established that these minority groups are often problematized. In British newspapers, refugees, asylum seekers, and immigrants are presented as a problem, emphasizing the migration issue instead of the people behind the stories (KhosraviNik, 2010). A cross-country analysis on news coverage on immigration (Germany, Italy, United Kingdom, and Dutch-speaking Belgium) concluded that immigrants are given little attention in the news and are often victimized (Masini et al., 2018). A large-scale content analysis of Flemish television news ($N = 1,630$ news items) revealed that almost all news about immigration was framed as a problem (Jacobs, Meeusen, & d'Haenens, 2016). Moreover, more than 70 percent of the news items had a negative tone and stated that immigrants are causing problems or seemed focused on the negative consequences of immigration. Although this negative representation of immigrants can be observed on both public and commercial broadcasters, the reporting on commercial broadcasters was generally found to be more negative than on public broadcasters (Jacobs et al., 2016). Studies have also found that people who mainly consume news on commercial television hold more negative attitudes toward minority groups than people who follow the news on public television (De Coninck et al., 2018; Jacobs et al., 2016).

Literature has shown that the way in which media represent immigrant groups influences public opinion on these groups in the general population and in journalists who report this news (Dixon & Williams, 2015). However, the (negative) impact of news media representations on public opinion can be reduced by direct intergroup contact—a final theory that we will turn to in the context of this chapter. On this matter, the contact hypothesis states that direct intergroup contact can reduce prejudice and stereotypes between groups. The absence of such direct contact may lead to greater sociocultural differences and interethnic conflict (Allport, 1954; Pettigrew & Tropp, 2006). Not just the frequency of interethnic contact, but also the perceived quality of that contact plays an important role in reducing prejudice (Ahmed, 2017). However, a majority of the population still does not have direct contact with migrant groups (Leavitt et al., 2015), which makes news media the primary source through which they form their attitudes (Van den Bulck & Broos, 2011).

Not only is the content of news media reporting important when considering attitudes toward minority groups, but the audience's trust in news media coverage also plays a role. When people mistrust mainstream news media, they will seek other sources of information such as alternative media (e.g., social media) or real-life information (Jackob, 2010). When we look at the Belgian and Swedish contexts, we find that trust in news media is high when compared to other European countries. According to the Eurobarometer results of 2016, 64 percent of Belgians and 77 percent of Swedes believe that their national media provide trustworthy information (European Commission, 2016). In comparison, the average European trust in news media is at 53 percent. Newspapers, radio, and television are considered reliable by respectively 71, 76, and 73 percent of the Belgian population and 70, 88, and 79 percent of the Swedish population, which is once again higher than the European average of 55 percent for both newspapers and television, and 66 percent for radio (European Commission, 2016).

Taking into account these considerations, we will attempt to provide an answer to the following research questions:

RQ1. Are there any differences between Belgium and Sweden with regard to attitudes toward immigrants and refugees?

RQ2. To what extent are news media consumption and trust related to attitudes toward immigrants and refugees in Belgium and Sweden?

RQ3. Do the issue importance of migration compared to other news topics and intergroup contact mediate the relation of news media consumption and attitudes toward immigrants and refugees?

Data and method

To answer our research questions, we used data from an online questionnaire distributed among the population aged between 18 and 65 years old in Belgium and Sweden. This took place in September and October of 2017, in cooperation with the Belgian polling agency iVOX and its partner company in Sweden, which drew a sample of 3,000 respondents (1,500 per country) out of its large-scale panels. We selected this methodology for its cost-effectiveness in cross-national research, and its efficient way of data collection. As public opinion on this subject can quickly be swayed by extreme events (e.g., a terror attack), it was important to gather the data in a timely fashion to ensure that such a scenario did not take place. Respondents were contacted though e-mail with the request to cooperate in a survey, without specifying a subject. Incentives in the form of coupons were provided, as respondents could enter a pool from which a limited number of winners were drawn. Our sample is representative for age and gender in both countries, and additionally for regions in Belgium. In table 7.1 we present a breakdown of our sample by country, age, gender, household income, migration background, and educational attainment.

Measures

Attitudes on immigrants and refugees
In order to measure the difference in public opinion on immigrants and refugees we adapted a scale used in the European Social Survey (ESS). This scale was developed to measure attitudes toward immigration and was included in round 1 (2002) and round 7 (2014) of the ESS. It consists of seven items, asking which groups of immigrants should be allowed to come and live in Belgium or Sweden: *"Immigrants of the same race or ethnicity as most of [country]'s population."*; *"Immigrants of a different race or ethnicity as most of [country]'s population."*; *"Immigrants of the richer countries in Europe."*; *"Immigrants of the poorer countries in Europe."*; *"Immigrants of the richer countries outside Europe."*; *"Immigrants of the poorer countries outside Europe."*; and *"Immigrants coming from Muslim countries who wish to work in [country]."*. Answer categories range from *"1 = Allow none"* to *"4 = Allow many"*. We used the scale in its original

Table 7.1. Descriptive results of socio-demographic variables (in %, unless otherwise specified)

	Belgium	Sweden	Total
Age (in years)	42.9	41.4	42.2
Gender	N = 1500	N = 1500	N = 3000
Male	50.3	50.0	50.1
Female	49.7	50.0	49.9
Household income	N = 1191	N = 1263	N = 2454
Less than €1500	14.7	13.8	14.2
€1500 – €2499	29.8	19.3	24.4
€2500 – €3499	24.5	18.6	21.4
€3500 – €4499	20.0	17.2	18.6
€4500 – €5499	6.1	15.5	10.9
Over €5499	5.0	15.7	10.5
Migration background	N = 1484	N = 1389	N = 2873
No migration background	90.8	74.4	82.9
Migration background	9.2	25.6	17.1
Educational attainment	N = 1421	N = 1362	N = 2783
No degree/Primary education	4.4	8.8	6.5
Secondary education	44.6	55.2	49.8
Tertiary education	50.6	35.1	43.0

Note: Respondents who did not want to reveal or did not know their household income (n = 546) were indicated as missing. In Sweden, household income was asked for in Swedish krona, with categories corresponding with Belgian categories in Euros.

form, but added an extra item concerning immigrants from Muslim countries. The reason for the inclusion of this item lies in the fact that a majority of immigrants and refugees entering Belgium and Sweden in the current refugee crisis originate from Syria, Iraq, or Afghanistan—predominantly Muslim countries (Pew Research Center, 2017). Before completing this block of items, we presented respondents with a definition of immigrants, as stated by the United Nations (UN). Later in the questionnaire we presented an alternate version of this scale in which the term 'immigrant' in the items was swapped for 'refugee.' Prior to completing each block, respondents were presented with the UN definition of immigrants and refugees respectively.

We clearly highlighted these two definitions so that respondents would be able to distinguish between immigrants and refugees.

News media consumption
Respondents were asked about their news media consumption patterns during the past month (*"To what extent did you watch/listen to news programmes on the broadcasters mentioned below in the past month?"*), with answer categories ranging from "*0 = Never*" to "*7 = Every day*". Both television and radio consumption were split into two groups: public and commercial. For the newspaper and online news consumption, the most commonly read newspapers and commonly visited news webpages in each country were included separately (*"To what extent did you read newspapers/online news mentioned below in the past month?"*). In order to provide a clear picture of the impact of newspaper and online news consumption, we calculated the country mean of quality and popular newspaper consumption, and quality and popular online news consumption separately. This newspaper typology is based on previous news media research that sets popular apart from quality papers (De Bens & Raeymaeckers, 2010; De Cock et al., 2018).

News media trust
We measured trust in the aforementioned news media brands by means of a five-point scale with answer categories ranging from "*1 = No trust at all*" to "*5 = A lot of trust*". Trust was measured separately for public and commercial television and radio. Trust in newspapers was aggregated into two groups: trust in quality newspapers (*De Standaard, De Morgen, De Tijd, Le Soir, La Libre, L'Echo, Dagens Nyheter, Svenska Dagbladet*) and trust in popular newspapers (*Het Laatste Nieuws, Gazet van Antwerpen, Het Belang van Limburg, Het Nieuwsblad, Metro, La Dernière Heure/Les Sports, L'Avenir, Métro, Aftonbladet, Expressen*), corresponding to the categories of news media consumption. Trust in news websites or apps was also measured on the same scale, but without the distinction between popular and quality online news consumption.

Importance of the migration theme
Based on previous categorizations of media themes (Carroll et al., 1997; De Bens & Paulussen, 2005; Diakopoulos & Naaman, 2011; Stempel III, 1988; Vandenberghe, 2017), we presented our respondents with 14 news media categories and asked them how important they considered each of these. Although previous typologies generally combine welfare and migration into a single category, we decided to split these because of the particular importance

of the migration theme in this chapter. The categories presented were: national politics; justice; crime; economy and trade; welfare; migration; environment; culture and entertainment; science, technology, and education; disasters; transport; war and peace; sports; and international and European politics. Respondents had to answer on a five-point scale, with answer categories ranging from "1 = *Not at all important*" to "5 = *Very important*".

Direct intergroup contact
In order to map direct intergroup contact, we again used a measure from the European Social Survey, asking how often respondents have contact with people of a different race or ethnic group when they are out and about (e.g., on public transport, in shops, on the street, or in their neighborhood). They could indicate this on a seven-point scale ranging from "1 = *Never*" to "7 = *Every day*".

Analytic strategy

To provide an answer to our research questions we will carry out t-test comparisons of mean scores on attitudes toward immigrants and refugees, news media consumption, news media trust, and the importance of the migration theme. Belgian and Swedish respondents are the two groups to be compared in the analyses. Subsequently, we will estimate linear regression models for each country and attitude separately using SPSS, to investigate which (if any) indicators on news media consumption, media trust, the importance of the migration theme, direct intergroup contact, or socio-demographic indicators are more important in relation to attitudes in Belgium than in Sweden, or vice versa. In order to use immigrant and refugee attitudes as dependent variables in the regression analyses, an exploratory factor analysis was carried out on the seven items for each set of attitudes. With Cronbach's alpha values of .94 (for attitudes toward immigrants) and .95 (for attitudes toward refugees), we can confirm that both scales are reliable. These factor scores will be the dependent variables in the linear regression analyses.

Results

The results of the independent samples t-tests in table 7.2 indicate that Belgium and Sweden differ significantly on attitudes toward immigrants and refugees, and on media use and trust. Swedes are found to hold significantly more positive attitudes on both immigrants and refugees than Belgians.

Table 7.2. Independent samples t-test on mean differences in immigrant attitudes and refugee attitudes, media consumption and trust, and the subjective importance of migration between Belgium and Sweden

	Belgium	Sweden	
	Mean values		T-values
Attitudes			
Immigrant attitudes (α = .94)	2.53	2.72	-6.69***
Refugee attitudes (α = .95)	2.54	2.72	-5.98***
Media consumption			
Public broadcast consumption – television	4.28	4.27	0.06
Commercial broadcast consumption – television	3.78	4.17	-3.98***
Public broadcast consumption – radio	4.02	3.23	8.06***
Commercial broadcast consumption – radio	3.10	3.20	-1.19
Quality newspapers	1.51	1.81	-6.16***
Popular newspapers	1.72	2.79	-17.50***
Quality online news	2.10	2.05	0.91
Popular online news	2.36	3.66	-18.05***
Media trust			
Public service television	3.79	3.31	11.29***
Commercial television	3.32	3.10	5.54***
Public service radio	3.73	3.31	9.97***
Commercial radio	3.27	2.62	17.56***
Quality newspapers	3.65	3.20	11.28***
Popular newspapers	3.23	2.62	16.04***
News websites/apps	3.40	2.86	14.78***
Importance of migration theme	3.45	3.58	-3.34**

*: $p < .05$; **: $p < .01$; ***: $p < .001$

Differences in attitudes toward immigrants and refugees cannot be found in either country. In terms of media consumption on television and radio, we observe that Belgians consume more public service news than Swedes, although this difference is only significant for radio. Swedes, on the other hand, are found to consume more commercial news than Belgians—particularly on television. For written and online media, we note that Swedes consume this more frequently than Belgians, with the exception of quality online news. It is also apparent that Swedes consume far more popular written and popular online media than quality (online) media. This is also the case for Belgians, but much less pronounced. Furthermore, Swedes and Belgians differ significantly on all types of media trust. T-tests show that Swedes have lower levels of trust in their media—for each media type under consideration—than Belgians. We do find, in both countries, that media trust is lower for commercial broadcasters and popular newspapers than it is for public broadcasters and quality newspapers. As for the importance of the migration theme, Swedes consider this issue to be significantly more important than Belgians.

The results of the regression analyses in table 7.3 show that in Belgium age is negatively associated with both sets of attitudes. Respondents with a migration background are found to hold more positive attitudes toward immigrants and refugees than those without a migration background. We observe that educational attainment is significantly related to attitudes toward refugees only: respondents with a tertiary degree hold more positive attitudes toward refugees than those with no degree or a primary degree. Neither gender nor household income is associated with attitudes. Three types of media consumption are related to attitudes. Firstly, we find that commercial television news consumption is negatively related to both sets of attitudes—with this association more pronounced for attitudes toward refugees than toward immigrants. Secondly, we also observe that quality online news consumption is positively related to both sets of attitudes. Thirdly, popular online news consumption is negatively associated with attitudes toward refugees only. For media trust, we note that trust in public service television news is positively associated with both sets of attitudes, whereas trust in commercial television news is positively associated with attitudes toward immigrants only. As for radio news, we find that trust in commercial radio is negatively associated with attitudes toward immigrants. A final finding on trust tells us that trust in popular newspapers is negatively associated with attitudes toward refugees. The importance of the migration theme proves to be a predictor of attitudes toward refugees, with a higher importance of the migration issue related to more positive attitudes toward refugees. Finally, we note that direct intergroup contact is positively related to both sets of attitudes.

In Sweden, age has a similar negative relation to both sets of attitudes as it does in Belgium. Gender does play a role here, as females are found to hold more positive attitudes on both minority groups than males. Educational attainment proves to be more important in Sweden than in Belgium: respondents with a secondary or tertiary degree are found to hold more positive attitudes on both immigrants and refugees than those with no degree or a primary degree. Migration background and household income are not related to attitudes. Media consumption is not found to play a role here, as popular online news consumption is the only type that exhibits a significant (negative) relation to attitudes. Media trust proves to be more important, however. Trust in public service television and radio is positively associated with both sets of attitudes. Trust in quality newspapers relates positively to attitudes toward immigrants only. The importance of the migration issue is not found to play a role here, but direct intergroup contact does. As in Belgium, the frequency of this contact is positively related to both sets of attitudes.

To summarize in terms of country differences, t-test results show that Swedes hold significantly more positive attitudes to both immigrants and refugees than Belgians. Regression results illustrate that gender, educational attainment, and media trust are important predictors of attitudes in Sweden, whereas in Belgium migration background, news media consumption, and the importance of the migration theme are more important. Age (negatively) and direct intergroup contact (positively) are associated with attitudes in both countries (RQ1). Furthermore, we can say that news media consumption is more strongly associated with attitudes in Belgium than in Sweden, whereas trust in news media is an important predictor of attitudes in both countries (RQ2). The importance of the migration theme is only related to attitudes toward refugees in Belgium, but direct intergroup contact is found to be positively associated with both sets of attitudes in both countries (RQ3).

Table 7.3. Linear regression models with attitudes towards immigrants and refugees in Belgium and Sweden as outcome variables and standardized beta's of independent variables

	Belgium		Sweden	
	Immigrant attitudes	Refugee attitudes	Immigrant attitudes	Refugee attitudes
Socio-demographics				
Age	-.13***	-.10***	-.12***	-.12***
Male	-	-	-	-
Female	-.01	.00	.06*	.06*
No degree/Primary degree	-	-	-	-
Secondary degree	-.01	.01	.13**	.11*

	Belgium		Sweden	
	Immigrant attitudes	Refugee attitudes	Immigrant attitudes	Refugee attitudes
Tertiary degree	.09	.14*	.18***	.18***
Low income	-	-	-	-
Average income	-.00	.00	-.04	-.04
High income	.03	-.02	-.01	-.03
No migration background	-	-	-	-
Migration background	.10***	.07**	.02	.00
Media consumption				
Public broadcast consumption – television	.06	.03	-.02	-.02
Commercial broadcast consumption – television	-.10***	-.14***	.01	.00
Public broadcast consumption – radio	-.02	-.02	-.02	-.01
Commercial broadcast consumption – radio	-.02	-.05	-.03	-.02
Quality newspapers	.02	.03	-.01	.03
Popular newspapers	-.03	-.04	.03	.04
Quality online news	.13***	.12***	.04	-.01
Popular online news	-.04	-.06*	-.08*	-.10***
Media trust				
Public service television	.13*	.12*	.18**	.21***
Commercial television	.11*	.05	-.07	-.07
Public service radio	.06	.07	.17**	.17**
Commercial radio	-.15**	-.06	-.03	-.03
Quality newspapers	.06	.05	.10*	.06
Popular newspapers	-.04	-.08*	.06	.03
News websites/apps	-.02	-.01	.01	.02
Importance of migration	.04	.05*	.02	-.02
Direct intergroup contact	.15***	.16***	.17***	.17***
Adjusted R-squared	.21	.23	.23	.21

*: p < .05; **: p < .01; ***: p < .001

Discussion

Recently, migration has become a prominent topic in Europe amongst scholars, the media, policy makers, and the public at large. One of the main drivers behind this is the scale of the refugee crisis, which many European countries are forced to cope with. Along with this increasing attention to the migration issue, we also note a growing polarization of public opinion on minority groups. Although news media are considered to be an important actor in influencing public opinion and building bridges within inter-ethnic societies (Mattelart & d'Haenens, 2014; Müller et al., 2017), news media are fairly negative and fall back on terminology of 'us' versus 'them', which can be seen as a mild form of cultural racism (Malik, 2014). In this study, we selected two groups (immigrants and refugees) to study the influence of Belgian and Swedish news media consumption and trust in these media on public opinion for the two groups in question. This chapter helps clarify the role of news media consumption and trust in media on the attitude formation on these groups in Belgium and Sweden.

Considering the discordance between media representations and public opinion, we find conflicting evidence. Literature suggests that, although news media in general are fairly negative in their portrayal of minority groups (KhosraviNik, 2010; Masini et al., 2018), public service media are more positive in their media representations of minorities than commercial media (Jacobs et al., 2016). Public opinion on these groups may therefore be influenced by the type of broadcasting the audience consumes (De Coninck et al., 2018). In Belgium, we find that commercial television consumption is negatively associated with attitudes toward immigrants and refugees, while public service consumption is positively (but not significantly) so associated. Quality online news consumption is positively related to both attitudes, whilst popular online news consumption is negatively related to attitudes toward refugees. In Sweden, the relationship between media consumption and attitudes seems much less pronounced. Here, the only media type which is associated with attitudes is popular online news consumption. This indicates that media representations are not necessarily linked to corresponding attitudes, particularly in Sweden. That means there is support for framing theory in the Belgian results only, as framing theory suggests that emphasizing or silencing specific aspects of reality in a news story (e.g., positive or negative aspects of the migration issue) can affect how news users interpret these events (Entman, 1993; Scheufele, 1999). However, a selection effect could also be at play here. We cannot make causal inferences based on our cross-sectional data, which means it is possible that individuals with positive attitudes on immigrants and refugees are drawn to public service/quality media, and those with negative attitudes consume more commercial/popular media. As news content on the refugee issue has been found to differ between media types and countries (see Chapter 3), individuals may select media which correspond to their existing preconceptions about this (or other) issues.

Media trust is found to play a role as well. We find that Swedes generally hold lower levels of trust in their news media than Belgians. In relation to attitudes, Belgians are mostly influenced by their trust in television news; trust in public broadcasting is positively related to both sets of attitudes, and trust in commercial broadcasting is positively related to immigrant attitudes only. Trust in commercial radio news and popular online media is negatively associated with respectively immigrant and refugee attitudes. In Sweden, the picture is much clearer. Trust in public service media, and quality newspapers to a lesser extent, is indicated to be an important driver in attitude formation. Trust in public television and radio is positively associated with immigrant and refugee attitudes. It is important to keep in mind in this regard that Swedes are found to consume public and commercial media equally, whereas in Belgium public service consumption is found to be much higher than commercial news consumption.

We find only limited support for the agenda-setting theory in our data. This theory suggests that news media can influence the public agenda by prioritizing certain topics in their reporting (McCombs & Shaw, 1972), which in turn may have an effect on public opinion on such topics (e.g., the overestimation of migration numbers due to the large-scale reporting on migration). We do find that the importance of the migration theme in Belgians is positively related to their attitudes toward refugees. The effect size is small, however, and for immigration attitudes in Belgium and both sets of attitudes in Sweden no relationship is found. Far more evidence can be found in support of the contact hypothesis, which states that direct intergroup contact can reduce prejudice and stereotypes, whereas the absence of such contact can lead to greater interethnic conflict (Allport, 1954; Pettigrew & Tropp, 2006). In Belgium and Sweden, direct intergroup contact is positively associated with both sets of attitudes. Previous literature on Belgium indicates that citizens of the Brussels Capital Region, where 34.8 percent of the population does not have Belgian nationality (Statistics Belgium, 2017), hold the most positive attitudes toward both minority groups of all three regions (Flanders and French-speaking Belgium being the other two) in Belgium, which underscores our findings that direct contact improves attitudes on immigrants and refugees.

Although this research is innovative in the sense that we investigated the association between news media consumption and trust—which we broke down in a detailed manner—and attitudes on two separate groups of newcomers in Belgium and Sweden, some limitations must be noted. We stressed the anonymity of the respondents' participation in the questionnaire, but it is still possible that certain items that measure sensitive attitudes (e.g., whether or not groups of immigrants/refugees should be allowed to enter the country) were subject to social desirability. Self-report questionnaires may suffer from other types of error as well. We measured direct intergroup contact by gauging how often respondents had random interactions with people from other ethnic groups. It is possible that respondents under- or overestimated their contact. Finally, we note that there are quite a large number of missing values for the household-income indicator. This is a common occurrence in the social sciences, as people are often hesitant to reveal their income. This may result in a biased image of Belgian and Swedish income distribution (Yan, Curtin, & Jans, 2010). We recommend that future research adopt an internationally comparative research design. By comparing our results with those of neighboring countries, or with attitudes of countries which are known to hold more negative views, further insight could be gained in how news media consumption affects attitudes toward both groups. Another addition could be through an effect study, in which an experimental design is used to further illuminate the link between media exposure, minority group framing, and both sets of attitudes (see also Chapter 9 in this book). Finally, connecting our quantitative survey data to a quantitative content analysis of news media reporting will also contribute to identifying the specific role of media representations of these minority groups on attitude formation.

In summary, in this chapter we have outlined the association between news media consumption and trust, and public opinion on immigrants and refugees in Belgium and Sweden. The attitudes under study were chosen because of their societal relevance, as migration issues are increasingly prevalent in the public domain, and public opinion on this issue is polarizing. News media consumption and trust were identified as two important elements that influence public opinion, while the subjective importance of the migration theme and direct intergroup contact were expected to have a mediating effect. Our results point to a larger influence of media consumption on public opinion in Belgium than in Sweden, while the reverse is found for media trust. The importance of the migration theme is only marginally related to attitudes, but having direct contact with people with a migration background is proven to affect both attitudes in a positive way in both Belgium and Sweden.

Acknowledgements

The authors would like to thank all respondents who completed the questionnaire for their cooperation.

References

Ahmed, S. (2017). News media, movies, and anti-Muslim prejudice: Investigating the role of social contact. *Asian Journal of Communication, 27*(5), 536–553.

Alba, R., Rumbaut, R. G., & Marotz, K. (2005). A distorted nation: Perceptions of racial/ethnic group sizes and attitudes toward immigrants and other minorities. *Social Forces, 84*(2), 901–919.

Allport, G. W. (1954). *The Nature of Prejudice*. Cambridge, MA: Addison-Wesley Pub. Co.

Campion, M. J. (2005). *Look who's talking. Cultural diversity, public service broadcasting and the national conversation*. Oxford, UK: Nuffield College.

Carroll, R. L., Tuggle, C. A., McCollum, J. F., Mitrook, M. A., Arlington, K. J., & Hoerner Jr, J. M. (1997). Consonance in local television news program content: An examination of intermarket diversity. *Journal of Broadcasting & Electronic Media, 41*(1), 132–144.

De Bens, E., & Paulussen, S. (2005). Hoe anders is de VRT? De performantie van de Vlaamse publieke omroep [How different is the VRT? The performance of the Flemish public broadcaster]. *Tijdschrift voor Communicatiewetenschap, 33*(4), 365–386.

De Bens, E., & Raeymaeckers, K. (2010). *De pers in België. Het verhaal van de Belgische dagbladpers. Gisteren, vandaag en morgen* [The press in Belgium. The story of the Belgian daily press. Yesterday, today and tomorrow]. Leuven, Belgium: LannooCampus.

De Cock, R., Mertens, S., Sundin, E., Lams, L., Mistiaen, V., Joris, W., & d'Haenens, L. (2018). Refugees in the news: Comparing Belgian and Swedish newspaper coverage of the European refugee situation during summer 2015. *Communications: The European Journal of Communication Research, 43*(3), 301–323.

De Coninck, D., Matthijs, K., Debrael, M., Joris, W., De Cock, R., & d'Haenens, L. (2018). The relationship between media use and public opinion on immigrants and refugees: A Belgian perspective. *Communications: The European Journal of Communication Research, 43*(3), 403–425.

Diakopoulos, N., & Naaman, M. (2011). *Towards quality discourse in online news comments*. Paper presented at the ACM Conference on Computer-supported Cooperative Work, Hangzhou, China.

Dixon, T. L., & Williams, C. L. (2015). The changing misrepresentation of race and crime on network and cable news. *Journal of Communication, 65*(1), 24–39.

Entman, R. M. (1993). Framing: Toward clarification of a fractured paradigm. *Journal of Communication, 43*(4), 51–58.

European Commission. (2016). *Media pluralism and democracy*. Retrieved from http://ec.europa.eu/commfrontoffice/publicopinion/index.cfm/General/index.

Fishbein, M., & Ajzen, I. (1977). *Belief, attitude, intention, and behavior: An introduction to theory and research*. Reading, MA: Addison-Wesley.

Hogg, M. A. (2016). Social identity theory. In S. McKeown, R. Haji, & N. Ferguson (eds.), *Understanding peace and conflict through social identity theory* (pp. 3–17). Cham, Switzerland: Springer.

Jackob, N. G. E. (2010). No alternatives? The relationship between perceived media dependency, use of alternative information sources, and general trust in mass media. *International Journal of Communication, 4*, 589–606.

Jacobs, L., Claes, E., & Hooghe, M. (2015). The occupational roles of women and ethnic minorities on primetime television in Belgium: An analysis of occupational status measurements. *Mass Communication and Society, 18*(4), 498–521.

Jacobs, L., Hooghe, M., & de Vroome, T. (2017). Television and anti-immigrant sentiments: the mediating role of fear of crime and perceived ethnic diversity. *European Societies, 19*(3), 243–267.

Jacobs, L., Meeusen, C., & d'Haenens, L. (2016). News coverage and attitudes on immigration: Public and commercial television news compared. *European Journal of Communication, 31*(6), 642–660.

KhosraviNik, M. (2010). The representation of refugees, asylum seekers and immigrants in British newspapers: A critical discourse analysis. *Journal of Language and Politics, 9*(1), 1–28.

Leavitt, P. A., Covarrubias, R., Perez, Y. A., & Fryberg, S. A. (2015). "Frozen in time": The impact of Native American media representations on identity and self-understanding. *Journal of Social Issues, 71*(1), 39–53.

Malik, S. (2014). Diversity, broadcasting and the politics of representation. In G. Titley, K. Horsti, & G. Hultén (eds.), *Public Service Media and Cultural Diversity in Europe* (pp. 21–42). Bristol, UK: Intellect Books.

Masini, A., Van Aelst, P., Zerback, T., Reinemann, C., Mancini, P., Mazzoni, M., Damiani, M., & Coen, S. (2018). Measuring and explaining the diversity of voices and viewpoints in the news: A comparative study on the determinants of content diversity of immigration news. *Journalism Studies, 19*(15), 2324–2343.

Mattelart, T., & d'Haenens, L. (2014). Cultural diversity policies in Europe: Between integration and security. *Global Media and Communication, 10*(3), 231–245.

McCombs, M. E., & Shaw, D. L. (1972). The agenda-setting function of mass media. *Public Opinion Quarterly, 36*(2), 176–187.

Müller, P., Schemer, C., Wettstein, M., Schulz, A., Wirz, D. S., Engesser, S., & Wirth, W. (2017). The polarizing impact of news coverage on populist attitudes in the public: Evidence from a panel study in four European democracies. *Journal of Communication, 67*(6), 968–992.

Pettigrew, T. F., & Tropp, L. R. (2006). A meta-analytic test of intergroup contact theory. *Journal of Personality and Social Psychology, 90*(5), 751–783.

Pew Research Center. (2017). *Europe's growing Muslim population*. Retrieved from http://assets.pewresearch.org/wp-content/uploads/sites/11/2017/11/06105637/FULL-REPORT-FOR-WEB-POSTING.pdf.

Scheufele, D. A. (1999). Framing as a theory of media effects. *Journal of Communication, 49*(1), 103–122.

Segijn, C., Bartholomé, G., Pennekamp, S., & Timmers, M. (2014). De afbeelding van statusverschillen in sekse en etniciteit in Nederlandse non-fictieprogramma's [The depiction of status differences in sex and ethnicity in Dutch non-fiction programmes]. *Tijdschrift voor Communicatiewetenschap, 42*(3), 305–320.

Semyonov, M., Gorodzeisky, A., & Glikman, A. (2012). Neighborhood ethnic composition and resident perceptions of safety in European countries. *Social Problems, 59*(1), 117–135.

Sides, J., & Citrin, J. (2007). European opinion about immigration: The role of identities, interests and information. *British Journal of Political Science, 37*(3), 477–504.

Statistics Belgium. (2017). *Bevolking naar woonplaats en nationaliteit* [Population by place of residence and nationality]. Retrieved from http://statbel.fgov.be/nl/statistieken/cijfers/.

Stempel III, G. H. (1988). Topic and story choice of five network newscasts. *Journalism and Mass Communication Quarterly, 65*(3), 750–752.

Strabac, Z. (2011). It is the eyes and not the size that matter: The real and the perceived size of immigrant populations and anti-immigrant prejudice in Western Europe. *European Societies, 13*(4), 559–582.

Tajfel, H., & Turner, J. C. (1979). An integrative theory of intergroup conflict. In W. G. Austin & S. Worchel (Eds.), *The social psychology of intergroup relations* (pp. 33–47). Monterey, CA: Brooks-Cole Pub. Co.

UNCHR. (2018). *Mediterranean Situation*. Retrieved from https://data2.unhcr.org/en/situations/mediterranean.

Van den Bulck, H., & Broos, D. (2011). Can a charter of diversity make the difference in ethnic minority reporting? A comparative content and production analysis of two Flemish television newscasts. *Communications: The European Journal of Communication Research, 36*(2), 195–216.

Van Klingeren, M., Boomgaarden, H. G., Vliegenthart, R., & De Vreese, C. H. (2014). Real world is not enough: The media as an additional source of negative attitudes toward immigration, comparing Denmark and the Netherlands. *European Sociological Review, 31*(3), 268–283.

Vandenberghe, H. (2017). *Diversiteit in de Vlaamse nieuwsmedia: een longitudinale en mediavergelijkende kijk* [Diversity in Flemish news media: A longitudinal and media comparative view] (Unpublished doctoral dissertation). Leuven: University of Leuven.

Vliegenthart, R., & Boomgaarden, H. G. (2007). Real-world indicators and the coverage of immigration and the integration of minorities in Dutch newspapers. *European Journal of Communication, 22*(3), 293–314.

Yan, T., Curtin, R., & Jans, M. (2010). Trends in income nonresponse over two decades, *Journal of Official Statistics, 26*(1), 145–164.

Chapter 8
Online News Consumption and Public Sentiment toward Refugees: Is there a Filter Bubble at Play? Belgium, France, the Netherlands, and Sweden: A Comparison

Stefan Mertens, Leen d'Haenens, and Rozane De Cock

Introduction

Pariser's seminal book, "The Filter Bubble: What the Internet Is Hiding from You," came out in 2011 and supporters and opponents are still debating whether there is such a thing as an online filter bubble. First of all, the term itself is not as universally used within the scholarly field as one might think. A number of academic investigations of the purported phenomenon use alternative terminology. Following in Sunstein's footsteps (2004), Garrett mentions "online echo chambers" (2009). Haim et al. refer to "partial information blindness" (2018). Others talk of "social polarization", "fragmentation," or "self-segregation" (Vaccari, Valeriani, Barberá, Jost, Nagler, & Tucker, 2016), or call on earlier communication studies' concepts such as the more widely applicable 'selective exposure' (Knobloch-Westerwick, & Meng, 2011). What's more, the actual matter under debate is in flux as well. While originally two clearly defined positions were pitted against one another, a third group of scholars now holds a more nuanced and complex position. As this chapter will show, online reality and its impact on viewpoints and opinions is more complex, less straightforward, and more difficult to pinpoint than originally thought by both proponents of the democratic power of online (news) media and opponents pointing at detrimental effects. We will investigate the role of traditional and online news consumption on public sentiment toward refugees, a topic that has seen intense media coverage in recent years (see Chapter 3) and a topic on which opinions are much divided (see Chapters 1 and 7). We will test the assumption that online news users have more clear-cut viewpoints on refugees owing to a narrower focus in their consumption, and we will do so in a cross-cultural setting (Belgium, Sweden, France, and the Netherlands).

Digital opportunities vs. online threats to democracy

In the early digital days, optimism about technological change within (news) media—cheap online publishing, SNS use and omnidirectional communication flows, permanent and unlimited online access to previously inaccessible information sources, the power of 'prosumers'—led to the firm belief that the public was going to benefit from ever-increasing exposure to highly diverse perspectives. No longer confined within a narrow inner circle of information, people would see their field of vision open up thanks to a wide and diversified news platform—from a myopic to a panoramic or hyperopic view. As the digital era went on, more pessimistic voices began to make themselves heard, but the optimists have remained strong, stressing the benefits of digital access, a broader social network, and unlimited access to online news. Such studies emphasize the increased exposure to heterogeneous viewpoints that comes with people being able to pick their information from a wider pool of voices: online social networks, recommendation systems, political fora (Garrett, 2009; Goel, Mason, & Watts, 2010). Results show, for instance, that friends tend to disagree more on a given topic than they think they do, resulting in a gap between perceived and actual agreement and lower political polarization than generally thought within inner circles of online social network groups (Goel et al., 2010). Garrett's study on selective exposure among online news users indicates that longer reading times are associated with opinion-challenging information, and thus contact with heterogeneous political ideologies. "People do not seek to completely exclude other perspectives from their political universe, and there is little evidence that they will use the Internet to create echo chambers", according to Garrett (2009: 279). These studies, though, are not based on representative samples. We attempted to fill this gap using four representative samples of the adult population between 18 and 65 years of age in four different countries (for more information, see methods section) to test the filter bubble hypothesis—both on representative population samples and through an intercultural comparative study model involving Belgium, France, the Netherlands, and Sweden.

Across from those who see online exposure to news, social networks, and news comments as a mostly positive development, others worry it may increase ideological segregation and generate effects that are detrimental to a democratic system built on a diversity of voices and opinions. Walter, Brüggemann, and Engesser (2018: 204) focus on the negative impact of online news use, stating that "User comment sections serve as echo chambers rather than as corrective mechanisms". Proponents of the filter bubble theory stress that within non-diverse, closed online groups where there is no room for alternative voices, opinions tend to 'echo', which locks users into their own—possibly false, but certainly limited—beliefs. Pariser (2011) warns against the rise of online 'micro-universes' of personalized information—bubbles that filter out any contradicting information, letting in only what we want to hear. People may thus be under the false impression that they have full control and responsibility over what comes in and what stays out of their news media menu. According to Pariser the public is unaware of any information that does not reach them due to obscure filtering mechanisms in global search engines, programmed algorithms, and digital recall of searching patterns, preferences, and interests. The result is a skewed information diet that only mirrors a user's preferences, harming the democratic equilibrium. Sunstein (2004) also clearly describes the filtering effect of online culture. While the Internet has proved highly useful—bringing people together over huge geographical distances, lowering the costs of distributing and consuming news, opening up countless avenues of self-expression—it also has negative effects. When people use online tools in ways that filter out alternative opinions, they isolate themselves and their inner group from the rest of society, in effect dwelling in "echo chambers" of like-minded people. Sunstein (2004) warns against excessive personalization, pleading for unplanned encounters of a diversity of information—a prerequisite for a healthy democracy. The danger is "cyberbalkanization"—increasingly segregated groups or ecosystems which are never exposed to one another. This favors the extremes within the filter bubble ingroups, jeopardizing democratic cooperation and understanding. Sunstein does not blame the medium as such but holds accountable both the people who use it and those who develop algorithms, personalization options, etc.: making constructive use of the Internet is up to them.

In a democracy, different sides of the political spectrum need to be aware of each other's standpoints to engage in fruitful debates that lead to societal solutions in the long run (Pariser, 2011). This is especially the case when a society wants to think out-of-the box and implement creative, innovative ideas—something that runs counter to repetitive filter bubble thinking patterns. A serious look at the core theme of this book and chapter—the refugee situation which Europe has been facing and which intensified from 2015 on—shows that our societies need to be more flexible in their approaches, not only for the sake of the refugees entering Europe, but also in the interest of the countries under study, their democratic values, their resilience, and their representations of themselves. Having available a wide range of views and reliable facts on the topic is a prerequisite for constructive thinking. Since a majority of the public is dependent on information on the refugee situation stemming from new and traditional media (see Chapter 7), the role of a possible online filter bubble functions as an important factor in the search for sustainable answers. Some of the previous studies testing the filter bubble hypothesis have zoomed in on other controversial yet highly socially relevant issues such as climate change (Walter et al., 2018), personal health (Holone, 2016), or elections (Vaccari et al., 2016). To our knowledge, it is the first time that the filter bubble hypothesis has been studied in the context of the refugee issue and in a cross-cultural sample (Belgium, France, the Netherlands, and Sweden).

Recent studies find partial support for both sides of the filter bubble debate, painting a more nuanced picture of the phenomenon (Dubois & Blank, 2018; Flaxman, Goel, & Rao, 2016; Haim et al., 2018; Resnick, Garrett, Kriplean, Munson, & Stroud, 2013; Vaccari et al., 2016). Haim et al. (2018) point to a possible "bursting of the filter bubble," but state in their conclusion that there is evidence in favor of both sides of the argument. While they found some "implicit personalization on content diversity" (p. 330), they did not find enough evidence in support of the filter bubble thesis. What they did find, though, was an overrepresentation of specific news brands and an underrepresentation of others by a global news aggregator. Flaxman et al. (2016) had mixed results as well when testing for links between social networks (SN) /search engines (SE) and potential filter bubbles. Both SN and SE are associated with a higher mean ideological distance between individuals, thus creating 'isles'. Counterintuitively, the authors also found that online news platforms were linked with an increase in people's exposure to their less preferred political side, a factor likely to widen their perspectives. In addition to finding that online news consumption mostly led people to the home pages of their mainstream, offline news outlets, Flaxman et al. mention the tempering (positive and negative) consequences of online technical innovations. This is in line with the outcome of the Twitter study by Vaccari et al. (2016), who state that the users of this highly successful social medium do engage more within likeminded networks, but that disagreement still plays an important role in conversations. In their opinion there is an immediate risk of viewpoint segregation. This is supported by Dubois and Blank's recent study (2018), in which they show that people interested in politics and exposed to a diverse media menu tend to avoid echo chambers.

To conclude, there is evidence in support of both sides of the filter bubble debate, and no final conclusion has been drawn. That said, recent studies pointing to the existence of filter bubbles mention relatively modest effects (Flaxman et al., 2016), and not everyone among the general public is likely to be susceptible to the lure of the echo chamber (Dubois & Blank, 2018). Our research makes use of an intercultural study to test for the existence of a potential filter bubble among online news consumers, affecting their attitudes toward refugees.

Method

In the Fall of 2017, to map out public sentiment on refugees in relation to news consumption patterns, we looked at media menus through an online survey of a representative sample of the adult population ($N = 6,000$) of four European countries: Belgium, France, Sweden, and the Netherlands ($n = 1,500$ in each country). We chose these as part of a focus on neighboring Western European countries—with the addition of Sweden, a country that is internationally recognized for its exemplarity in the refugee debate. The 'Swedish exception' refers to Sweden's extraordinary tolerance of cultural diversity. As such, Sweden may be an example for other European countries pursuing interculturalism and social cohesion (Schierup & Ålund, 2011). Next to Belgium and Sweden, the key countries in the IM²MEDIATE project, France and the Netherlands, are interesting added cases, because they represent two different policy orientations (Willem, 2010: 47). France has historically chosen an assimilationist integration policy while the Netherlands have chosen a multicultural integration policy.

Measures

Respondents were asked to indicate gender, birth year, total net household income, and educational attainments. To measure their media consumption, we asked them to report how many minutes they tended to devote each day to four news channels: television, radio, newspapers, and online platforms. In all four countries television was the most popular news source in terms of time spent, with an average of 54.13 minutes. Radio came in second with 42.50 minutes on average. Online news was third with a daily average of 32.25 minutes. Newspapers (in printed form) were found to be the least popular news channel, with an average of only 22.14 minutes a day. Cross-country differences among medium-specific consumption profiles are presented in Table 8.1. The Swedes tend to be the keenest users of print and online platforms, while the French were clearly the most avid television viewers. Belgium follows Sweden as the second most online and print news oriented country, while registering the lowest mean score of television news consumption. The Netherlands scored highest for radio news consumption, coming in second for television and third for online and print channels. While Belgium scores higher than the Netherlands for print and online news, the difference between the two countries is very small. In summary, Sweden scores high for print and online channels, while France is more television oriented and Belgium and the Netherlands tend to be more middle-of-the-road.

Table 8.1: Media consumption patterns in four countries with mean of minutes spent on the consumption of each medium

	Television	Radio	Print	Online
Belgium	47.05	41.17	21.20	32.40
Sweden	50.15	44.02	26.56	36.13
France	68.32	40.33	19.10	27.40
The Netherlands	50.22	45.29	21.13	32.28

Cross-country differences as to radio news consumption are not statistically significant according to an ANOVA test ($F(3,5595) = 1.432, p > .05$). Cross-country differences as to television news consumption ($F(3,5595) = 27.023, p < .001$), print news consumption ($F(3,5595) = 8.923, p < .001$, and online news consumption ($F(3,5595) = 5.298, p < .001$) do reach the level of statistical significance.

A 13-item scale (Arlt & Wolling, 2018) was used to measure the degree to which respondents feel more or less favorable toward refugees. Each item was used as a question with five potential answers: "do not agree at all," "somewhat disagree," "neutral," "somewhat agree," and "fully agree." Fully agreeing with an item was coded as 5 in all items, except for items 10 and 11, two items formulated in the other direction to make the scale less repetitive. The last items were subsequently recoded. The degree of coherence between items proved to be very good (Cronbach's alpha = .850). These are the 13 statements:

1. Educated refugees should be given the chance to use their degree here.
2. My country can do more to provide dignified accommodation for refugees.
3. Each country in Europe should accommodate its share of refugees.
4. There ought to be binding rules that determine how many refugees each country can accommodate and how they need to be sheltered.
5. The media blow problems out of proportion and neglect positive aspects in the refugee debate.
6. We cannot leave the care for refugees in Europe solely to Greece and Italy.
7. The way in which Europe treats refugees is humiliating.
8. While their applications for refugee status are being considered, refugees should be allowed to work in the country.
9. The government should be generous in judging people's applications for refugee status.

10. Most applicants for refugee status aren't in real fear of persecution in their own countries.
11. While their case is being considered, applicants should be kept in detention centers.
12. While their case is being considered, the government should give financial support to applicants.
13. Refugees whose applications are granted should be entitled to bring in their close family members.

The mean score of positivity was the highest in Sweden (3.23). The Netherlands came in second with a mean positivity of 3.17 on a scale of 5. Belgium had a mean positivity of 3.13, while France had the lowest positivity with a mean of 3.01. This cross-country difference was significant in an ANOVA test ($F(2,5595) = 19.525, p < .001$). Moreover, additional Chi-square testing (not presented in detail here) showed statistically significant differences across the countries on each of the 13 statements.

Research Questions and Hypotheses

We begin with testing for positive or negative sentiment in relation to different types of news consumption. While the main interest of this research relates to nonneutrality, the latter's 'directions' (i.e., positivity or negativity) are obviously important aspects.
RQ1: Does the number of minutes spent on news consumption on different media types correlate with more positive or more negative sentiment?
After having shown the direction, i.e., the positive or negative sentiment, we will focus on this study's core hypothesis on neutrality. Increased online news consumption is expected to coincide with less neutral opinions. These less neutral opinions might be either more positive or more negative. This assumption is tested by correlating the time spent on news consumption on four media types with the number of statements regarding which respondents choose a neutral stance. We argue that the more time people will spend reading news online, the less often they will choose neutral statements to illustrate their opinions on refugees.
H1: People who consume more online news will tend to hold non-neutral views.
This media-specific assumption implies that people with less neutral sentiment will on average devote less time to radio, television, or print media for their news consumption.

H2: People who tend to consume less radio, television, and print news will hold non-neutral views.

Furthermore, we will test how a neutral sentiment might be correlated with socio-demographic characteristics (Hypotheses 3a, 4a, 5a, and 6a). We know from prior research that online news platforms have more appeal to people depending on their specific demographics (e.g., Media Insight Project, 2014; Preston, 2015; Jensen, 2017). Hence, we will test this dimension further (Hypotheses 3b, 4b, 5b, and 6b). Our other hypotheses (Hypotheses 3c, 4c, 5c, and 6c) pertain to attitude, suggesting more positive sentiment among women, younger people, highly educated and more affluent people.

We will calculate correlations to provide more insight on the relations found. We performed a stepwise regression with two dependent variables— i.e., the number of items with a neutral response (measuring the degree of neutrality) and the mean direction of sentiments (i.e., the degree to which respondents express a positive or a negative sentiment). This provided answers to the second research question: do socio-demographic characteristics outweigh the importance of media consumption variables, or is it the other way around when it comes to sentiment toward refugees?

H3a: Men hold less neutral opinions.
H3b: Men consume more online news than women.
H3c: Men hold less positive opinions.
H4a: Younger people hold less neutral opinions.
H4b: Younger people consume more online news than older people.
H4c: Younger people hold more positive opinions.
H5: Higher educated people hold less neutral opinions.
H5b: Higher educated people consume more online news than less educated people.
H5c: Higher educated people hold more positive opinions.
H6a: More affluent people hold less neutral opinions.
H6b: More affluent people consume more online news than less affluent people.
H6c: More affluent people hold more positive opinions.
RQ2: Are socio-demographic characteristics more influential than media consumption variables in the formation of the opinions expressed based on a) the number of items to which a neutral answer was given and b) the degree to which respondents hold positive or negative opinions on refugees?

Since we rely on a cross-country database (Belgium, France, Sweden, and the Netherlands), a final research question deals with differences between these countries.

RQ3: In what way are these significant results (types of news media consumption on the one hand and positive and neutral opinions on refugees on the other hand) country-specific?

Apart from the last research question that deals with international differences the main focus of the article is on outweighing the influence of media and demographic variables and their relation with the neutrality of sentiments toward refugees and the direction of sentiments toward refugees. The direction of sentiments could be both positive and negative. For the sake of clarity a figure integrating all the hypotheses and research questions on media and/or demography is presented.

Figure 8.1: Hypotheses and research questions

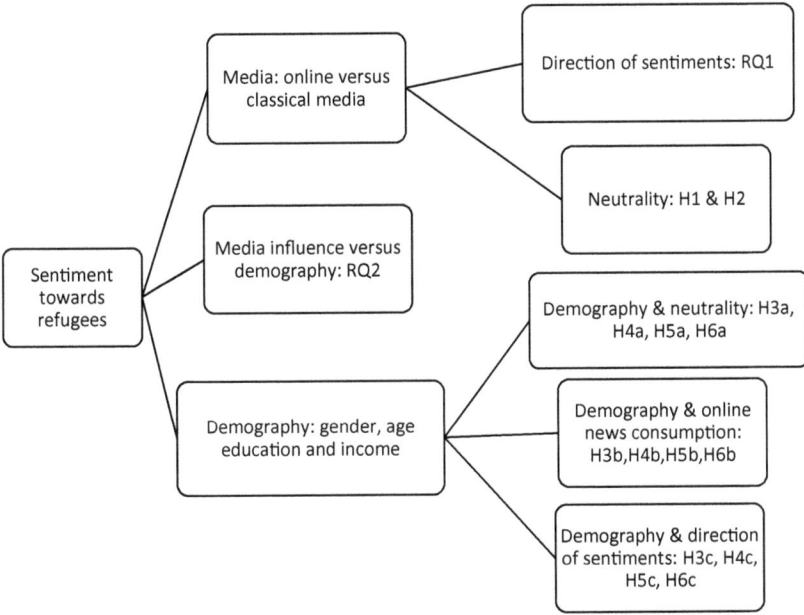

Results

Table 8.2 shows the correlations between time spent on different types of news and negative or positive sentiment (1 is negative and 5 is positive). The 13 items were merged into one mean score. The two items that were negatively formulated were recoded.

The only type of news consumption that significantly correlates with the refugee sentiment is television news consumption ($r(5998,2) = -.057$, $p < .001$). People who consume more news on television hold significantly more negative views on refugees. The other types of news consumption do not correlate with opinions on refugees.

Table 8.2: Correlations between time spent on news media platforms and sentiment on refugees

News consumption platform	Sentiment on refugees
Television	-.057***
Radio	-.016
Newspapers	.003
Online	-.002

Note: * $p < .05$, ** $p < .01$, ***, $p < .001$

Table 8.3: Correlations between time spent on news media platforms and number of neutral opinions on refugees

News consumption platform	Neutral opinions on refugees
Television	-.020
Radio	.001
Newspapers	-.009
Online	-.058***

Note: * $p < .05$, ** $p < .01$, ***, $p < .001$

Furthermore, people who consume online news tend to hold the most polarized opinions on immigration ($r(5998,2) = -.058, p < .001$), meaning that their sentiment happens to be the furthest removed from a neutral stance. A similar correlation was not found for the other news platforms under study. As we intended to measure not only neutral and nonneutral sentiment, but slightly negative/positive views as well, we recoded neutral answers as 3, rather positive and rather negative answers as 2, and positive and negative answers as 1, which resulted in Table 8.4.

Tellingly, two types of news media consumption imply less than neutral opinions. Television news consumption ($r(5998,2) = -.050, p < .001$) is related to less neutral opinions, reflecting the relative prevalence of negative opinions associated with it. Another significant correlation emerges between online news consumption and degree of neutrality ($r(5998,2) = -.057, p < .001$), although (see Table 8.3) online news is not related to negativity as such, but rather to more clear-cut (as opposed to neutral) opinions on either side of the

Table 8.4: Correlations between time spent on media types for news consumption and degree of neutrality among respondents

News consumption platform	Degree of neutrality in opinions on refugees
Television	-.050***
Radio	-.014
Newspapers	-.019
Online	-.078***

Note: * $p < .05$, ** $p < .01$, *** $p < .001$

Table 8.5: Background variables and online news consumption: correlations

Variable	Correlation with online news consumption	Correlation with number of items to which a neutral answer was given	Correlation with the direction of sentiments
Age	-.053***	-.032*	-.064***
Gender	-.102***	.045***	.081***
Educational attainment	-.010	-.049*	.173***
Income	.000	.014	.013

Note: * $p < .05$, ** $p < .01$, *** $p < .001$

spectrum. Radio and newspaper news consumption does not hold significant relations with the degree of neutrality.

Table 8.5 provides results on hypotheses 3b, 4b, 5b, and 6b regarding the correlations between online news consumption and socio-demographic background variables. Individual characteristics such as age and gender prove to be explaining variables, while educational attainment does not. Younger age goes together with higher consumption of online news (confirming hypothesis 4b $(r(5998,2) = -0.053, p < .001)$. Hypothesis 3b also gets confirmed, implying that men are keener consumers of online news $(r(5998,2) = -.102, p<0.001)$ There are no education $(r(5998,2) = 0.010, p > .05)$ or income $(r(5998,2) = 0.0, p > .05)$ related differences in the amount of online news consumed, refuting hypotheses 5b and 6b.

Table 8.5 shows the correlation between background variables (age, gender, highest educational attainment, net income) and the number of items to which respondents responded in a neutral fashion. Hypothesis 5a is confirmed

($r(5998,2) = -.049, p < .001$), while for hypothesis 4a the opposite is true with older people holding less neutral opinions ($r(5998,2) = -.0.32, p < .001$). Hypothesis 3a is confirmed since women tend to hold more neutral opinions. ($r(5998,2) = .045, p < .001$). There is no relation with income level, which refutes hypothesis 6a ($r(5998,2) = .014, p > .05$).

A third correlation analysis deals with the relationship between socio-demographic factors and direction of sentiment (i.e., positive or negative). The results on direction of sentiment once again prove the importance of gender (confirming hypothesis 3c ($r(5998,2) = .081, p < .001$), age (confirming hypothesis 4c ($r(5998,2) = -.064, p < .001$), and educational attainment (confirming hypothesis 5c, $r(5998,2) = .173, p < .001$). There is no link between level of affluence and sentiment toward refugees (which refutes hypothesis 6c, $r(5998,2) = -0.013, p < .001$). Women have more positive attitudes, and the same holds for higher educated and younger people.

Furthermore, a stepwise regression was performed. All the socio-demographic variables (age, gender, educational attainment, income) as well as all the media consumption variables (online news consumption, television news consumption, radio news consumption, newspaper consumption) were included as independent variables. The number of items on which a neutral answer was given was the dependent variable. The highest R-square reached was only .011 in a model with five variables. The most influential variable on neutrality is the degree of online news consumption (added $R^2 = .003$), again confirming our basic hypothesis. Further variables adding additional explained variance included educational attainment (added $R^2 = .002$), age (added $R^2 = .002$), gender (added $R^2 = .002$), and newspaper consumption (added $R^2 = .001$).

A second stepwise regression was added with the same independent variables and the direction of sentiments as a dependent variable. Once again the total explained variance was very low, with an R-square of .038. Only three variables were important for this model: educational attainment proved to be the most influential variable (added $R^2 = .030$), followed by gender (added $R^2 = .007$) and the already reported small influence of television news consumption on the development of less positive attitudes toward refugees (added $R^2 = .001$).

To further probe the relationship between online news consumption and less neutral opinions, we tried to see whether it also holds within both age groups and the age and education quartiles in which we divided the sample. The results are shown in Table 8.6.

The results show that the relationship between online news consumption and less neutral opinions exists among both men ($r(2,5598) = -0.40, p < .05$) and women ($r(2, 5598) = -.074, p < .001$). A division in age groups also shows a similar trend across all age groups. The relationship between the two phenomena

Table 8.6: Subgroups and correlation between online news consumption and neutral sentiment

Subgroup	Correlation between online news consumption and neutral sentiment	p-value
Men	-.040	.028*
Women	-.074	.000***
Age quartile 1 (18-31)	-.061	.017*
Age quartile 2 (32-44)	-.065	.013*
Age quartile 3 (45-54)	-.049	.060
Age quartile 4 (55-65)	-.068	.008**
Education quartile 1 (lowest)	.019	.722
Education quartile 2	-.073	.074
Education quartile 3	-.021	.696
Education quartile 4 (highest)	-.239	.001**

Note: * $p < .05$, ** $p < .01$, *** $p < .001$

does not hold only in the third quartile of the age categories (45-54 years old). Among the other age groups statistical significance is reached.

On table 8.6 the most interesting result is to be found in the education quartiles divisions. The relationship between online news consumption and less neutral sentiment does not hold in the three less educated quartiles, but is especially strong in the highest education quartile ($r(2,5598) = -.239$, $p < .01$). The relationship between online news consumption and diminishing neutrality—which is indicative of the presence of a filter bubble—is especially strong among highly educated media consumers, and non-existent among the three less educated quartiles.

We further calculated the correlations between the direction of opinions and the amount of online news consumption. The negative correlation between sentiment on refugees on the one hand and online news consumption ($r(2,5598) = -.170, p < .05$) on the other hand implies that there is indeed a filter bubble in the case of highly educated people who consume a lot of online news and have negative views toward refugees.

Finally, let us move on to the analysis of the cross-country differences in our dataset. The basic assumption that online news consumption and less neutral opinions go together is confirmed in the complete data set, but a country-by-country analysis proves that Sweden is an exception as this correlation is not

Table 8.7: Cross-country comparison of correlations between media use (television and online) and direction (positive or negative) of sentiment towards refugees

Country	Correlation between television news consumption and direction of sentiment	Correlation between television news consumption and neutral sentiment	Correlation between online news consumption and direction of sentiment	Correlation between online news consumption and neutral sentiment
Belgium	-.087**	-.065*	.002	-.073**
Sweden	-.095***	-.003	-.068**	.013
France	-.024	-.033	.048	-.092***
The Netherlands	.026	-.042	.002	-.062*

Note: * $p < .05$, ** $p < .01$, *** $p < .001$

present there ($r(2,5598) = .013, p > .05$). In Belgium ($r(2,5598) = -.073, p < .05$), France ($r(2,5598) = -.092, p < .001$), and the Netherlands ($r(2,5598) = -.062, p < .05$) the basic assumption (RQ 3) is confirmed.

Sweden is also an odd case as far as the relation between positive opinions and online news consumption is concerned. Indeed Sweden ($r(2,5598) = -.068, p < .05$) is the only country where more online news consumption and more negative opinions on refugees go together. As is the case in the total cross-country dataset, for the other countries there is no correlation between positivity or negativity of opinions on refugees on the one hand and online news consumption on the other hand ($r(2,5598) = .002, p > .05$ in Belgium; $r(2,5598) = .048, p > .05$ in France, and $r(2,5598) = .002, p > .05$ in the Netherlands).

Belgium is the outlier when it comes to the relationship between television news consumption and neutral opinions on refugees, because it is only in Belgium that higher television news consumption goes hand in hand with less neutral opinions ($r(2,5598) = -.065, p > .05$). Sweden ($r(2,5598) = -.003, p > .05$), France ($r(2,5598) = -.033, p > .05$), and the Netherlands ($r(2,5598) = -.042, p > .05$) follow the trend of the total cross-country dataset in this respect.

Finally, it should be added that while in the total cross-country dataset a higher television news consumption correlates with more negative opinions, the country picture is more differentiated. Belgium ($r(2,5598) = -.087, p < .05$) and Sweden ($r(2,5598) = -.095, p < .001$) significantly follow the trend of the total cross-country dataset, but France ($r(2,5598) = -.024, p > .05$) and the Netherlands ($r(2,5598) = .026, p > .05$) do not.

Conclusion

Notwithstanding the prominent place that refugees take in news and political discussions both in Europe and around the world, public opinion is split (if not negative) and generally uninformed or misinformed on the issue, tending to overestimate both the numbers of the newcomers and any association with crime and terrorism. This chapter explored the perceptions of refugees by the general population of four European countries (Belgium, France, Sweden, and the Netherlands) through a look at news media menus. We compared the views of the public regarding these cross-border flows of people as well as the underpinning of such views by looking at neutral versus positive and negative sentiment toward refugees.

There is ample evidence that negative sentiment is growing (see Chapter 1): people in Europe worry that newcomers may not integrate successfully in their host countries, and that they may not be able or willing to adopt 'European values', however fluid the interpretation of the concept may be. Europeans are not uniform in their sentiment toward refugees: The Swedes are the most positive, and the French the least positive, while the Belgians and the Dutch sit in the middle of the Migrant Policy Index (MIPEX), established to document countries' immigration policies (see Chapters 1 and 2). As indicated by the latest MIPEX report (2015), politicians and policy makers either resist anti-immigrant sentiment or cultivate it and thrive on it: "Political will may matter more than a country's tradition of immigration, since more inclusive integration policies may encourage more immigrants to settle permanently and the public to trust immigrants more" (MIPEX quoted in Adams, 2017: 29).

Furthermore, perspectives on the refugee issue in our four-country study vary somewhat across age groups, with more negative sentiment most widely voiced by older people, by men, and by the less educated. We also know from other survey research (see Chapter 7) that people with a migration background (which colors their expectations regarding refugees) tend to be more positive.

Looking at media use in particular, Chapter 7 assesses the crucial role of the public service broadcaster in shaping people's news media menus as well as their overall trust in those news sources that mediate their sentiment toward immigrants and refugees. Studies found that people who mainly consume news on commercial television hold more negative attitudes toward minority groups than people who follow the news on public television (De Coninck et al., 2018; Jacobs et al., 2016). Both the content of news media reporting (see Chapters 3, 4, and 5) and the audience's trust in such coverage play a crucial role.

This research tapped into the debate about the ontology of the filter bubble. We empirically tested its existence with respect to news about refugees, in the sense that heavy online news users tend to be exposed to a less diverse offer which merely echoes their ideological preferences and interests, which may foster less open, less diverse, and less neutral views about refugees. Notably, two types of news media consumption implied less neutral sentiments: television news consumption and online news consumption. This bears explaining: while television news consumption reflects the relative prevalence of negative sentiment, online news is not related with negativity as such, but rather with more clear-cut (as opposed to neutral) sentiment on either side of the spectrum. Radio and newspaper news consumption does not link to type of sentiment in a statistically significant way. Interestingly, our results point to the presence of a filter bubble among highly educated people who consume a lot of online news and hold negative sentiments toward refugees. Nevertheless, in line with recent, more nuanced findings on the filter bubble issue (Flaxman et al., 2016; Haim et al., 2018), our study uncovered rather small but statistically significant evidence pointing to the importance of a diverse online and traditional news consumption pattern.

As far as the country policy and media use context is concerned, this was only a four-country study focusing on Western Europe, which showed remarkable differences as to news media use linked to types of sentiment on refugees. Consequently, we recommend more cross-country research, especially looking at more countries in Central, Southern, and Eastern Europe. The latter countries are known to hold a more uniform negative sentiment toward 'the other' regardless of their socio-demographics, so that further insight could be garnered in how news media menus—with a focus on legacy and social media use—are profoundly impacted by digital disruption (e.g., algorithms steering news users in certain directions based on their preferences) and drive people's and political responses in quite opposite directions, characterized by a growth of both radical left- and right-wing populist movements, at the expense of a fractured centrist consensus (see also Michael Adams, 2017).

References

Adams, M. (2017). *Could it happen Here? Canada in the Age of Trump and Brexit*. New York: Simon & Schuster.

Arlt, D., & Wolling, J. (2018). Bias wanted! Examining people's information exposure, quality expectations and bias perceptions in the context of the refugees' debate among different segments of the German population. *Communications: The European Journal of Communication Research, 43*(1), 75–99.

De Coninck, D., Matthijs, K., Debrael, M., Joris, W., De Cock, R., & d'Haenens, L. (2018). The relationship between media use and public opinion on immigrants and refugees: A Belgian perspective. *Communications: The European Journal of Communication Research, 43*(3), 403–425.

Dubois, E., & Blank. (2018). The echo chamber is overstated: the moderating effect of political interest and diverse media. *Information, Communication & Society, 21*(5), 729–745.

Garrett, R.K. (2009). Echo chambers online? Politically motivated, selective exposure among Internet news users. *Journal of Computer-Mediated Communication, 14*(2), 265–285.

Goel, S., Mason, W., & Watts, D.J. (2010). Real and perceived attitude agreement in social networks. *Journal of Personality and Social Psychology, 99*(4), 611–621.

Haim, M., Graefe, A., & Brosius, H-B. (2018). Burst of the filter bubble? *Digital Journalism, 6*(3), 330–343.

Holone, H. (2016). The filter bubble and its effect on online personal health information. *Croatian Medical Journal, 57*(3), 298–301.

Knobloch-Westerwick, S., & Meng, J. (2011). Reinforcement of the political self through selective exposure to political messages. *Journal of Communication, 61*(2), 349–368.

Jacobs, L., Meeusen, C., & d'Haenens, L. (2016). News coverage and attitudes on immigration: Public and commercial television news compared. *European Journal of Communication, 31*(6), 642–660.

Jensen, M. (2017). *Digital news report: Gendered spaces of news consumption.* http://www.broadagenda.com.au/home/gendered-spaces-of-news-consumption/

Media Insight Project (2014). *The personal news cycle.* http://www.americanpressinstitute.org/wp-content/uploads/2014/03/The_Media_Insight_Project_The_Personal_News_Cycle_Final.pdf.

Pariser, E. (2011). *The Filter Bubble: What the Internet is hiding from you.* London: Penguin UK.

Preston, A. (2015) Generational Gaps – UK News Consumption and the Impact of Age. http://www.digitalnewsreport.org/essays/2015/generational-gaps/.

Resnick, P., Garrett, R.K., Kriplean, T., Munson, S.A., & Stroud, N.J. (2013). *Bursting your (Filter) Bubble: Strategies for Promoting Diverse Exposure*, Conference on computer supported cooperative work companion, San Antonio, Texas, USA, 23 February 2013, pp. 95–100.

Schierup, C.U., Ålund, A. (2011). The end of Swedish exceptionalism? Citizenship, neoliberalism and the politics of exclusion. *Race & Class, 53*(1), 45–64.

Sunstein, C. (2004). Democracy and filtering. *Communications of the ACM, 47*(12), 57–59.

Vaccari, C., Valeriani, A., Barberá, P., Jost, J.T., Nagler, J., & Tucker, J.A. (2016). Of echo chambers and contrarian clubs: Exposure to political disagreement among German and Italian users of Twitter. *Social Media + Society, 2*(3), 1–24.

Walter, S., Brüggemann, M., & Engesser, S. (2018). Echo chambers of denial: Explaining user comments on climate change. *Environmental Communication, 12*(2), 204–217.

Willem, C. (2010). *Young People from diverse ethno-cultural Backgrounds constructing their Identities using digital Media.* Universidad de Barcelona: doctoral thesis.

Chapter 9
The Effects of Dominant versus Peripheral News Frames on Attitudes toward Refugees and News Story Credibility

Willem Joris and Rozane De Cock

Introduction

Earlier in this book, authors stipulated that news media are one of the key factors having an impact on the public's negative opinions and attitudes toward minority groups such as refugees and immigrants (e.g., Müller et al., 2017; Van Klingeren et al., 2017). News media provide citizens with frames enabling them to know exactly how to understand and make sense of policy themes (Brewer & Gross, 2010). Moreover, Gamson and Modigliani (1989) argued that media use their power of influence by interpreting reality as a way to emphasize specific frames and downplay others. As news media are highly interconnected with politics and public perception (e.g., Entman, 2003; 2004; Orgad, 2012), they contribute to or combat stereotyping of minority groups (see also Chapter 7 in this book; De Coninck et al., 2018).

Typically, in crisis situations such as the current refugee issue, people start looking for information about causes and effects more than they usually do (Coombs & Holladay, 2004). As the majority of citizens have limited real-life contact with refugees, media are their main source of information on this topic (e.g., Bleich, Bloemraad, & de Graauw, 2015; Jacobs, Hooghe, & de Vroome, 2017). Not only do the media select the topics they report on, they also define the way they cover them when it comes to news angle, tone of voice, etc. Through the information made available and the way it is accessed (Scheufele & Tewksbury, 2007) the media shape the perception of events. The news coverage of the refugee issue (see also Chapter 3 in this book) has created highly prominent portrayals, which may have substantial implications for public opinion formation toward minority groups and ordinary citizens' understanding of the refugee issue. Therefore, research into the effects of frames on attitudes is greatly needed since coverage of the current refugee issue may have a tangible effect on public opinion. In contrast to Chapter 7 in this book, which distinguishes between attitudes toward migrants and refugees, we focused only on the attitudes toward refugees as a minority group.

How do frames affect individuals' opinions and attitudes?

The news framing approach is central to our study. Frames are schemes of interpretation that may be used to organize information and to manage it efficiently (Lecheler & de Vreese, 2012). As defined by Entman (1993: 52), to frame is to *"select some aspects of a perceived reality and make them more salient in a communicating context, in such a way to promote a particular problem definition, causal interpretation, moral evaluation, and/or treatment recommendation."* Thus, frames are certainly not neutral (Berinsky & Kinder, 2006). A frame might cause significant changes in attitudes when participants are exposed to them separately in different experimental conditions (Chong & Druckman, 2007).

As we use Entman's definition (1993), built around ideas of selection and salience, the frames under study are salience or emphasis frames (Cacciatore, Scheufele, & Iyengar, 2016). This refers to the identified elements in the news that are emphasized by the communicator. In other words, this suggests that news framing functions by making some aspects of an issue or event more accessible, visible, or salient to the public. With a focus on salience, the frame analysis in this study is related to agenda-setting and priming which are also related to accessibility.

Frames in the news coverage of the refugee issue can be considered as properties of informational texts that condition the processes of both news reception and news impact (Igartua & Cheng, 2009). The framing effect refers to two differentiated processes. News frames about immigration not only induce cognitive channeling effects (frame-setting), they also affect attitudes and beliefs with regard to a topic. For example, Brader, Valentino, and Suhay (2008) discovered that a news item focusing on the negative consequences of migration, in contrast to an item pointing out its benefits, encouraged more negative attitudes toward migrants, higher levels of anxiety, and a greater perception of threat. Furthermore, a study by Cho, Gil de Zuniga, Shah, & McLeod (2006) pointed out that reading a news article in which Arab citizens are described as both immigrants and extremists stimulated a negative opinion on Arabs and consequently a rejection of immigration. In addition, Van Gorp (2005) asserted that the media play a critical role in generating public support for or condemnation of the immigration policy. Focusing for example on women and children that are left behind, being unprotected and traumatized, would eventually recall sentiments such as compassion with innocent people (Information Center about Asylum and Refugees, 2012). These findings indicate that the way refugees, migrants, and/or asylum seekers are portrayed in news media directly (by frame-setting) and indirectly (by forming judgments on the topic) influences attitudes toward these minority groups among media audiences (Igartua & Cheng, 2009).

The framing effect has been linked to the concept of accessibility (memory-based model), but also to the applicability of the knowledge triggered by the news story (e.g., Igartua & Cheng, 2009; Matthes, 2007; Nelson, Oxley, & Clawson, 1997; Scheufele, 2000). Petty and Cacioppo's Elaboration Likelihood Model (ELM) (1986) can be considered as a general model for understanding the effect of news stories. Within ELM the effects of framing are explained as the result of peripheral route processing. ELM theorizes a dual route describing attitudinal change: *central* and *peripheral* route processing. Central route processing means that the receiver of the news message tries to make a critical and exhaustive evaluation of it. This process is mainly rational and conscious. As arguments are fundamental, this central route involves a high level of elaboration. Peripheral route processing is automatic and based on peripheral cues (e.g., credibility of the source) instead of arguments. As the peripheral route does not require a high level of elaboration, durable change in attitudes is less likely to occur than when the central route is activated.

Shen (2004) found that the framing effect is moderated by an individual's level of knowledge and awareness of the topic under study. For example it is more difficult to persuade a person of a different angle on a topic if he or she is motivated or has the ability to process the message (Petty & Cacioppo, 1986). However, taking into account the role of diverse individual-level moderators, news reception is usually presided over by a low level of capability and/or motivation. So, the framing effect is usually governed by peripheral route processing (Igartua & Cheng, 2009).

Six dominant frames in the coverage of the refugee issue

This contribution measures the effects of the six most dominant frames in the news coverage of the refugee issue, based on research of Philo, Briant, and Donald (2013) and Joris, d'Haenens, Van Gorp, and Mertens (2018). Philo et al. (2013) identified eight frames to explain public reactions toward asylum seekers in the United Kingdom. These frames are seen as the most comprehensive set of frames encompassing all the frames that were mentioned previously. These eight frames include (1) representing asylum seekers as illegal immigrants or economic migrants, (2) exaggerated numbers ("we take too many"), (3) asylum seekers as a burden on the job market and the welfare system, (4) asylum seekers as potential criminals and terrorists, (5) advocating stronger controls and deportation of failed refugees, (6) positive impacts of immigration on economy and culture, (7) problems and suffering faced by migrants, and (8) the role of the West and its responsibility in the refugee crisis.

The first five frames entail an intruder frame and threats to the economy, security, and/or identity. The three other frames aim to look at the issue in a different way. The sixth frame stresses the resilience and the potential of refugees, their positive characteristics which may result in benefits for society as a whole instead of describing them in black-and-white terms such as mere victims or criminal welfare scroungers. Lastly, the seventh ('asylum seeker as a victim') and the eighth frame ('role of the West') incorporate respectively the victim frame, and the solidarity and responsibility frame.

A quantitative content analyzis by Joris et al. (2018) examined the relative occurrence of the eight frames identified by Philo et al. (2013) in the Austrian, Belgian, British, French, and German press coverage of the refugee issue between 1 June 2015 and 31 December 2015. The "asylum seeker as a victim" frame turned out to be the most frequently used frame, followed by the "role of the West," "we take too many/exaggerating numbers," "increased insecurity," "burden on welfare and the job market," and "benefits of immigration" frames. The "increasing deportations" and "abuse of the asylum system by illegal immigrants" frames were hardly present. Overall, the news coverage of the refugee issue was rather negative. However, the study by Joris et al. (2018) showed that the use of the "'role of the West" frame claimed that the European and national governments need to shoulder their responsibilities and solve the crisis.

In this study we examined the influence of frames on individuals' opinions and attitudes, assuming that the frames in the coverage of the refugee issue may affect ordinary citizens' attitudes along the same lines as the reasoning reflected in these frames. The general research question thus reads as follows:

RQ: Do news frames of the refugee issue affect readers' opinions and attitudes in accordance with the reasoning as reflected in these frames?

The frames under study go beyond what is often done in studies on framing effects, that is using a one-sided design with two or more contrasting experimental conditions (Chong & Druckman, 2007; Igartua & Cheng, 2009): positive versus negative, black versus white. Most of these studies have found that clearly opposing frames have a significant impact when compared to one another. In our research, the six frames (i.e., 'asylum seeker as a victim,' 'role of the West,' 'we take too many,' 'increased insecurity,' 'burden on welfare and the job market,' and 'benefits of immigration') are not opposing frames. This more subtle approach of providing alterations in news reporting wants to do justice to the nuances of a complex reality and is more in line with actual reporting on the issue. Overall, we expect that the participants will more often express their opinions about the refugee issue with a reference to the frame elements activated in their experimental condition.

H1: News frames on the coverage of the refugee issue will sway people's opinions in the direction of the frame.
In recent years, the public and scholarly attention for 'fake news' and what is perceived by the public as fake news is on the rise. In this regard, framing effects are also interrelated with important news concepts such as news credibility (Fico, Richardson, & Edwards, 2004; Tsfati & Cappella, 2005) and its anti-pole, perceived story bias. Framing effects can be the result of both conscious and unconscious mental processes, but when readers fail to believe the story they are reading, this may have immediate impact on their willingness to go along with the story's content and to adopt the included frame. This might hinder the public's reception of new, nonmainstream news angles and points of view. In the abovementioned studies on the actually used news frames on the refugee issue, we see that predominantly negative news frames come to the fore and only a small fraction of positive frames are present in the newspaper coverage on refugees. Therefore, we formulate the following hypothesis:

H2: More peripheral news frames on the refugee issue will result in lower levels of news credibility and higher levels of story bias perception of the news story among readers.
Although the media are the main source of information on the refugee issue for the majority of Europeans (Jacobs et al., 2017), the news coverage of the crisis evidently does not affect all citizens equally. The potential effects may be moderated by individual-level factors as well as contextual moderators (e.g., Lecheler & de Vreese, 2011; Shen, 2004; Waheed, Schuck, Neijens, & de Vreese, 2015). Furthermore, the degree to which people rely on the media for understanding and interpreting events and surroundings affects the perceptions of the news (Morton & Duck, 2001): the higher the media dependency, the higher the magnitude of the media effect.

In our study, we added 'awareness of the refugee issue' as an individual-level moderator, measured by the extent to which the participants came across news on refugees and the extent to which refugees came up in conversations with others during the past year. As it is more difficult to persuade a person who is motivated or has the ability to process the message (Petty & Cacioppo, 1986; Shen, 2004), the frames will have less effect on individuals who can rely on more awareness of the refugee issue. The ability to process the message may also be dependent on the level of education. Therefore, hypotheses 3 and 4 are formulated as:

H3: News frames will affect readers with more awareness of the refugee issue to a lesser extent than participants with lower levels of awareness of the refugee issue.

H4: News frames will affect readers with higher educational attainment to a lesser extent than participants with a lower educational attainment.

Method

Design

We conducted a randomized post-test only between-subjects survey experiment (see, among others, Brewer & Gross, 2010). Besides the six framing conditions, a control group was included, exposing participants to the news story without frame elements. The control group provided a reference point against which to judge the influence of the six frame conditions. Consequently, the design resulted in seven experimental conditions.

Participants

The data collection occurred between June 26 and July 11, 2018. In total, the online survey experiment included 1,400 Flemish participants (aged 18 to 65), carefully recruited by iVOX, a Belgian research company (ww.ivox.be), controlling for different attributes of the members of the sample, and representing the adult population in Flanders: 699 women (49.9 percent) and 701 men (50.1 percent); aged 18 to 34 (32.3 percent), 36 to 54 (44.2 percent), and 55 to 65 (23.5 percent). After completing an initial questionnaire, these participants were randomly assigned to one of the six frame conditions and a frameless control condition: control condition ($n = 208$), conditions 'victim' ($n = 217$), 'benefits of immigration' ($n = 193$), 'increased insecurity' ($n = 198$), 'role of the West' ($n = 207$), 'we take too many' ($n = 183$), and 'burden on welfare and the job market' ($n = 194$).

Stimulus material and manipulation

The participants in both samples received an e-mail message with a link to the online survey. First, questions were asked to measure the media use and the prominence of the refugee issue in the daily lives of the participants: (1) How important is following current events to you personally?; (2) How often did you come across news on refugees during the past year?; (3) How often did refugees come up in conversations that you had with others during the past year?; (4) To what extent do you use the following media to follow current events: print (newspapers, magazines), audiovisual (television, radio), and online (digital newspaper, social media)? The first question used a five-point Likert scale, going from 'not important at all' to 'very important'; the other questions used an eight-point Likert scale, going from 'never' to 'every day'. After completing these questions, participants were randomly assigned to one of the seven conditions and asked to read through a news story dealing with the refugee issue. The core of the news story was identical, except for the frame elements of the corresponding frame conditions. The sentences and frame elements in the article are actually used in the news coverage of the refugee issue, based on previous content analyses on this topic (e.g., Joris et al., 2018; De Cock et al., 2018). In this way, the news story gave the impression of a realistic news article.

The effect measurement of the frames consisted of two components: evaluation of the news story on the one hand, and opinion and attitudes toward refugees on the other hand. These components will be presented in what follows.

Evaluation of the news article
Two types of questions were asked of the participants: (1) To what extent do you find the article you read incredible/credible, heartless/understanding, biased/objective, lacking quality/of high quality, pessimistic toward the future/positive toward the future, complex/simple, all using a five-point semantic differential scale with antonymic adjectives; (2) What was the stance of the article toward refugees? A five-point Likert scale was used going from 'very negative regarding refugees' to 'very positive regarding refugees.'

Opinion on and attitude toward refugees
Furthermore, the effects of framing on the opinion on and attitude toward refugees were measured. The first question asked 'to what extent do you think refugees mentioned below should be allowed to come over and live here?', using a five-point Likert scale ranging from 'allow none to live here' to 'allow many to live here'. This question contained seven types of refugees: (1) refugees of the same race or ethnicity as most of Belgium's population; (2) refugees of

a different race or ethnicity than most of Belgium's population; (3) refugees of the richer countries in Europe; (4) refugees of the poorer countries in Europe; (5) refugees of the richer countries outside Europe; (6) refugees of the poorer countries outside Europe; (7) refugees coming from Muslim countries.

Next, twelve statements with five-point Likert scales were used to measure the frame effects, ranging from 'strongly disagree' to 'strongly agree':

1) Educated refugees may strengthen our labor market.
2) Belgium can do more to provide dignified accommodation for refugees.
3) Each country in Europe should accommodate its share of refugees.
4) There ought to be binding rules that determine how many refugees each country can accommodate and how they need to be sheltered.
5) We cannot leave the care for refugees solely to Greece and Italy in Europe.
6) The way in which Europe treats refugees is humiliating.
7) The government should be generous in judging people's applications for refugee status.
8) Most applicants for refugee status are in real fear of persecution in their own countries.
9) While their cases are being considered, applicants should be kept in detention centers within Europe.
10) While their cases are being considered, applicants should be kept in detention centers outside Europe.
11) While their cases are being considered, the Belgian government should give financial support to applicants.
12) Refugees whose applications are granted should be entitled to bring in their close family members.

Finally, the study made use of six questions with an 11-point semantic differential scale to measure the frame effects:

1) Have Belgium's crime problems increased or decreased by refugees coming to live here from other countries?
2) Would you say that refugees who come to live here generally take jobs away from workers in Belgium, or generally help to create new jobs?
3) Many refugees who come to live here work and pay taxes. They also use health and welfare services. Do you think refugees who come here take out more than they put in or put in more than they take out?
4) Would you say it is generally bad or good for Belgium's economy that refugees come to live here from other countries?
5) Would you say that Belgium's cultural life is generally undermined or enriched by refugees from other countries coming to live here?
6) Refugees make the country a worse or better place to live in.

Results

Preliminary analyses

No significant differences were observed among the seven experimental conditions in the variables gender ($X^2(6) = 5.853, p = .440$), age ($F(6,1392) = .689, p = .659$), the extent to which they came across news on refugees during the past year ($F(6,1392) = .620, p = .715$), and the extent to which refugees came up in conversations with others ($F(6,1392) = .971, p = .444$). Neither were there statistically significant differences in the consumption of print news ($F(6,1392) = .458, p = .839$), audio-visual news ($F(6,1392) = 1.368, p = .224$), and online news ($F(6,1392) = .872, p = .514$).

Table 9.1: Description of participants by frame condition (in Mean, unless otherwise specified)

Condition	Gender: Male %	Age (in years)	News on refugees*	Conversations on refugees*	Print media use*	AV media use*	Online media use*
Control condition	46.5	44.8	5.6	2.9	3.9	6.5	6.3
Benefits of immigration	52.4	45.1	5.5	3.1	3.7	6.4	6.7
Increased insecurity	56.8	46.2	5.8	3.0	3.9	6.7	6.5
Victim	50.2	43.7	5.8	3.2	3.7	6.2	6.4
Role of the West	49.2	44.9	5.6	3.1	3.9	6.5	6.4
We take too many	46.9	45.5	5.7	2.9	3.6	6.7	6.3
Burden on welfare / job market	48.7	45.8	5.5	2.8	3.6	6.5	6.4

*(1 = never – 8 = every day)

In order to verify the effectiveness of the experimental manipulation, we analyzed the evaluation of the news story in the different conditions. To verify experimental manipulation, we analyzed the evaluation of the news story, based on the question 'what was the stance of the article toward refugees?' using a five-point Likert scale going from '1 = very negative regarding refugees' to '5 = very positive regarding refugees.' A significant difference in stance across the frame conditions was found, $F(6,1392) = 39.832, p < .001$. As would be expected, the news stories in the 'increased insecurity' condition ($M = 2.90$) and 'burden on welfare and the job market' condition ($M = 3.18$) turned out to be perceived as the most negative toward refugees, followed by the control condition ($M = 3.54$), 'we take too many' ($M = 3.69$), and the 'victim' frame conditions ($M = 3.77$). The participants assessed the 'role of the West' ($M = 3.81$) and 'benefits of immigration' frames ($M = 3.98$) as most positive regarding refugees. This is in line with the set-up and intention of the experiment. The frames were thus adequately designed and perceived by our audience sample.

Different opinions across frame conditions?

To answer hypothesis 1, which postulated that frames in the coverage of the refugee issue will sway people's opinions in the direction of the presented frame, the mean scores on all statements in the survey experiment will be compared between the frame conditions. First, no significant differences were found across the conditions on the question *'to what extent do you think refugees mentioned below should be allowed to come and live here?'*. However, one steady pattern could be noticed, namely that participants exposed to the 'role of the West' frame condition were always more willing to allow refugees to come and live in Belgium (see table 9.2).

Furthermore, the twelve statements to measure the frame effects were compared across the frame conditions. No statistically significant differences were observed in ten of the twelve statements considered. There were two exceptions: only the statements *'each country in Europe should accommodate their share of refugees'* ($F(6,1392) = 2.746, p < .05$) and *'most applicants for refugee status are in real fear of persecution in their own countries'* ($F(6,1392) = 2.997, p < .05$) differed significantly. Participants in the 'increased insecurity' ($M = 4.04$), 'we take too many' ($M = 4.02$), and 'role of the West' conditions ($M = 3.95$) significantly more often found that each country should accommodate its share of refugees, whereas participants in the 'burden on welfare and the job market' ($M = 3.67$) and 'refugees as victim' conditions ($M = 3.71$) more often disagreed with this statement. Regarding the statement on the *'real fear of persecution'*, the participants exposed to the 'increased insecurity' condition agreed significantly more than those taking part in the control condition, $t(403,604) = -3.502, p < .001$.

To measure the frame effects, this study included six questions with an eleven-point semantic differential scale regarding the impact of the refugee issue on criminality, the job market, health and welfare services, the economy, cultural life, and living conditions. No significant differences were found

Table 9.2: Attitudes toward refugees' acceptance by frame condition on a five-point scale (1-5) (in Mean)

	Control condition	Victim frame	Role of the West	We take too many	Increased insecurity	Burden on welfare	Benefits of immigration
Refugees of same ethnicity as most Belgian citizens	3.18	3.27	**3.35**	3.16	3.23	3.27	3.24
Refugees of different ethnicity	2.83	2.78	**3.00**	2.88	2.94	2.74	2.89
Refugees of the richer countries in Europe	2.69	2.87	**2.95**	2.71	2.85	2.89	2.69
Refugees of the poorer countries in Europe	2.87	2.91	**3.08**	2.93	2.97	2.86	3.02
Refugees of the richer countries outside Europe	2.59	2.65	**2.98**	2.64	2.77	2.61	2.58
Refugees of the poorer countries outside Europe	2.86	2.71	**2.99**	2.90	2.96	2.72	2.95
Refugees coming from Muslim countries	2.57	2.51	**2.79**	2.53	2.63	2.49	2.57

Note: no significant differences, respectively $F(6,1392) = .649, p = .691$; $F(6,1392) = 1.257, p = .275$; $F(6,1392) = 1.528, p = .165$; $F(6,1392) = .949, p = .459$; $F(6,1392) = 1.752, p = .106$; $F(6,1392) = 1.835, p = .089$; $F(6,1392) = 1.336, p = .238$.

across the seven frame conditions of the survey experiment. These findings regarding the effects of the different framing conditions point out that the first hypothesis is mainly not confirmed. Only two statements turned out to be significantly different.

Do more peripheral news frames lead to other evaluations?

Statistically significant differences were found in five of the six evaluative attributes measured: criteria 'incredible/credible' ($F(6,1392) = 3.291, p < .001$), 'heartless/understanding' ($F(6,1392) = 14.920, p < .001$), 'biased/objective' ($F(6,1392) = 5.032, p < .001$), 'lack of quality/high quality' ($F(6,1392) = 5.425, p < .001$), 'pessimistic toward the future/positive toward the future' ($F(6,1392) = 11.045, p < .001$). As would be expected, the news stories that used the 'burden on welfare and the job market' frame or the 'increased insecurity' frame were assessed more as pessimistic toward the future and heartless. Furthermore, these two news frames were also more frequently perceived as biased. In contrast, the 'role of the West' frame was evaluated more as positive toward the future, objective, and understanding. However, this does not automatically mean that the readers agree with this frame.

The participants in the 'benefits of immigration' frame condition significantly more often assessed the news story being told as incredible than the stories told in the other six conditions. This might be explained by the fact that this frame is a less frequently used, atypical news frame in comparison with the other frames under study. Besides the fact that previous content analyses of the refugee issue (e.g., Joris et al., 2018, Philo et al., 2013) found only one positive news frame (i.e., benefits of immigration), the study by Joris et al. (2018) showed that this frame was least used in comparison to the other five frames in the survey experiment. Consequently, the 'benefits of immigration' frame might diverge from the news coverage in the previous months and years that focused more on the other predominantly negative news frames under study. As readers are mainly confronted with negative frames in the coverage of the refugee issue, they are less inclined to believe a news story in which journalists use the 'benefits of immigration' frame or another peripheral positive frame. As the positive 'benefits of immigration' frame is clearly not mainstream, this more peripheral frame does not seem to be working, in that it is not considered a credible story. These findings regarding the influence of peripheral news frames on the level of news credibility and story bias perception among readers point out that the second hypothesis is partly confirmed: peripheral news frames on the refugee issue significantly result in lower levels of news credibility, whereas these peripheral frames do not lead to higher levels of story bias perception of the news story.

Role of individual-level moderators

Similarly to previous research (e.g., Chapter 7 of this book), educational attainment is significantly related to refugee attitudes (for each statement or question under study). Participants with a higher level of education hold more positive refugee attitudes than those with a lower educational attainment. However, if we check for the individual-level moderators under study, it appears that there is no significant effect of the level of education nor the awareness of the refugee issue on the frame effect on the attitudes toward refugees' acceptance. Besides, statistically significant framing effects were observed neither regarding the twelve statements on attitudes on refugees using a five-point Likert scale, nor regarding the six questions with an eleven-point semantic differential scale. We may conclude that hypotheses 3 and

4 are not confirmed in this study. Although educational attainment and the awareness of the refugee issue have a significant effect on the attitude toward refugees, these individual-level moderators do not have an effect on the framing effect.

Conclusion and discussion

In a survey experiment among the general public between 18 and 65 years old in Flanders (Dutch-speaking part of Belgium) ($N = 1,400$), we analyzed the possible effects of a set of commonly used and peripheral, atypical news frames on individuals' opinions and attitudes on refugees.

Similarly to Chapter 7 in this book that only found limited support for the agenda-setting theory, in this chapter only two of the statements or questions of the survey experiment proved to be significantly differently received across the framing conditions. This means that an overall direct effect on attitudes toward refugees in the same direction as suggested by the frame was not found. A possible explanation for this result might be related to the continued year after year exposure of our Flemish participants to predominantly negative news coverage on refugees in the Flemish newspapers (see Chapter 3 in this book; Joris et al., 2018; Philo et al., 2013). Ideally intercultural comparative experimental studies should test this assumption in the future as other media landscapes such as the Swedish and French-speaking press in Belgium have been writing in a more positive way, and this for several years, resulting in an overall more positive sentiment toward refugees, as seen in Chapter 7 in this book. News consumption is only one factor in the complex attitude formation process, but repeated exposure to negative framing of refugees in the long term is difficult to counter by other frames offered in a short-term experiment such as this study. This survey experiment was performed almost three years after the peak of the refugee crisis (summer 2018 versus fall 2015). This might have influenced the results of our study, since framing effects are less likely to happen on established or long-term topics (Chong & Druckman, 2007).

Furthermore, when exposed to a more positively framed story contradicting the viewpoint one is usually exposed to in the media our results show this has a negative impact on readers' willingness to adopt this atypical frame. Readers fail to believe the story presenting clear economic and cultural benefits of migration and attribute a lower level of credibility to the story. Seen from that angle, non-dominant frames seem to hinder the public's reception of nonmainstream points of view on the refugee issue. This can only be countered by holding an intensive plea for a sustained more diverse news menu and offer of a variety of news angles in investigative journalism pieces, offering other takes and viewpoints than the dominant ones, in an effort to avoid a media-driven spiral of silence feeding a negative public sentiment, irrespective of sociodemographics. Future research therefore must continue to perform long-term content analyses including frame-shift studies combining public opinion and media effects measurement.

Moreover, our study found no evidence that individual-level variables' 'awareness of the refugee issue' and 'level of education' moderated the frame effect. These results are in contrast to previous research (e.g., Igartua & Cheng, 2009; Shen, 2004; Petty & Cacioppo, 1986) that found that individuals' level of knowledge and awareness moderate the framing effect, as people who are motivated or have the ability to process the message are less affected by framing. The already long-lasting attention for the topic in the news might play a role in this matter, resulting in a dimming of otherwise crucial characteristics. Furthermore, the data collection was based on an online nonprobability survey that may raise questions about accuracy. In future research, traditional probability-based surveys need to confirm our findings. Another explanation may be found in a possible weakness of our study: the measurement of awareness of the refugee issue by using self-reports. For future studies, we recommend incorporating more objective measurement forms of factual knowledge on the topic.

References

Berinsky, A.J., & Kinder, D.R. (2006). Making sense of issues through media frames: understanding the Kosovo crisis. *The Journal of Politics*, 68(3), 640–656.
Bleich, E., Bloemraad, I., & de Graauw, E. (2015). Migrants, minorities and the media: Information, representations and participation in the public sphere. *Journal of Ethnic and Migration Studies*, 41(6), 857–873.
Brader, T., Valentino, N.A., & Suhay, E. (2008). What triggers public opposition to immigration? *American Journal of Political Science*, 52(4), 959–978.
Brewer, P.R., & Gross, K. (2010). Studying the effects of issue framing on public opinion about policy issues. In P. D'Angelo & J.A. Kuypers (Eds.), *Doing news framing analysis: Empirical and theoretical perspectives* (pp.159–186). New York: Routledge.
Cacciatore, M.A., Scheufele, D.A., & Iyengar, S. (2016). The end of framing as we know it ... and the future of media effects. *Mass Communication and Society*, 19, 7–23.
Cho, J., Gil de Zuniga, H., Shah, D.V., & McLeod, D.M. (2006). Cue convergence: Associative effects on social intolerance. *Communication Research*, 33(3), 136–154.
Chong, D., & Druckman, J.N. (2007). A theory of framing and opinion formation in competitive elite environments. *Journal of Communication*, 57, 99–118.
Coombs, W.T., & Holladay, S.J. (2004). Reasoned action in crisis communication: An attribution theory-based approach to crisis management. In D.P. Millar & R.L. Heath (Eds.), *Responding*

to *Crisis Communication Approach to Crisis Communication* (pp. 95–115). Hillsdale: Lawrence Erlbaum Associates.

De Cock, R., Mertens, S., Sundin, E., Lams, L., Mistiaen, V., Joris, W., & d'Haenens, L. (2018). Refugees in the news: Comparing Belgian and Swedish newspaper coverage of the European refugee situation during summer 2015. *Communications: The European Journal of Communication Research, 43*(3), 301–323.

De Coninck, D., Matthijs, K., Debrael, M., Joris, W., De Cock, R., & d'Haenens, L. (2018). The relationship between media use and public opinion on immigrants and refugees: A Belgian perspective. *Communications: The European Journal of Communication Research, 43*(3), 403–425.

Entman, R.M. (1993). Framing: Toward clarification of a fractured paradigm. *Journal of Communication, 43*, 51–8.

Entman, R.M. (2003). Cascading activation: Contesting the White House's frame after 9/11. *Political Communication, 20*(4), 415–432.

Entman, R.M. (2004). *Projections of power: Framing news, public opinion, and U.S. Foreign Policy.* Chicago: University of Chicago Press.

Fico, F., Richardson, J.D., & Edwards, S.M. (2004). Influence on story structure on perceived story bias and news organization credibility. *Mass Communication & Society, 7*(3), 301–318.

Gamson, W.A., & Modigliani, A. (1989). Media discourse and public opinion on nuclear power. A constructionist approach. *American Journal of Sociology, 95*(1), 1–37.

Igartua, J., & Cheng, L. (2009). Moderating effect of group cue while processing news on immigration: Is the framing effect a heuristic process? *Journal of Communication, 59*, 726–749.

Information Centre about Asylum and Refugees (ICAR). (2012). *Asylum seekers, refugees and media.* London: ICAR.

Jacobs, L., Hooghe, M., & de Vroome, T. (2017). Television and anti-immigrant sentiments: The mediating role of fear of crime and perceived ethnic diversity. *European Societies, 19*(3), 243–267.

Joris, W., d'Haenens, L., Van Gorp, B., & Mertens, S. (2018). The refugee crisis in Europe: A frame analysis of European newspapers. In S.F. Krishna-Hensel (Ed.), *Migrants, Refugees, and the Media. The New Reality of Open Societies* (pp.59–80). London: Routledge.

Lecheler, S., & de Vreese, C.H. (2011). Getting real: the duration of framing effects. *Journal of Communication, 61*, 959–983.

Lecheler, S., & de Vreese, C.H. (2012). News framing and public opinion: A mediation analysis of framing effects on political attitudes. *Journalism & Mass Communication Quarterly, 89*(2), 185–204.

Matthes, J. (2007). Beyond accessibility? Toward an on-line and memory-based model of framing effects. *Communications: The European Journal of Communication Research, 32*(1), 51–78.

Morton, T., & Duck, J. (2001). Communication and health beliefs. Mass and interpersonal influences on perceptions of risk to self and others. *Communication Research, 28*(5), 602–626.

Müller, P., Schemer, C., Wettstein, M., Schulz, A., Wirz, D. S., Engesser, S., & Wirth, W. (2017). The polarizing impact of news coverage on populist attitudes in the public: Evidence from a panel study in four European democracies. *Journal of Communication, 67*(6), 968–992.

Nelson, T.E., Oxley, Z.M., & Clawson, R.A. (1997). Toward a psychology of framing effects. *Political Behavior, 19*(3), 221–246.

Orgad, S. (2012). *Media representation and the global imagination.* Cambridge: Polity Press.

Petty, R.E., & Cacioppo, J.T. (1986). *Communication and persuasion: Central and peripheral routes to attitude change.* New York: Springer-Verlag.

Scheufele, D.A., & Tewksbury, D. (2007). Framing, agenda setting, and priming: The evolution of three media effects models. *Journal of Communication, 57*, 9–20.

Shen, F. (2004). Effects of news frames and schemas on individuals' issue interpretations and attitudes. *Journalism and Mass Communication Quarterly, 81*(2), 400–416.

Tsfati, Y., & Cappella, J. N. (2005). Why do people watch news they do not trust? The need for cognition as a moderator in the association between news media skepticism and exposure. *Media Psychology, 7,* 251–271.

Van Gorp, B. (2005). Where is the frame? Victims and intruders in the Belgian press coverage of the asylum issue. *European Journal of Communication, 20*(4), 485–508.

Van Klingeren, M., Boomgaarden, H. G., Vliegenthart, R., & De Vreese, C. H. (2014). Real world is not enough: The media as an additional source of negative attitudes toward immigration, comparing Denmark and the Netherlands. *European Sociological Review, 31*(3), 268–283.

Waheed, M., Schuck, A., Neijens, P., & de Vreese, C.H. (2015). The effects of news frames and political speech sources on political attitudes: The moderating role of values. *Communications: The European Journal of Communication Research, 40*(2), 147–169.

PART IV

REFUGEES' EXPERIENCES

Chapter 10
Beyond Victimhood: Reflecting on Migrant-Victim Representations with Afghan, Iraqi, and Syrian Asylum Seekers and Refugees in Belgium

Kevin Smets, Jacinthe Mazzocchetti, Lorraine Gerstmans, and Lien Mostmans

Introduction

How do refugees and asylum seekers experience and react to the way they are being represented? Such is the central question addressed in this chapter, where we will share stories of a group that is rarely heard from in discussions about migration. Visuality and visibility have become central themes in studies on media and migration, and humanitarianism more broadly (Chouliaraki & Stolic, 2017). There is a wealth of research on visual representations of refugees and how their Otherness is constructed by presenting them as social, economic, or security threats or as victims (Chouliaraki & Zaborowski, 2017; Wright, 2002). In humanitarian communication, a growing genre of the field, the "regime of pity" and its negative representation strategies are dominant (Ongenaert & Joye, forthcoming). This current study moves beyond the traditional analysis of media content, since it is important to recognize that media (mis)representations might be experienced as harmful by historically disempowered groups such as refugees (Perez Portilla, 2018). We are inspired by Horsti's call to "refract our analytical gaze" on media representations and to study how people engage with the images and texts that circulate. She pleads for a co-analytical perspective in which researchers *listen to* and *see with* migrants (Horsti, forthcoming). Thus, we will concentrate on how asylum seekers and refugees make sense of how they are represented, and how those representations connect to broader issues of victimization, recognition, and identity. The stereotypes embedded in these representations are very powerful, as they have an influence on social representations and practices. As Machillot (2012: 81-82) argues, stereotypes harbor a power of structuration, which "through the language and practices they carry" are "a force acting on practices."[9]

While there are plenty of content analyses focusing on representations of cultural others, research rarely includes the perspective of those (supposedly) being represented. This is striking, given the continued calls by scholars and civil society actors to include the perspective of vulnerable and voiceless groups into knowledge production and mediated discourses (Georgiou, 2018; Rajaram, 2002). Aiming to make a humble contribution to this matter, this chapter presents findings from voice-centered, participatory research with asylum seekers and refugees living in Belgium. The study, conducted with forty-four Afghan, Iraqi, and Syrian men and women who arrived in Belgium after 2015, included biographic interviews as well as participatory visual workshops regarding migrants and refugee media representations.

Early on in our conversations, it became clear that participants were highly critical of two main tropes, i.e., the refugee as a (political, economic, religious or cultural) threat, and the refugee as a victim. These two stereotypes echo recent research on discourses on refugees (Bozdag & Smets, 2017; Chouliaraki & Stolic, 2017; De Cleen et al., 2017). In this chapter, we have chosen to focus on the figure of the refugee-victim, as this turned out to be a theme that was also connected to how participants experience their lives in Belgium. Although *a priori* more positive than the refugee as a threat, the refugee-victim trope also conceals painful and problematic experiences for refugees, as it is regarded as a limiting marker that prevents them from being seen as full-fledged citizens and individuals.

In the first part of this chapter, we briefly describe the methodological setup of the study. The second part is devoted to the analysis of the participants' accounts. We first discuss the political context and asylum procedures in Belgium and Europe, showing that suffering has become an integral part of legitimate asylum applications, and that this 'selection process' is increasingly grounded in a division between good migrants (real victims) and bad migrants (parasites and cheaters). Next, we explore how participants' experiences are articulated along a so-called triple violence: the violence faced with in the national contexts they fled, the violence encountered during their journeys to Europe, and the insecurity and precariousness during the asylum procedures. Analytically, we distinguish between lived sufferings, representations of the self and others, and the enclosure within the refugee-victim figure. In the third part, using the results

---

9   All translations from French sources are the responsibility of the authors.

of our participatory visual study, we analyze how participants perceived, probed, and deconstructed mainstream representations of refugees. The findings reveal their counter-discourses on a range of topics such as asylum, their countries of origin, host societies, and suffering itself. Finally, the fourth part of the chapter focuses on the challenge for our interlocutors to recognize suffering while not being confined by it. We show that this challenge requires a meticulous deconstruction of the representation of the refugee as a complete 'Other'.

Before continuing, it is important to clarify certain terms used throughout the chapter. When discussing findings from our own study, we refer to refugees and asylum seekers because this best describes our participant sample. Throughout other sections of the chapter we usually use the terms preferred by the authors we cite, for instance, migrants, refugees, forced migrants. When referring to the 'victim position' or 'victimization' of refugees, we specifically mean the discursive structure with which participants describe or accentuate episodes of their migration during which they experienced suffering, injustice, or mistreatment. When using the figure of the 'migrant-victim' then, we particularly point at the perspective whereby refugees and asylum seekers are reduced to victims. This concept echoes strongly the way in which migrants are represented in certain media and political discourses as well as in public opinion. Through the rich and personal accounts of how asylum seekers and refugees experience their journeys and their reception in a sometimes-hostile society, we mainly focus on how victimization is perceived and deconstructed and how it is negotiated in the context of asylum procedures.

Methodological approach

Overview and participant sample

This study is the result of an interdisciplinary collaboration between two research teams, respectively rooted within media studies and anthropology, from two different Belgian universities. This collaboration was fruitful and led to an interesting methodological interdisciplinarity that enabled complementary methodological approaches and accents. Regular interaction and exchange guaranteed the development of a shared, coherent approach. Reflecting the interdisciplinarity within the research team, we used various participant selection processes based on formal and informal strategies. As a result, some members of our team organized the majority of individual interviews, combined with a few collective workshops, while the other part of the team organized the focus group interviews. Most of our data were collected between July 2017 and February 2018.

We selected research participants by contacting several major agencies, organizations, and NGOs working with and for refugees (e.g., providing moral support, integration, or language classes etc.) in Brussels and Wallonia. We also reached out to smaller, more informal organizations in our own Dutch- and French-speaking networks. In other cases, for instance in the search for (female) Afghan and Iraqi participants, we wrote a social media post in Arabic and English, explaining the aim of the study on a publicly available Facebook group supporting refugees and asylum seekers in their daily life in Belgium. Finally, a number of participants were found through snowball sampling, a widespread sampling technique in social sciences whereby informants recruit future participants amongst their own networks and acquaintances (Bryman, 2012: 202-203). That way, we ended up working with ten organizations based in Wallonia or Brussels. The recruitment process via these organizations was intensive, taking, on average, three months between the first contact and the first interviews. These efforts resulted in fifteen focus group interviews and individual interviews with another fifteen participants (several of whom were interviewed a number of times), which took place in locations chosen by the participants themselves (i.e., their homes or public spaces such as cafés).

In total, forty-four asylum seekers and refugees participated in the research. They all came from Syria (24), Afghanistan (11), and Iraq (9) and have been living in Belgium since 2015. The participants were thirty-one men and thirteen women, between the ages of 17 and 60 (Appendix 10.1). The majority of the participants in our sample had gone through higher (post-secondary) education. However, some of the younger participants had been unable to finish secondary or post-secondary education.

Interview procedures

Our study combined both focus group interviews and individual ethnographic interviews (Beaud, 1996), and was inspired by participatory visual methods. Generally speaking, the focus group interviews consisted of three parts. In the first part, we explained the research project to the participants and introduced ourselves. In the second part, participants were invited to talk about their lives prior to coming to Belgium, decisions they had to make related to migration, experiences with migration journeys, with life in Belgium and the role of media in their everyday lives now and before. Some participants shared relatively 'rich' stories, while others found it more difficult to discuss precise details. The third part of the focus group interviews then consisted of probing participants' views on the roles of media in processes of migration and integration, and a conversation on stereotypes and prejudices about refugees and migrants in everyday life as well as in the media.

Two participatory visual methods, photo elicitation and photovoice, inspired these collective interviews. Such methods allow for more bottom-up perspectives and alternative, non-verbal, output. They also enable participants and researchers to produce stories together. Firstly, photo elicitation implies the use of images to elicit thoughts, feelings, and ways of talking that are more difficult to address through talk-based interviews with participants (Rose, 2014). It has been argued that visual methods provide participants with power and choice because they can choose what to capture and how to express their experiences. Participants were asked to categorize and interpret widely used photos from major press and photo agencies (Reuters, Associated Press, Belga, Time, Magnum) that had accompanied articles in major national and international newspapers, and that represented key themes in the press coverage of refugees and the refugee 'crisis.' These were selected based on a review of key literature and content analyses regarding media coverage of refugees and migration (see e.g., Berry et al., 2015; Bozdag & Smets, 2017). We identified fourteen recurring themes, each representing migration and refugees in a particular way, and selected twenty-nine photos. Participants were asked to categorize the photos on a continuum that ranged from 'negative media coverage' to 'positive media coverage' (*What do you think of this photo? What story or message does this photo contain? Do you think it is a rather 'good' or a rather 'bad' story or message? Why so?*) and to collectively discuss this continuum.

Secondly, photovoice is a participatory research process through which people can "identify, represent, and enhance their community through a specific photographic technique" (Wang & Burris, 1997: 369). Participants did not produce their own images but were asked to select one of the twenty-nine photos used during the photo elicitation exercise they found most striking. Once a photo was chosen and discussed, participants were invited to identify with at least one character in the photo and give the selected character a 'voice' through messaging or making use of text balloons (*If the character(s) in the photo could speak to the photographer about this photo, what would they say?*) and postcards (*If the character(s) in the photo could speak to the Belgian people about this photo, what would they say?*). The participants were specifically asked to address the photographer (i.e., the media professional) and the wider Belgian population.

In the individual ethnographic interviews, we employed an informal structure. Although we had prepared a topic guide for all individual ethnographic interviews, the priority was to let people express themselves freely about their own migration and life stories. As they were previously informed about the research, the conversations often led us to discuss the main theme of prejudices, stereotypes, and racism in daily life in Belgium. The less formal character of these conversations resulted in rich personal accounts, to which we sometimes added participatory visual exercises for additional depth.

The majority of the interviews were conducted in a combination of English, Dutch, and French, depending on the languages spoken by the participants. In some cases, a translator was present during the interviews. For example, a team member of a center for language learning and integration attended the focus group there, and translated parts of the interview in Arabic. In other instances, the translator was a friend of the participants, which helped in making them feel comfortable during the interview.

Ethical issues

Given the highly sensitive nature of some topics discussed with the participants, the research was based on informed participation. Prior to the interviews, informed consent was established through a thorough discussion of the main elements of common informed consent procedures, including research aims, potential implications of the project results and participation, duration of participation, and issues such as privacy, anonymity, and confidentiality. Moreover, we paid particular attention and care when formulating questions that probed for sensitive or highly personal information. Participants were asked to share only as much as they felt comfortable with. The names of all organizations and participants have been replaced by pseudonyms. Participants did not receive financial compensation, but in several cases they were treated to lunch with the researchers after the interviews.

Visual participatory methods raise specific ethical concerns. In our study, for example, some pictures appeared to be violent for participants and they sometimes brought them to relive their own traumas or reminded them of their current insecurity and psychological difficulties. While we avoided such direct confrontations, we did pay significant attention to assuring the wellbeing of all participants during the interviews.

Critical analysis of migrant-victim representations

Asylum and the suffering body

What has become known as the 2015 refugee crisis[10] should be situated within long-term shifts in the perceptions of asylum seekers in Europe (De Cleen et al., 2017). These shifts are notable for the growing climate of suspicion and the emergence of a distinction between real and false refugees and asylum applicants (Bohmer & Shuman, 2018; Fassin & Rechtman, 2007). This distinction has become a leading paradigm in European politics (Valluy, 2004: 17). Currently, only families of "real victims", those whose lives are under threat and who come from countries officially recognized as war zones are welcome to enter through the asylum process. According to Lacroix, this selection lies at "the heart of the liberal paradox", for it is built as a "conditional opening for some, a closing for others, all against the backdrop of deregulated exchanges and of the free flow of capital, goods and information" (Lacroix, 2016: 14). At the same time, we have seen an increased convergence between criminal law on the one hand and immigration policy on the other, giving rise to what Stumpf (2006) coined as "crimmigration." The convergence between the two spheres again marks divisions between new categories of people: "innocent versus guilty, admitted versus excluded or, as some say 'legal' versus 'illegal'" (Stumpf, 2006: 380).

As a consequence, the mediated figure of the refugee has been re-imagined quite profoundly. The romanticized and heroic image of the 1960s and 70s has ceded to an image of the refugee as extremely vulnerable, "stripped off everything, without a name, without an opinion" (Vanoeteren & Gehrels, 2009: 494). While the figure of the migrant-hero—the activist who, at great pains, finally came to reach his host country—still prevails among, for instance, social workers (Kobelinsky, 2007), it seems in total discordance with the legal and administrative realities of current asylum procedures. We have, as Vrancken argues, shifted from "a history mainly devoted to the celebration of winners ... to the narrative of hurt memories" (2010: 52).

The amplification of these categories reflects a general climate of suspicion (Vianna, 2007), within which displaced persons have to demonstrate the legitimacy of their presence and requests. The asylum procedure is an ordeal ("une mise à l'épreuve", Vrancken, 2010) articulated around a central question: how

---

10   We use the term here in full awareness of the critical stance many scholars have taken toward the "crisis vocabulary" and the powerful practice of labelling humanitarian events and populations as "crisis". See Carastathis et al. (2018), Dines et al. (2018), and Sigona (2018), among others, for more elaborate discussions.

can one prove that one *merits* asylum? Procedures require a declaration, and display of hardships, which become the indisputable evidence for legitimate asylum demands. For policy makers, these are mostly articulated around "… the impact on physical and mental health of experiencing persecutions, torture, exile and related traumas", which increasingly necessitates medical and psychological expertise supporting asylum procedures (Vanoeteren & Geherels, 2009: 495). Moreover, the body has become the ultimate evidence of the threats migrants endure (Vrancken, 2010). Increasingly then, refugee status becomes granted on the basis of humanitarian and health reasons rather than political ones (Fassin, 2005: 368). A large group of people have become reduced to their suffering bodies, rather than being citizens with rights, much in the same way as Agamben (1998) defines the "bare life." Not surprisingly, the body occupies a central role in analyses of the spectatorship of suffering (Chouliaraki, 2006) and in studies on the visual representation of refugees (Bleiker et al., 2013).

The triple encounter with violence of refugees

The description of suffering is part and parcel of the asylum procedure, and it is established legally and institutionally. Acquiring refugee status becomes an individual responsibility, whereby the utterance of suffering alone may lead to "the right to have rights" (Mazzocchetti, 2017a: 111). The good, "real", refugee is the one who can prove their suffering and capitalize on victimhood. Although a certain "staging" of suffering is taking place (Mazzocchetti, 2017a; 2017b), physical and psychological wounds are not imaginary. The trajectories of the individuals encountered during this study were marked by multiple traumatic episodes. Suffering and trauma are related to decisions to migrate, and amplified by the brutality of protected boundaries (Agier, 2018). They are anchored often in both the bodies and the minds of refugees. Our participants often described how difficult it was to simply continue to *live*. We argue that these lived sufferings should not be ignored, but taken into account in a non-exclusivist, non-classifying, and non-discriminatory way.

While our participants' individual routes differed significantly (e.g., length, means of transportation), the risks, violence, and harm related to land and sea crossings have been widely reported. Many participants have also talked about discrimination, degradation, and neglect. To capture the scope of these sufferings and the different types of (symbolic) violence, we refer here to a "triple violence" experienced by participants: the violence of the country fled (violent conflicts and its effects on society), the violence of the perilous journey (often including serious life risks), and the violence of unstable and uncertain new lives (see also Kobelinsky, 2012). References to this triple violence were interlaced in our participants' accounts. More specifically, many of the conversations focused on the third, more symbolic layer of violence that is experienced when one has little certainty during asylum procedures. This discourse was particularly strong among Iraqi and Afghan participants whose trajectories had been more chaotic, as several had already been refused asylum once or twice. This was the case, for instance, for Amir, a 32-year old Iraqi. Having arrived in Belgium in late 2015, his asylum application had already been refused twice. When we met him, he had just prepared a new application, as he had been able to accumulate more evidence of the threats he faced in Iraq, where he had denounced one of his military superiors:

> I want security, and to continue my life. I am a person like... all others. What I want is to continue living a *normal* life. But Belgium, unfortunately, deprives me of that. It has *shackled* me, *broken my wings*. [silence] What do we do? [very long silence] It's sad... my life experience. I wish Belgium would have been more generous. That it would... *give* me what I *deserve*. But unfortunately that's not the case. ... And so, psychologically, waiting is... painful. Two years and three months is a lot, it's too much. ... I lost everything and I want to restart with simple things... but those simple things are not available. ... The problem is that my memories are scarred in this body. And when I think of that... my... body trembles. *Because I could have been dead with the others*. My situation is not very different from someone who has been killed.[11]

Most of our interlocutors tried desperately to re-humanize themselves, and legitimize their presence in Belgium by demonstrating their individual and collective sufferings. Their search for legitimacy went through three discourses, reflecting the triple violence of asylum seekers and refugees previously mentioned: the impossibility of simply continuing their lives in their countries of origin, the difficulties encountered during their journey, and the inhumane uncertainties experienced in the host country; either institutional or interpersonal. As Vida, a 30-year old Afghan participant, stated particularly on that last point:

> And they [refugees] are suffering in these conditions. And these are *also humans*, they also had their goals, and their dreams and ambitions and now

---

11   Our translation from French. Italics in this and following quotes indicate insistence in the original conversation.

it's all being blocked, the world should see this ... these are people from all over the world, from all different families, that have come *not because they want to* but as a necessity, to try to make a better life. But now, what the world has done is *block* these people, so their living conditions *are worse* than they've ever been...

Other participants also referred to suspicion and the lack of understanding they experienced after arriving. Turan, an Afghan man in his thirties stated "... people here do not understand. ... For me it's important to show how we have arrived in Belgium. ... It's really *hard*." As we will develop further below, this narration of various lived sufferings does not have a restrictive character per se. Talking about the three different layers of (symbolic) violence is above all an attempt to claim a subject position with rights (legal status, housing, employment). This means having the right to a dignified life and not being reduced to particular types of suffering.

Counter-discourses: toward 'realistic' representations

Despite the centrality of the triple violence in the lives of the participants, there was a strong pushback by asylum seekers and refugees of being reductively thought of solely as victims. Instead, they formulated more nuanced counter-discourses regarding the humanity of refugees, their countries of origin and arrival, and the suffering of asylum. We will explore and illustrate these counter-discourses below.

First of all, for many participants the dominant victim position has a connotation of inability or inferiority. This sometimes leads to feeling ashamed about being a refugee, and developing ways to conceal their status or make it less prominent. A case in point is Hicham, a 27-year-old Syrian from Damascus who came to Belgium with a student visa. Although he was already working as a professional for more than a year in Syria, he started over again in Belgium, now studying two master programs at the same time:

> ... I feel like I'm looked at better if I'm a student than a refugee. So this is really direct and it... it really directs me to introduce myself as... I'm Hicham and I'm a student in KU Leuven ... just in order to not be looked at... *a low position* [low voice tone].

While the victim position legitimizes refugees' presence and legal recognition, as described earlier, it also hinders the feeling of being someone, or to have been someone before—an individual, embedded in a social and family life and with a vast array of assets (see Kisiara, 2015). Losing that sense of being someone comes with a certain "mourning of the self," as Métraux (2011) has described it. The socio-economic situation of refugees, too, is perilous in many cases, and often linked to the non-equivalence of diplomas, which hinders them in continuing their previous profession. How the dominant discourse of victimization deters refugees from a humane and subjective position can be illustrated with the story of Nour and Vida.

When we met the sisters Nour and Vida for the first time, they had been residing in a Fedasil center (i.e., the federal agency for the reception of asylum seekers) for nearly two years. Coming from a family of nine, they were 30 and 32 years old respectively. They had lived in Kabul, Afghanistan, all their lives but decided to flee after the death of their mother. Both sisters completed university education against their father's will, and saw themselves becoming double victims, both of their status as women as well as highly educated graduates. It proved impossible for them to find decent jobs, and after having been chased from their home by their father, they decided to leave their country together with one of their brothers. During several of our conversations, Nour and Vida argued for a recognition of their suffering instigated by their migration plans as well as restrictive European border policies. However, according to both sisters, such recognition should not lead to an exclusive labeling as a victim in an inferior position. As Nour explained:

> When people come, you should not make them feel like victims, because you should… say, ok, like "something was done to… bring you guys the situation and now… … you are given the resources to *make the way right*". But not… to make them feel so *small, and so little and incapable*. … And people see us as very lazy. … [But] you know, I know people are not dumb or lazy or incapables [sic]. It's the situation that… that made it this way. (Nour, Afghan, 32)

In the next part of the interview, Nour and her sister Vida discussed how a violent context—be it political, economic, or social—pushes people to leave their home countries. The act of migration itself becomes not simply an individual choice; it also becomes part of a more collective or even global story. At the same time, by emphasizing such universality, they plead for humanity and compassion.

A second counter-discourse refers to the countries of origin. Within the dominant discourse of the victim-migrant, refugees' countries of origin are seen as underdeveloped—the scene of nothing but misery, war, and terror. Our participants deconstructed the stereotypes of their fellow Afghans, Iraqis, or

Syrians as uncivilized nonintellectuals by insisting on the fact that, despite the difficult national contexts, there are many university-educated people. Trying to reverse the dominant image of the migrant who is nothing and who comes from nothing, several interlocutors reminded us of the similarity of our academic trajectories. Searching for common ground or a more universal outlook was often a way to overcome boundaries and show an image that extended beyond victimhood. Thus, new images transpire, notably that of (rather) young individuals with an open outlook to the world and with transnational backgrounds.

However, certain participants also held more ambiguous or negative views toward their countries or regions of origin. For many, those in power—the Taliban in Afghanistan, President Bashar al-Assad in Syria, conflicting Shiites and Sunnis in Iraq—have threatened them in a violent way, either physically or mentally. For them, arrival in Belgium symbolizes the end of a difficult and chaotic trajectory. Still, while some see this arrival and the ensuing asylum procedure as a positive experience, others spoke of a strong deception. Take for instance Adnan, a 41-year-old business administrator from Baghdad. After a long journey across the Middle East, the Mediterranean Sea, and the European mainland, he thought he had arrived in "the capital of human rights". But, unfortunately, his hopes were crushed the moment he arrived in Brussels:

> As an Iraqi, for me, Brussels represented the center of Western democracy, I knew it from the Iraqi and Arabic news channels as the city with all the human rights organizations and institutions, the NATO headquarters, the European Parliament. When the war started, I knew that's where I wanted to live. … When I stepped into Brussels North Station, police razzias were taking place, and I was arrested together with a bunch of others and sent to a closed detention center outside of Brussels. It was horrible. I was detained for a couple of days …. The atmosphere was grim, and people were aggressive. I saw a lot of violence, people had knives and fights broke out between groups. Some people had been there for a longer time. I quickly learned that democracy does not come without a price and that human rights are not distributed equally, even in the West.

After a couple of days, Adnan was released and he was able to start asylum procedures. He now has temporary residence status, but was still visibly shaken when recounting his first acquaintance with the world's "capital of human rights." Such accounts of disappointment, as well as testimonials of hostile or unjust reception in Belgium constitute a third counter-discourse, which is part of nuancing the dominant discourse of the refugee-victim from uncivilized regions arriving in the "superior" Western European host regions.

It is important to note that these counter-discourses relate very much to how participants experience representations of migration, and refugees in particular, in the media. They want their suffering to be represented, but not in the way it is now. In general, participants were disturbed by one-sided emphases in the press on either the threats posed by refugees or their suffering, and deemed it necessary for more balanced representations—in words and in images—to be produced and circulated. They believe that this would lead to a less suspicious but also less *miserabilist* approach to refugees. Participants largely confirm what previous content analyses on media coverage have demonstrated: the key themes in representation and the key discourses are negatively connoted. However, it also became clear that asylum seekers and refugees might interpret photographic media coverages differently. While the associations and suggestions that are made in some photos (for example between law enforcement, disorder, criminality, and refugees), or by some of the elements in the pictures (including health masks, balaclavas, and weapons), can be disturbing, the asylum seekers and the refugees themselves saw and 'read' the importance of showing how dangerous refugee experiences can be. Or, as Younes, a 38-year-old business administrator from Iraq, said: "It is important to show 'the ugly truth'. Such media coverage shows the reality of what refugees are going through and it informs and prepares those who still want to leave their countries".

In general, the importance of showing 'the ugly truth' was emphasized by participants throughout our study and across the interviews. They all underlined the importance of a 'realistic' representation of the difficult and dangerous journey refugees have to take. Photos that are brutally hard, for instance showing physical suffering, were often experienced and categorized as 'positive' media coverage. Firas, a 22-year old Syrian, for instance, emphasized that these photos were important, not only as messages to other refugees, but also to confront 'detached' European audiences and remind them about notions of humanity, human rights, and solidarity. For Nour, the 32-year old Afghan woman who was already introduced above, more realistic and sometimes harsh visual representations might not only stimulate empathy but provoke real change. When discussing the pictures used during our participatory visual workshop, she stated that:

> You should know *how*… it's so hard to tell someone without seeing a picture or experiencing it, the difficulties… they *should know*. How many nights we've been sleeping in the streets, how many nights we've had *hunger*, how much pain and stress we saw on our way here and… they [European people], they *need* to see those images because no words could bring it…

> ... but these pictures, the point of them is that *they should make a change,* they should make the general public to make a change. Not just to see a picture and say "Ow...".

Being *seen* can thus be regarded as a condition for real understanding. It is precisely this connection that we will investigate further in the next section, as we will explore how participants' experiences of dominant representations and their alternative suggestions are connected to a deep-rooted need for recognition within Belgian society.

From pity to empathy: the need for recognition

We will complete the analysis section of this chapter by weaving together the participants' experiences of suffering, the triple violence experienced as a refugee, and their counter-discourses to how refugees are represented. Linking these themes, we argue that participants solicit a paradigmatic shift in the way refugees are approached from pity to empathy. Our participants feel the need to be acknowledged as victims, not in general, but at a particular moment and in a particular context. Their violent experiences in their countries of origin or on the road to Europe are vastly different from the victimization often experienced in their daily lives as well as in the context of international protection more generally. As the victimization of refugees takes place in a context of suspicion, classification, and competition among refugees, it leads to a certain loss of individual identities. Participants have a strong desire for an empathic gaze to re-value and re-humanize themselves and seek connections with others. This is expressed well by Salima, a 48-year old Syrian who was a lawyer in her country:

> Sometimes I feel that I'm in the middle of the sea... and I have no boat, I can't swim... ... [silence]. *What can I do?* [low tone voice]. You feel like... The people... are against you. There is no money, there is no job, there is no... your family is not here... you feel cold... you feel... depressed... The language is different, *everything is different*. And... *extra*, people are coming saying ... "why are you here?"... [long silence]. ... The important thing that I can say [to people in Belgium] is *"Please try to put yourself in my situation"*. What can I do? [silence].

Yet, empathy needs to be distinguished from pity. As Kobelinsky, following Hannah Arendt, argues that compassion, or empathy, consists of "being struck by the others' suffering as if it was contagious" (Kobelinsky,

2007, s.n.), while pity "is not stricken in the flesh and keeps its sentimental distance" (Arendt, 1990: 89). Kobelinsky adds that compassion "cannot be inspired by the suffering of an entire class. It cannot go further than the suffering of a single individual without ceasing to be what it is by definition: a co-suffering" (2007: s.n.) Thus, while empathy supposes a relation of proximity with the person suffering, pity generalizes and is "felt from a distance of the one suffering" (2007: s.n.). This is a highly relevant observation, and distinction: when analyzing participants' accounts, it is clear that while many strive for a more universal recognition of refugees and asylum seekers, they also have an individual battle to fight. The demand for a balanced visibility of suffering seems to be the symptom of a more profound wish to be recognized as a human being. In the words of Hicham, a 27-year old Syrian:

> … And we should stop think that… yeah, … I mean,… we should really deliver the message that we are not less successful or less human. We can be as… any as other human if we… feel safe enough. Emotionally and also physically. Physically we started to feel it, completely. Emotionally… we should work on ourselves and our ideas and then to deliver this message it will… it will need time.

Recognition thus becomes a central node in many of the conversations we had. The work of Honneth (2001) is particularly enlightening in this context, as he argues that processes of recognition are intimately related to (in)visibility. Distinguishing literal and figurative invisibility, he states on the one hand that figurative (or metaphorical) invisibility links to the human capacity to "show our disregard to persons who are present by behaving toward them as if they were not actually there in the room" (Honneth, 2001: 112). He refers to the expression of "looking *through* something": the other is intentionally not watched. This form of invisibility is part of a complex social situation (rather than being a cognitive "fact"). Physical invisibility, on the other hand, can be analyzed by looking at physical *visibility* first. The latter supposes basic individual identifiability. This is why the feeling of being figuratively invisible supposes a visibility in the literal sense. "The subject must have already made the assumption that he has been taken cognizance of as an individual within the spatio-temporal order" (Honneth, 2001: 114). Consequently, Honneth links physical visibility to "cognizing", and figurative visibility to "recognizing", i.e, "an expressive act through which this cognition is conferred with the positive meaning of an affirmation" (Honneth, 2001: 115).

Making suffering visible becomes a gateway for our participants to express frustration, or at least disappointment, with the fact that there is a lack of realistic media representations about their histories and individual trajectories. This connects to a broader sense of societal misconceptions about refugees. It is not so much the question of suffering as such, but the wish to be made visible, in the metaphorical sense described by Honneth. The refugees among our participants, on the one hand, want to simply exist, as legitimate and dignified individuals. Perhaps even more than other forms of recognition (such as affective or legal recognition), they need genuine solidarity—or social esteem, as Honneth (2004: 351) calls it. Those who were applying for asylum while living in reception centers, on the other hand, saw this somewhat differently and stressed the wish to be recognized legally and to survive physically and mentally. Making their suffering visible to the Belgian society fulfills a more critical goal of survival. Those with refugee status, who felt they had more time to accustom to Belgium and had the possibility to exercise their rights, emphasized the need for social esteem. Participants felt that this need for recognition was considerably discordant with the perceived hostile and skeptical political climate. For many participants, the road to recognition and legitimacy departs from a strong personal commitment and, crucially, the search for employment. The following quotation by Hakim, a 29-year old Syrian, shows how recognition, visibility, and identity are interconnected in very concrete ways for our participants:

> I try to *construct* this legitimacy... by integrating codes, references, by learning the *language* ... being somehow indebted to this country. ... For me personally, it is impossible to say I feel invisible... But maybe, psychologically, I have been searching this visibility, I committed myself a lot. My main motivation is *ethical*. But I told myself: "I want to…" and there is a kind of mission given to me… to make a little bridge between the misunderstandings. (Hakim, Syrian, 29 years old)

The visibility of suffering is thus a complex issue, as it is both 'formatted' discourse and counter-discourse. It is inscribed into the framework where suffering requires proof and merits a certain status. The victim position and the tensions it entails are, however, not intractable. Participants clearly take issue with the misinterpretation of victim as a pan-identity for refugees, which strips them of dignity and agency.

Conclusions

One of our key aims when we embarked on this study was to give voice to those who often remain voiceless, and to reflect on representations of migration together with those supposedly being represented. A nuanced picture has emerged that shifts the dominant perspective of discussion on migration. Rather than analyzing media content *in abstracto*, we have started reflecting on regimes of representation with asylum seekers and refugees. Our central focus on suffering and the thorny issues of legitimacy and recognition was prompted by the accounts of the participants. If we leave aside the utterly hostile representations and portrayals of refugees as (cultural, economic, or security) threats, the 'refugee as a victim' is a very dominant media figure. This powerful image hinders refugees from being seen as reflexive agents, and only grants them legitimacy with proof of suffering. It also leads to feelings of inferiority vis-à-vis the members of the host society. How to move beyond that, while at the same time recognizing the real suffering experienced by refugees? The stories of participants show that despite being trapped in legal, administrative, economic but also *symbolic* immobility, they are above all individuals with capabilities, dreams, and future plans. By reducing them to a suffering, anonymous population—or suffering bodies, rather—it becomes difficult for them to show their abilities and resilience.

The participants in this study sense that the dominant image of the refugee-victim is being perpetuated by mainstream media representations. In order for them to feel more legitimate, and thus recognized as actors with agency in new societies, more realistic media representations are needed. The harsh realities of refugees' different struggles ought to be shown, but they should not be all-encompassing. We have discussed several counter-discourses formulated by refugees that, according to them, could lead to more nuanced representations such as providing more refined representations of refugees' personal stories and questioning the dichotomy of civilized versus uncivilized countries. Participants expressed the hope that this will enable a shift from pity and victimization to empathy and recognition. These findings, despite their simplicity, are not banal. The study demonstrates that reflecting on representations with asylum seekers and refugees is a useful and necessary exercise that touches upon issues fundamental to their experienced well-being. Studies conducted among journalists reporting on refugees (Pantti & Ojala, 2018) and the Syrian conflict (Vandevoordt, 2017) as well as press officers of refugee organizations (Ongenaert & Joye, forthcoming) point at structural constraints and difficulties to change regimes of representation, but also offer signs of hope for more reflexive media representations. Raising awareness among media producers, policy makers, and public opinion about the impacts of those representations for refugees, and considering possible alternatives to current representations therefore remains crucial.

References

Agamben G. (1998). *Homo sacer: Sovereign power and bare life*. Stanford, CA: Stanford University Press.
Agier, M. (ed.) (2018). *Entre accueil et rejet: ce que les villes font aux migrants*. Lyon: Le Passager Clandestin.
Arendt, H. (1990, first edition 1963). *On Revolution*. London: Penguin Books.
Beaud, S. (1996). L'usage de l'entretien en sciences sociales. Plaidoyer pour l'entretien ethnographique. *Politix. Revue des sciences sociales du politique*, 9(35), 226–257.
Bleiker, R., Campbell, D., Hutchison, E., & Nicholson, X. (2013). The visual dehumanization of refugees. *Australian Journal of Political Science*, 48(4), 398–416.
Bohmer, C., & Shuman, A. (2018). *Political Asylum Deceptions: The Culture of Suspicion*. Houndmills: Palgrave Macmillan.
Bozdag, C., & Smets, K. (2017). Understanding the images of Alan Kurdi with "small data": a qualitative, comparative analysis of tweets about refugees in Turkey and Flanders (Belgium). *International Journal of Communication*, 11(1), 4046–4069.
Bryman, A. (2012). *Social Research Methods (4th edition)*. Oxford: Oxford University Press.
Carastathis, A., Spathopoulou, A., & Tsilimpounidi, M. (2018). Crisis, what crisis? Immigrants, refugees, and invisible struggles. *Refuge: Canada's Journal on Refugees*, 34(1), 29–38.
Chouliaraki, L. (2006). *The spectatorship of suffering*. London: SAGE.
Chouliaraki, L., & Stolic, T. (2017). Rethinking media responsibility in the refugee 'crisis': a visual typology of European news. *Media, Culture & Society*, 39(8), 1162–1177.
Chouliaraki, L., & Zaborowski, R. (2017). Voice and community in the refugee crisis: A content analysis of news coverage in eight European countries. *International Communication Gazette*, 79(6-7), 613–635.
De Cleen, B., Zienkowski, J., Smets, K., Dekie, A., & Vandevoordt, R. (2017). Constructing the 'refugee crisis' in Flanders. Continuities and adaptations of discourses on asylum and migration. In M. Barlai, B. Fähnrich, C. Griessler, & M. Rhomberg (Eds.), *The migrant crisis: European perspectives and national discourses* (pp.59–78). Berlin: LIT Verlag.
Dines, N., Montagna, N., & Caccelli, E. (2018). Beyond crisis talk: interrogating migration and crises in Europe. *Sociology*, 52(3), 439–447.
Fassin, D. (2005). Compassion and repression: the moral economy of immigration policies in France. *Cultural Anthropology*, 20(3), 362–387.
Fassin, D., & Rechtman, R. (2007) *L'Empire du traumatisme: enquête sur la condition de victime*. Paris: Flammarion.
Georgiou, M. (2018). Does the subaltern speak? Migrant voices in digital Europe. *Popular Communication*, 16(1), 45–57.
Honneth, A. (2001). Invisibility: On the Epistemology of 'Recognition'. *Proceedings of the Aristotelian Society*, Supplementary Volumes 75, 111–139.
Honneth, A. (2004). Recognition and justice: outline of a plural theory of justice. *Acta Sociologica*, 47(4), 351–364.

Horsti, K. (forthcoming). Refracting the analytical gaze: studying media representations of migrant death at the border. In K. Smets, K. Leurs, M. Georgiou, S. Witteborn, & R. Gajjala (Eds.), *The Handbook of Media and Migration*. London: SAGE.

Kisiara O. (2015). Marginalized at the centre: how public narratives of suffering perpetuate perceptions of refugees' helplessness and dependency. *Migration Letters, 12*(2), 162–171.

Kobelinsky, C. (2007). Le jugement quotidien des demandeurs d'asile, *Recueil Alexandries*, Collections Esquisses. Retrieved July 17, 2018, from: http://www.reseau-terra.eu/article559.html.

Kobelinsky, C. (2012). Des corps en attente. Le quotidien des demandeurs d'asil. *Corps, 10*(1), 183–192.

Lacroix, T. (2016), *Migrants. L'impasse européenne*. Paris: Armand Colin.

Machillot, D. (2012). Pour une anthropologie des stéréotypes: Quelques propositions théoriques. *Horizontes Antropológicos, 18*(37), 73–101.

Mazzocchetti, J. (2017a). Mises en scène, souffrances et quêtes de dignité. Quelle humanité dans les parcours d'asile? In C. Mayneri (Ed.), *Entre errances et silences* (pp. 99–133). Louvain-la-Neuve: Éditions Academia L'Harmattan.

Mazzocchetti, J. (2017b). Dire la violence des frontières dans le rapport de force que constitue la procédure d'asile. Le cas d'Ali, de l'Afghanistan en Belgique. *Revue Européenne des Migrations Internationales, 33*(2-3), 91–114.

Métraux, J. C. (2011). *La migration comme métaphore*. Paris: La Dispute.

Ongenaert, D., & Joye, S. (forthcoming). Selling displaced people: a multi-method study of international refugee organizations' public communication strategies towards the Syrian displacement crisis. *Disasters*.

Pantti, M., & Ojala, M. (2018). Caught between sympathy and suspicion: journalistic perceptions and practices of telling asylum seekers' personal stories. *Media, Culture & Society*. doi: 0163443718756177.

Perez Portilla, K. (2018). Challenging media (mis)representation: an exploration of available models. *International Journal for Crime, Justice and Social Democracy, 7*(2), 4–20.

Rajaram, P. K. (2002). Humanitarianism and representations of the refugee. *Journal of Refugee Studies, 15*(3), 247–264.

Rose, G. (2014). On the relation between 'visual research methods' and contemporary visual culture. *The Sociological Review, 62*(1), 24–46.

Sigona, N. (2018). The contested politics of naming in Europe's 'refugee crisis'. *Ethnic and Racial Studies, 41*(3), 456–460.

Stumpf, J. (2006). The crimmigration crisis: migrants, crime and sovereign power. *American University Law Review, 56*(2), 367–419.

Valluy, J. (2004). La fiction juridique de l'asile. *Plein droit, 4*(63), 17–22.

Vandevoordt, R. (2017). Why journalists covered Syria the way they did: on the role of economic, social and cultural capital. *Journalism, 18*(5), 609–625.

Vanoeteren, A., & Gehrels, L. (2009). La prise en considération de la santé mentale dans la procédure d'asile. *Revue du droit des étrangers, 155*, 492–543.

Vianna, P. (2007). Du soupçon à la mise à l'écart: le droit d'asile en danger. *Migrations société, 1*(109), 79–91.

Vrancken, D. (2010). Des corps souffrants, corps parlants dans le nouvel ordre protectionnel. *Le sujet dans la cité, 1*(1), 50–58.

Wang, C., & Burris, M. A. (1997). Photovoice: concept, methodology, and use for participatory needs assessment. *Health Education & Behaviour, 24*(3), 369–387.

Wright, T. (2002). Moving images: the media representation of refugees. *Visual Studies, 17*(1), 53–66.

Appendix

Appendix 10.1: overview of participants (pseudonyms) according to sex, age and country of origin

Pseudonym name	Sex	Age	Country of origin
Omar	Male	47	Syria
Asma	Female	41	Syria
Haya	Female	28	Syria
Lina	Female	31	Syria
Adnan	Male	41	Iraq
Fathi	Male	37	Iraq
Hussein	Male	43	Syria
Najib	Male	18	Afghanistan
Dawood	Male	18	Afghanistan
Farid	Male	18	Afghanistan
Saleh	Male	18	Afghanistan
Firas	Male	22	Syria
Younes	Male	38	Iraq
Mohammed	Male	33	Syria
Mounir	Male	29	Iraq
Karim	Male	In his thirties	Syria
Abdel	Male	36	Syria
Soran	Male	21	Iraq
Hicham	Male	26	Syria
Malek	Male	In his thirties	Syria
Zohra	Female	In her thirties	Syria
Rania	Female	23	Syria
Raed	Male	21	Syria
Vida	Female	30	Afghanistan
Nour	Female	32	Afghanistan
Hakim	Male	29	Syria
Salima	Female	48	Syria
Selim	Male	26	Iraq

Pseudonym name	Sex	Age	Country of origin
Jasmine	Female	In her thirties	Syria
Nawal	Female	28	Syria
Farida	Female	28	Iraq
Loubna	Female	Late forties	Afghanistan
Mehdi	Male	20	Syria
Ahmed	Male	19	Syria
Samir	Male	19	Syria
Fouad	Male	18	Afghanistan
Amir	Male	32	Iraq
Shabir	Male	17	Afghanistan
Zinedine	Male	Late forties	Syria
Oualid	Male	29	Syria
Nacer	Male	19	Syria
Shaima	Female	22	Iraq
Turan	Male	In his thirties	Afghanistan
Ashkan	Male	In his fifties	Afghanistan

Conclusion

François Heinderyckx

Immigration defines our time. People moving across national borders, once seen as a welcome benefit of European integration and worldwide globalization, is again the focal point of attention and an exceptionally efficient tool in the hands of fearmongers who successfully thrive on ethnic bigotry and antagonism. Migrants, refugees, and other visible minorities have proved to be the perfect scapegoats for the scourge of the moment: economic crisis, unemployment, poverty, criminality, terrorism, health hazards, cultural homogenization; populists of all sorts have, once again, effectively convinced a sizeable portion of the people, of a causal link between the presence (let alone the influx) of populations of foreign origin and most of the issues Western societies are grappling with.

A great many underlying factors are shaping our representation of immigration and our capacity to understand the extent to which it is, or isn't, related to current issues and concerns. In spite of the major systemic transformation prompted by digital information and communication technologies, traditional news media are still front and center in nurturing our representations of the world. The events that make it through the mysterious mazes of gatekeeping, the way that they are framed, and the interpretation that they are given weave the fabric of the backdrop against which we see our world, shape the public debate and the policy agenda and, ultimately, we vote (or decide not to).

In Western Europe, a surge of refugees coming from war zones (prominently from Syria, Afghanistan, and Iraq recently), in conjunction with a steady flow of economic immigration and an increased mobility of workers and students, combine to create a confused impression of demographic and cultural pressure on autochthonous populations (or rather on those who perceive themselves as such). Political figures, intellectuals, civil society organizations, and loud mouths of all kinds are wrestling for attention in the public sphere, resulting in patterns of representation that are diverse and unpredictable in their shape, their substance and their reach.

Analyzing the image of immigrants and refugees is key to untangling the nexus of perceptions and attitudes toward 'the other' and alterity in general. By combining a study of representation in the media and among the population, including among the refugees themselves, with an investigation within news production, the research presented in this volume provides a much-needed set of facts supporting a better understanding of how contemporary immigration is shaping public opinion, politics, and policy. Such understanding is all the more important, knowing that political tensions surrounding the refugee crisis develop above layers of tension regarding European integration itself and how it puts national identities and cultures at risk (see Chapter 2).

Combining existing and original data on migration, policy, public opinion, media content, and the work of journalists, and mobilizing the conceptual and theoretical arsenal of gatekeeping, agenda-setting, and framing, this research offers a novel glimpse comparing in particular depth the situation in Belgium with that in Sweden, while including other countries on specific aspects. The deep focus on two countries does not seek to extrapolate generalizations. Instead, by showing significant differences between these two small Western-European countries of similar population size which were once emigration countries but became immigration countries (we call them 'divergent cases'), the study signals the potential magnitude of differences within Europe. The social, political, economic, and cultural contexts are so diverse across Europe (some countries initially organizing themselves to welcome or even attract refugees, while others deploy spectacular measures to deter them), as are the nature and magnitude of immigration, that no one-size-fits-all analysis can possibly grasp such a complex issue at the level of the continent.

What has soon been referred to as a 'refugee crisis' does show some similarities in newspaper coverage in Belgium and Sweden (e.g., the over-representation of Syrian refugees: see Chapter 3). Analysis of left-wing quality newspapers in Belgium and The Netherlands shows a shared caution not to cast refugees as intruders or malicious individuals, but also a striking lack of voice and agency for those refugees (see Chapter 5). News media exposure has more influence on public opinion in Belgium than it does in Sweden, but trust in news media shows a stronger correlation in Sweden. Within Belgium, an analysis of television news coverage compared the main commercial channel and the main public service channel, revealing some differences (fewer but longer segments on public service and more focus on emotions on the commercial channel) and many similarities (see Chapter 4). French-speaking Belgian journalists also appear to feel more strongly that they should promote tolerance and cultural diversity than their Dutch-speaking colleagues. Significant differences within such a small country as Belgium are a reminder of the factors at play in understanding and perceiving immigration and the refugee crisis, and the ensuing expectations for policy making and political action, are deeply embedded in a complex mesh of cultural values and attributes. These observations revealing signs of multidimensional diversity are humbling at a time when all eyes are on European Union institutions for concerted efforts, policy, and action.

Attitudes toward immigration and perception of the magnitude and nature of the refugee crisis show intriguing differences even among neighboring countries. Trying to identify regional clusters showing some convergence in interventionist journalism culture promoting tolerance in various contexts of public opinion and policy only reveals more signs of multidimensional diversity as the clusters of countries vary in shape and size depending on the variables under consideration (see Chapter 6). Unexpectedly, countries where journalism culture substantially promotes tolerance tend to display less emancipative values and migrant friendly policies.

In Belgium, public service television news consumption is more associated with a positive attitude toward immigrants and refugees than commercial television (Chapter 7). This is not the case in Sweden, but there, the overall attitude toward immigrants and refugees is more positive than in Belgium. Signs were also found showing that exposure to television news is associated with more negative views on refugees (Chapter 8), while online news consumers tend to be more polarized on the topic, particularly among people with higher levels of education. There are signs of a filter bubble among highly educated heavy consumers of social media for online news consumption who hold negative views toward refugees.

Furthermore, an experiment conducted among the population of Flanders showed how positively framed news stories (which is unusual in a context where, for many years, the dominant news framing is rather negative) tends to meet resistance as audiences find these unusually positive news stories less credible (Chapter 9). This finding does not mean that positive news framing is useless, but rather that a better balance between positive and negative news framing would leave people more open to nuanced opinions.

As for refugees and asylum seekers themselves, our research reveals that they resent being portrayed as threats, but also as victims, even though proving their suffering as victims is key to their being recognized as legitimate refugees (Chapter 10). They regret not being portrayed and recognized enough as reflexive agents with skills, ambitions, and dreams of their own. Journalists would presumably be welcome to approach them to tell that side of the story and add an element of positive and constructive news framing to their representation in the news media and, consequently, within the broader population.

Whether or not news media are part of the problem, a number of findings gathered in this volume seem to indicate that there is a real potential for them to be part of the solution. By deliberately avoiding clichés and going beyond classic newsworthiness provided by stories and framing oriented toward immigrants as threats and victims to enhance abilities, projects, and ambitions, news sources in their newly expanded diversity would improve the relevance of their coverage while pleasing their audience. For although it is assumed that individuals find cognitive comfort in news stories that are consonant with their representations and world views, many will also find comfort in associating such anxiety-provoking topic with glimpses of hope, positive outcomes, and happiness. Faced with the challenge of representing a complex reality, journalists must resist the line of least resistance of reproducing the clichés. Instead, they must strive to convey the rich diversity otherwise hidden behind a wall of shallow, simplistic stereotypes.

List of authors

Leen d'Haenens (PhD, Political and Social Sciences, University of Ghent, Belgium) is Full Professor at the Institute for Media Studies – Faculty of Social Sciences, KU Leuven, Belgium. She holds an MA in Romance Languages, an MSc in Press and Communication Sciences (University of Ghent), and an MSc in Information Studies (University of Toronto). Her current areas of research include journalism studies (frame analysis of immigrant and refugees in the news, longitudinal studies on news diversity), media and ethnic minorities (e.g., ethnic discussion forums as a source of social capital for ethnic minorities), digital media and youngsters, and media governance and accountability mechanisms.
E-mail: leen.dhaenens@kuleuven.be

Rozane De Cock (PhD 2007) is Assistant Professor in Communication Sciences and Journalism Studies at the Institute for Media Studies – Faculty of Social Sciences, KU Leuven, Belgium. She holds an MA in Communication Sciences and an MA in Post-graduate teacher training (KU Leuven) and is director of the Brussels Center for Journalism Studies. Rozane has published on newsroom practices and news content, children and news, adolescents and media use, and problematic internet and gaming use.
E-mail: rozane.decock@kuleuven.be

David De Coninck (MSc, Sociology, University of Antwerp, Belgium) is a PhD student at the Center for Sociological Research – Faculty of Social Sciences, KU Leuven, Belgium. His current areas of research include multi-methodical approaches on media and migration attitudes (e.g., media consumption as a source for attitude formation on immigrants or refugees), threat perspectives, fear dynamics, and policy analysis. He also investigates subjective wellbeing and family attitudes among Flemish youngsters.
E-mail: david.deconinck@kuleuven.be

Lorraine Gerstmans is a graduate in sociology and anthropology at Université Catholique de Louvain, Belgium. At the end of her master's degree, she obtained a complementary university certificate in "Mental Health in Social Contexts: Multiculturality and Precariousness" (UCL).
E-mail: lorraine.gerstmans@gmail.com

François Heinderyckx is Full Professor at Université libre de Bruxelles (ULB) where he teaches media sociology and political communication. His research interests include journalism and news media, political communication, audience studies, and media literacy. He is the Dean of the Faculty of Letters, Translation and Communication. He was a Chang-Jiang Scholar Professor at Communication University of China (2013-2018). He was among the founding members of the European Communication Research and Education Association (ECREA) in 2005. He was the President of ECREA from its creation until 2012. He was also the 2013-2014 President of the International Communication Association (ICA).
E-mail: francois.heinderyckx@ulb.be

Willem Joris (PhD, Social Sciences, KU Leuven, Belgium) is postdoctoral researcher at the Institute for Media Studies – Faculty of Social Sciences, KU Leuven, Belgium, and Guest Professor in Communication Sciences at CEMESO, Vrije Universiteit Brussel (VUB). He holds a master's degree in Communication Sciences and a master's in Public Management and Policy (KU Leuven). His research focuses on media and diversity, journalism studies (e.g., frame analysis of immigrant and refugees in the news), political communication, Europe.
E-mail: willem.joris@kuleuven.be

Lutgard Lams (PhD, Linguistics, University of Antwerp, Belgium) is Professor of Pragmatics, Media Discourse Analysis and Intercultural Communication at the Faculty of Arts at the KU Leuven Campus Brussels. She holds an MA in Germanic Philology (KU Leuven), and an MA in Literary Theory (Carnegie Mellon University, Pittsburgh). Her research interests include journalism studies (framing and positioning social actors in media narratives), political communication in the Asia-Pacific region, and democracy studies (official language strategies in authoritarian regimes, discourses about democracy).
E-mail: lut.lams@kuleuven.be

Koen Matthijs is Full Professor of Sociology and Demography at the University of Leuven (Belgium). He is head of the research group *Family and Population Studies* (https://soc.kuleuven.be/ceso/fapos), directing the integration of historical demographic research on long-term, sociodemographic trends with contemporary sociological studies on current family structures and processes. He has published widely on (historical) fertility, marriage, divorce, family forms, migration, and mortality. He is an elected member of the *Royal Flemish Society of Belgium for Science and Arts*.
E-mail: koen.matthijs@kuleuven.be

Jacinthe Mazzocchetti is a graduate in Applied Communication (IHECS – Institut des Hautes Etudes en Communications Sociales, Brussels). She then obtained an MA and a PhD in Anthropology at UCL (Université de Louvain). Currently she is Assistant Professor at UCL, head of the Anthropology Department and member of the Laboratory for Prospective Anthropology (LAAP). Since 1997, she has conducted field research (ethnography) in Belgium, France, and Burkina Faso on topics related to youths (socialization, recognition...) as well as issues related to migration. Since 2012, she has also led research in Malta and Belgium on policies about migration and asylum, on the related institutional practices and their impact on migration strategies.
E-mail: jacinthe.mazzocchetti@uclouvain.be

Stefan Mertens (PhD, Catholic University of Brussels) is postdoctoral researcher at the Institute for Media Studies – Faculty of Social Sciences, KU Leuven, Belgium. He is also partner for the Dutch speaking part of Belgium in the international Worlds of Journalism Project (http://www.worldsofjournalism.org). His research interests include quantitative and qualitative content analysis, media and diversity, media policy analysis, survey research, research on cultural values and journalism cultures and audience reception studies.
E-mail: stefan.mertens@kuleuven.be

Valériane Mistiaen has been a joint PhD candidate since 2019 at the Faculty of Letters, Translation and Communication (LTC) of the Université libre de Bruxelles (ULB) and at the Faculty of Social Sciences & Solvay Business School of the Vrije Universiteit Brussel (VUB). She is a member of the Center for Research in Information and Communication Sciences (ReSIC – ULB) and of the Center for the Study of Democracy, Signification and Resistance (DESIRE – VUB). Her research focuses on the denomination of people on

the move in Belgian French- and Dutch-speaking media since the beginning of the so-called refugee crisis (April 2015).
E-mail: vmistiae@ulb.ac.be

Lien Mostmans wrote a doctoral thesis (2017, VUB, Belgium) about the moral conceptions of children concerning online self-disclosure, funded by FWO (Fund for Scientific Research in Flanders). Additional research efforts focused on young people's changing media landscape and their overall media behaviors, attitudes, and cultures. She was also a member of the IM²MEDIATE project at VUB, focusing on refugees' experiences. Lien holds masters' degrees in Germanic languages (Vrije Universiteit Brussel, 2007) and cultural sciences (Vrije Universiteit Brussel, 2008).
E-mail: lien.mostmans@ehb.be

Paul Puschmann (PhD Social Sciences, KU Leuven, Belgium) is an Assistant Professor in Economic, Social and Demographic History at the Radboud Group for Historical Demography and Family History, Radboud University, Nijmegen, the Netherlands and a Postdoctoral Fellow at *Family and Population Studies*, KU Leuven, Belgium. He is Co-Editor-in-Chief of Historical Life Course Studies and Research Program Director of the Life Courses, Family and Labor Network of the N.W. Posthumus Institute, the Research School for Economic and Social History in the Netherlands and Flanders. His research focuses on long-term changes in migration, social inclusion, partner choice, marriage and family formation in Europe, the Middle East, and North Africa.
E-mail:p.puschmann@let.ru.nl

Kevin Smets is Assistant Professor in media and culture at Vrije Universiteit Brussel (Belgium). He obtained his PhD in Film Studies and Visual Culture from the University of Antwerp (2013) and was a visiting fellow at, among others, Bilgi University Istanbul, the School of Oriental & African Studies (London), and the University of Oxford. He is the vice-chair of the Diaspora, Migration & the Media section of the European Communication Research & Education Association. His research focuses on relations between media, diaspora, conflict, and migration in the European, Turkish, and Middle Eastern contexts.
E-mail: kevin.smets@vub.be

Olivier Standaert is Assistant Professor at the Louvain School of Journalism (Université Catholique de Louvain, Belgium). His research and teaching focus on methodological issues in journalism studies, journalism cultures, professional identities, careers and labor markets of media workers. As a former freelance journalist, he previously worked for various Belgian newspapers and magazines.
E-mail: olivier.standaert@uclouvain.be

Ebba Sundin (PhD, Journalism and Mass Communication, University of Gothenburg, Sweden) is Associate Professor at the School of Health and Welfare, Halmstad University, Sweden. She is currently Program Director for the Master Program in Nordic Welfare, an interdisciplinary program with a focus on social challenges in the Nordic region. Her current research areas include journalism studies (e.g., refugees in the news), young children and digital practices, and digital health issues.
E-mail: ebba.sundin@hh.se

Hanne Vandenberghe (PhD, Social Sciences, KU Leuven, Belgium) is both postdoctoral researcher and lecturer at the Institute for Media Studies (Faculty of Social Sciences, KU Leuven). She is also part-time researcher at the Center of Expertise for Social Innovation (Vives University College, Kortrijk). Her research interests include the conceptualization of diversity, the representation of women and ethnic minorities, gender stereotyping in news, the journalist-source relationship, and news audience demographics.
E-mail: hanne.vandenberghe@kuleuven.be